T0149747

Not Just Any Bag of Bones

Jonathan Peter Studebaker

authorHOUSE®

AuthorHouse™
1663 Liberty Drive
Bloomington, IN 47403
www.authorhouse.com
Phone: 1 (800) 839-8640

Published by AuthorHouse 06/27/2018

ISBN: 978-1-5462-4664-0 (sc)
ISBN: 978-1-5462-4663-3 (e)

Library of Congress Control Number: 2018907081

Print information available on the last page.

Contents

Dedication

This book is dedicated to our parents, Henry and Cynthia Studebaker, and Shriners Hospitals for Children, whom are prominently mentioned.

10% of all profits from sale of this book will be donated to Shriners International.

Acknowledgements

I would like to thank my wife, Donna Studebaker, and my sisters, Amy Dennison and Rebecca Downing, for their editorial advice and assistance.

About the Cover

The photo on the front cover is of Jonathan with his trademark grin, taken in August 1990. He included the photo in a letter he wrote to his parents:

8-7-90

Dear Mom & Dad,

I thought you might be interested in having a picture of this good looking guy in a blue sweater. I think you might be able to recognize him. Well, he wanted me to tell you that even though he doesn't get a chance to see you very often, it doesn't mean that he doesn't think of you. Hopefully, you'll get a chance to see him in person real soon, but as for now, he wanted you to have this picture. Besides, this picture could be worth something someday.

I love you! ! !

Love, your son—

Jonathan

Foreword

In August 1996, I visited my younger brother, Jonathan Studebaker, at his home on Orient Street in Chico. I had flown out to California to help our parents move back to the Midwest. They tasked me with taking some boxes of Jonathan's belongings to him. Little did I know that I would be returning with his greatest treasure, his recently completed autobiography.

To the best of my knowledge I was the sole recipient of his book. Why he gave it to me still mystifies me. Why he didn't publish it himself mystifies me even more.

At the time I was in the middle of publishing my first book, *Wisdom for a Lifetime,* and was distracted by that project. I made a cursory read of his book, but eventually set it aside only for it to languish on the hard drives of several computers for the past twenty years, until now.

I finally reread his book and realized what a disservice I had done by ignoring it for so long. I also discovered what a good writer he was, especially given his hodgepodge of an education.

If you take the time to read *Not Just Any Bag of Bones* you will come away with a clear and honest understanding of what it is like to be disabled and how to make the most of it. Jonathan was born with half the bones in his body broken, was put in an incubator, and given only a couple weeks to live. Our father even made his funeral arrangements. They weren't needed.

He lived. Wow, did he live!

In spite of spending half of his childhood in Shriners hospitals receiving treatment for osteogenesis imperfecta, or OI, he managed to attend a college, pledge a fraternity, serve as a college football coach, and receive his degree in just four years. None of his siblings were able to accomplish that feat. Was he disabled? Yes, he was, but not where it counts, within his mind and heart.

You will discover upon these pages the soul of a dragon with a roar the size of the Grand Canyon. He was relentless throughout his life in demanding that the world treat him as a normal human being, not a pathetic anomaly of nature. One can only imagine how his life and notoriety would have expanded had he lived during the time of social media.

Sadly, Jonathan passed away on April 3, 2001, a couple of months shy of his thirty-sixth birthday. No doubt his love of life extended his lifespan well beyond the accustomed length of someone with an acute case of OI. In celebration of his life, I was privileged to officiate at his memorial service in a place he truly loved, the Chico State University Stadium, home of the Wildcats. Years later, his ashes were scattered by Arrowhead Stadium in Kansas City and in Bidwell Park in his adopted hometown of Chico, California.

Alden Studebaker

Introduction

Most people write their autobiographies after they've accomplished a spectacular feat that nets them some notoriety. Others write their memoires in the twilight of life. They've amassed a series of successes that compel them to articulate the who, what, where, when, why, and how they did it.

This is one perspective.

It is not often that you will find a book written by someone who is currently receiving government assistance at a time in his life where he should be working at a full-time job, just like the rest of us. To write a book and stop and smell the roses at age thirty would probably rank right up there with being a couch potato and watching eight hours of daytime T.V. talk shows while snacking on chips and salsa. Hard working people scoff at others' laziness.

This is another perspective.

As I finished this book, I realized that the time I spent writing became a full-time job. For the most part, it was a labor of love. I mean, I didn't have any cash advances sitting in my mailbox. There was no one at my door with big book deals and contracts ready to sign.

While it may not be spectacular writing a book, no matter what it is, it is an accomplishment. It is a sight to behold.

Alright, so I have written a book that was a labor of love and an accomplishment. So what?

Well, I have a story to share.

This story is not intended to make you cry, rather, it is supposed to make you feel—something.

This is not a purely inspirational story. Yet, if this book inspires you, great!!

I hope that after reading this story, you will take a few minutes to stop and smell the roses and take stock in your own life.

*Who Am I? And Why Am I Here?** in part chronicles the first thirty years of my life. It takes you through, in great detail, the peaks that became valleys as well as the valleys that would become peaks.

Moreover, this book discusses topical as well as unfamiliar issues that bring with it a unique perspective.

How does having a disability affect my views on abortion, healthcare, and euthanasia?

How much, if any, does my disability affect my own identity?

How am I different from others? In what ways am I not different from other people?

Are my hopes and dreams the same as anyone else's?

Do politics and religion play a role in my life? Or, am I so occupied with questions like who is going to help me in the bathtub? Or, what are you going to do the next time your wheelchair breaks down?

While there are no right or wrong answers, these questions, along with a few others, are discussed in this book.

Really though, *Who Am I? And Why Am I Here,** is an extension of me that often times I don't get a chance to reveal to others. While it was difficult to write at times, overall, it was a very enjoyable experience.

Whether you are a parent of a disabled child, educator, policy-maker, disabled person, or just you, reading this book will provide you with a unique perspective about living with a disability as well as osteogenesis imperfecta.

Enjoy.

*Jonathan's original title of the book, renamed, *Not Just Any Bag of Bones.*

There Are Places I Remember

An automobile would be the best way I could describe my family in terms of our relationships with one another. Coming from a Studebaker, you may think it's funny, but it's true.

From my perspective, my parents are basically the guts of the car itself. Each of us children represent a wheel that when put together, make it go.

Though the car still runs today with all of us well into adulthood, it goes in different directions and at different speeds, depending on what wheel you're looking at. We're all trying to carve out our own niches, all the while holding on to the values that our parents taught us as children.

To look at the same car from my parent's perspective, I would see a vastly different picture. It definitely wouldn't be a car. In fact, it may just be one wheel. A wooden wheel likened to the old Studebaker wagon that sat outside my cousins' house in Indianapolis.

In this wheel, my parents are at the center, or hub, and each of us is a spoke that is connected to the rim of the wheel that the tire sits on. This wheel has put on a lot of miles and weathered some treacherous roads along the way. It may have broken once or twice, only to be put back together.

Perhaps I am a bit selfish when I choose not to spend a holiday with the family at the designated location. After all, this wheel is turning alright.

When I get the phone call wishing me a Merry Christmas, or Happy Easter, I am reminded of the closeness of our family. I am reminded of the love, joy, faith, and inner strength that kept us together. I am reminded of that wooden wheel.

The story of my family took a series of dramatic twists and turns from the moment I was born.

At the time, my father Alden Henry and his wife Cynthia had been married almost ten years and had three children, Alden Jr., Becky, and Amy. My mother's family had moved to the town of Dune Acres from Hammond, Indiana in 1950. My Grandpa Elster worked for Lever Brothers as a buyer of fats and oils while Grandma Elster was a school teacher.

They lived in a house nestled amongst the sand dunes along the shore of Lake Michigan in northern Indiana. Dune Acres was not only my father's childhood home, it was the town where his father, Alden Koch Studebaker, had built many of the older houses including my father's boyhood home at 32 Crest Drive. The brown, 1920's style bungalow was occupied by my manic depressive grandmother who was still grieving over the loss of my grandfather. He had committed suicide almost ten years earlier.

Despite this tragedy, my father was on the road to writing his own success story about how a depression-era baby, that served his country during two wars, was living out the American Dream deep in the heart of Middle America.

My father was moving up the corporate ladder at Standard Oil and was poised to become a corporate exec. If all things had gone according to plan, at this moment he'd be sitting on a boat fishing on Lake Michigan. He likes fishing.

Along with his job at Standard Oil, my father was the clerk treasurer for the town of Dune Acres, thus carrying on the family's legacy. Though by definition, he doesn't consider himself a politician, my father is civic minded.

Some people might have thought I was a premature baby. In fact, I was late. My mother endured a lot of pain upon my entrance into this world, and those in the delivery room weren't exactly sure what to do with this "bag of bones."

It took the doctors about half an hour to diagnose that I had osteogenesis imperfecta, a genetic disease caused by a lack of collagen in the bones. They had to look it up in one of those medical dictionaries. I was born with several fractures, including those that had healed while I was still in the womb. I also had some paralysis on one side.

The doctors gave me a week to live. After that week passed, came another, and then, another. With each passing day, I was defying the experts.

While I was busy working on being a medical miracle, my parents soon discovered that modern medicine came with a huge price tag. My father's substantial health insurance policy from Standard Oil ran dry and my family was left with few options.

It was at this point where my father had to abandon his plans of spending the rest of his life in Middle America. We began a journey that would take us from place to place, with several stops in between.

When my father told my Grandma Elster we were moving to Hawaii, the land of warm sun and gorgeous women, she was horrified.

"Len, they're leaving!" she cried in between belts of whiskey.

Grandma Elster got over it though and they even made a trip out to the islands to visit us.

We spent most of our ten-year stay in the Aloha State living in the Aina Haina neighborhood of Honolulu. Our home was a one story, flat roofed, concrete block house that sat on a quarter acre lot. It had five bedrooms, a large dining room with an adjoining family room, a kitchen with a breakfast nook, and a huge living room.

Next to the two-car carport was a grove of banana trees. We were never short on bananas.

In the front yard stood two tall coconut palm trees. Near the street was a mock orange hedge. Our dog, Ilio, spent most of his time chasing birds and husking coconuts.

We'd come home from school and I'd try to throw coconut husks for him. Since the coconuts were normally too big for me to throw, the other members of the family took up the task.

When Ilio was through ripping off the husks, he'd try to crack open the coconut with his teeth.

The front yard was his domain.

Ilio, or "dog" in Hawaiian, was an 85-pound German Shepherd who was around for most of my childhood. When Ilio first came into our family, he was a very well-behaved dog, almost too well behaved. He did almost everything you told him to do, and had almost no personality. His previous owner took him on a lot of business trips where Ilio was taught some pretty hefty manners.

As Ilio got used to a change in atmosphere, he became another member of the family.

While living in Hawaii, I used to watch him chase the birds in the front yard and play with the toads around our swimming pool in the back yard.

One thing about Ilio that you could count on was that he was a protector. He ruled the house and the entire neighborhood. Every dog and human knew it.

Once when my father came to check on me, Ilio growled at him. I could see the whites of his fangs so clearly in the dark. My father had to tell Ilio who he was, or the dog was going to sink those pearly whites into his flesh and have a late night snack.

Ilio also put all the other dogs on notice that he was king of the neighborhood.

While out on his late night walks with my father, he got into scraps with every dog on Nenue Street. Ilio always won.

Along the side yard we had lime trees and a lone avocado tree. There may have been a papaya tree tucked away somewhere as well.

The enclosed backyard came complete with a swimming pool. Amy had a playhouse and we even housed some pet mice. A lot of things went on in the backyard. We had countless pool parties. Mom went swimming almost every day. I took baths outside using a bar of soap and the hose. In Hawaii, they were called Nanakuli baths, named after the town of the same name. Even my father took Nanakuli baths.

My favorite thing we did in the back yard was when my father, Ilio, and I used to play with the "buffos," or toads, just after the sun went down. That was good sport.

My father's first job was working for one of his old buddies from Dune Acres, Roland Force, the Director of the Bishop Museum. He was the Assistant to the Director for Operations, or the number two man, and was responsible for keeping the books and making sure things ran smoothly.

Growing up, I was probably closest to my sister Amy. She and I played a lot together, both after school and on weekends. Even when I was in the hospital, she used to come by almost every day.

We used to play house where of course, she was the mother. She used to dress me up in funky outfits. I didn't mind. I mean, how could I? I was her baby brother and it wasn't like I could get up and run, or beat her up. We used to set up "tents" with blankets and umbrellas in the front yard, or play in her playhouse.

We played school together where she was the teacher and I was the student. I think my parents liked this especially because unlike going to school, they thought I was actually learning a thing or two.

One of our favorite things we used to do was go to the Aina Haina Shopping Center and raid both the candy and grocery stores, sometimes on the same trip. We'd buy Icee's, Pixie Stix, and candy bars to satisfy our sweet tooths. Then, we'd get little smokie link sausages, Cheeze Whiz in a bottle, and crackers to satisfy our other cravings. We always ate it there. Sometimes, it was a little tough leaving a half empty plate at dinner. I don't know why.

Aina Haina was a nice area with many single family houses. Our neighborhood had families with lots of children. There was always a group of us playing outside.

Though I did go out and play with all the neighborhood kids, my fondest times were the visits I would make to the St. Sure's house just across the street.

The St. Sure's were Cissy and Katherine St. Sure, both sisters, who were married to twin brothers, George and Robert. They had grand children who were just a bit younger than me.

I used to go over to their house and have a blast talking with Cissy and Kakie.

That's what everyone called her. They were from Alabama and loved to talk about the Crimson Tide football team and their coach, Paul "Bear" Bryant. Like everyone who followed the career of the man with the houndstooth hat, they spoke highly of him.

I also used to play Chinese checkers and paper football with their sons, Buff and Bill. They were quite a bit older than me, but age didn't seem to matter.

The St. Sure's were a lot like the rest of our neighbors on Nenue Street. They were generous people who treated you like family.

On rare occasions, they would make lunch for me to take to school. They made the lunches for all of their grandchildren and once in a while they would surprise me with a lunchbox big enough to feed an army division. It would take me at least two days to polish off one of their lunches.

I haven't been to Hawaii since we left in 1976. Growing up on an island with warm sun and tropical rains, I probably took this majestic beauty for granted. It wasn't until we were about to leave Hawaii that I began to appreciate the things that made the islands so special.

I learned a lot about the Hawaiian culture and its history. We used to sing Hawaiian songs in school and study the language. I tried to play the ukulele but wasn't very good at it. The culture of the islands, which includes those of other countries, is something to behold and appreciate.

How can you not talk about Hawaii without mentioning the food? There is nothing like the taste of kalua pig, laulau, poi, lomi-lomi salmon, haupia, fresh fruit, and your favorite beverage while listening to Hawaiian music. You haven't been to a luau unless you go to one in Hawaii.

One of my favorite things we used to do when we lived in the islands was going to Hawaii Islanders games at Honolulu Stadium. The "Termite Palace," as we affectionately called it, was the home of the Pacific Coast League baseball club before they moved to Aloha Stadium. Today, both the Islanders and Honolulu Stadium are gone.

My mother got me a booster club pass and I went to several games and sat in my wheelchair on the other side of the right field fence. The rest of the family was perched in their usual spot, just behind me in the wooden bleachers. Mom went to practically all of the games. She was a die-hard Islanders fan in those days.

There was something romantic about the stadium which is now but a memory.

From where I was sitting, I could push my wheelchair to the bullpen and talk to the players. There was no problem getting autographs. Sitting so close to the action, you could talk to the outfielders, and sometimes they'd talk back.

I'll never forget the time during a game, a Phoenix Giants outfielder went to make a play on a fly ball that was heading toward the fence. Going all out for the ball, he slammed right into the fence. There was no padding in those days. The guy ended up in a heap, lying still for several moments.

"Is he going to be alright?" I asked a player.

A crowd of players and team personnel went to work on him.

"Yeah, he'll be alright," the player responded.

In 1972, my father left the Bishop Museum and opened his own business consulting firm. The business never really flourished and subsequently led to our family's biggest challenge since my birth. He recalls it being the most economically devastating decision he ever made.

As Alden was getting ready to graduate from high school, my father had money tied up in a financial deal to put a movie studio in Hawaii. The deal went sour and left him with a lawsuit from one of the investors who had put money into the project.

My father felt responsible for what happened even though he wasn't the one who caused the deal to falter. He was dealing with some shady Hollywood types and the Samoan Mafia.

In 1976, my father started to fall apart. Rather than just blowing off what happened with the movie deal, he attached his identity to it and it started to eat away at him. He got behind on our house payments and a realtor offered to sell the house. After paying off the mortgage, it left us with about twenty-thousand dollars. We moved into another house in Lower Manoa near the University of Hawaii where we lived for about six months.

My father continued his downward slide by lying around a lot. He was afraid to show his face downtown because he was sure that everyone would see what a failure he had become.

At this time, Alden started to emerge as the de-facto captain of the team. He became my father's counselor and gave him countless pep talks. While giving him moral support for the most part, Alden chided my father for doing stupid things like missing payments on a storage unit. A lot of our family's mementos, including my brother's high school yearbooks were thrown away.

In the summer of that year, Alden and my father took a trip to the West Coast to find a new place for the family to live. When they came back, it was decided that we were moving to Spokane, Washington. The movers tagged our belongings for the Pacific Northwest.

Then, one night we had some church friends over to the house. They were also contemplating a move to the mainland. After some discussion, it was decided that we were either going to move to San Diego, or San Francisco.

So, what happened next?

Well, it came down to heads, or tails. As three coins went up and came down, tails won over heads and we decided to move to the San Francisco Bay Area.

After playing heads or tails, we moved to a sort of pin the tail on the donkey to decide exactly where we were going to live. The Rand McNally Atlas was brought out and opened to the Bay Area map. Someone took a pencil, closed their eyes, and dropped it on the map. A mark was left in the bay off Coyote Point in San Mateo. We told the movers to send our things to the Bay Area and not Washington State.

We rented a house in the southern part of San Mateo, because that's where all the good schools were according to the test scores at the county education office. It also had a nice view of the bay which made my mother happy. She loves water.

Everyone had their own bedroom in this house. Well, sort of. I had my own bedroom which happened to be a linen closet. It was alright. I mean, I wasn't in it very much because I spent a lot of time at Shriners Hospital during those days.

My father was continuing his downward slide and Alden was busy trying to keep the family afloat. He got a job as a janitor/dishwasher at a nearby restaurant. It didn't pay a lot but it was a steady job. Foodwise, it was great. He would bring home ribs, steaks, potatoes, veggies, anything that was edible for us to eat. This helped to cut down on our grocery bills.

Alden spent many nights counseling my father. I remember them very well because my mother always sent me to another room so they could talk.

"I have to make two-thousand a month or it's not worth working," my father would say to him. Alden thought that any money he brought home would be great.

The money from the sale of our house eventually dried up. Alden was barely making enough money to pay the rent on the house. We were borrowing money from friends and relatives just to survive. One time, an anonymous cashier's check arrived in the mail for two hundred dollars.

Life went on like this for about a year. My mother was strong, but would break down in Alden's presence. On one occasion she saw a garden hose in the back of my father's Chevy station wagon and panicked. He thought about killing himself like his father did back in '55.

Fortunately, he didn't.

With my father unable to find a job in the "Golden State," we started looking at other options. It should be pointed out that California was having its share of problems as well. The state's unemployment rate was one of the highest in the nation, and it was hard enough for anyone to find a job, much less my father.

In the late fall of 1977, our family split up. Alden moved to Santa Cruz and went to college, while Becky moved north to Seattle. My mother, father, and Amy moved to the Midwest and lived with my cousins in Indianapolis. Uncle Art and Aunt Jan had three daughters, Lisa, Gayle, and Heidi.

My father worked for my Aunt Jan's mother fixing all of her rental houses. Most of them were in the seedy parts of town. He made three bucks an hour.

Amy, my father, and Ilio went by truck across the country while my mother and I followed shortly after by Greyhound bus. It was a fun trip.

It wouldn't surprise me if I said I was the only one excited about the move.

I mean, my father certainly hadn't envisioned this line of work at age fifty. He should have been approaching the back nine of his career as a top level executive solving complex engineering problems, not wading through sludge fixing broken sewer pipes.

Amy had to leave all of her friends in the Bay Area, and, my mother had to trade in her bay view for cold temperatures and snow.

Snow? What's that? Since I hadn't seen the stuff since I was born, I had only known it through pictures. I was finally going to see it for real.

I was looking forward to the change in scenery and a household where I wasn't the youngest. I was a year older than Heidi.

The cookie cutter red brick ranch house in the community known as Devonshire was in an up-scale part of town. My Aunt Jan was the matriarch of the family. She gave the orders in that household. Sitting in her chair in the living room with a cigarette in one hand and a coffee cup at arm's reach, I can recall her ordering my uncle around like a drill sergeant. Though her voice was quiet, it was perfectly audible to him. He followed every order on command.

I couldn't help but feel bad for him. For starters, here was a guy who, as I got to know him, was a gentle man who would do just about anything for you without hearing a please or thank you. When my father was out of town, he took care of me like I was his own son.

On top of that, he was married to a woman who would likely finish a close second to Elvis when it came to taking mind altering drugs. I used to watch her arrange her pills for the month, all of them in a tray with compartments for each day. It didn't take this twelve year old very long to figure out that my aunt was not an ordinary person. She was a walking pharmacy.

Once again, I found my sleeping quarters to be another linen closet. As far as linen closets go, it wasn't too bad. It was in a hallway where almost all the action took place.

To one side were Heidi's room and the bathroom. Next to Heidi's room, on one corner of the house, was the master bedroom. Not far to the other side, were two more bedrooms. Amy went back and forth staying in both Lisa's and Gayle's rooms. My parents and Ilio stayed in a room down in the basement.

Alright, so it's not really exciting to have everyone walk past your room on their way to the bathroom. And even though I could hear Tom Snyder late at night on my aunt's television, it wasn't loud enough for me to listen.

But when Uncle Art threw out one of my cousin's suitors on a Saturday night after he had climbed in through a window, I heard everything.

"Lisa! Lisa!" my aunt cried out. Her voice rang with a hysterical shrill. I cracked the door open just a little more so I wouldn't miss anything.

"Mom, I was just giving him a haircut," Lisa replied.

Meanwhile, my uncle ushered out the unwanted visitor and the melee continued until I fell asleep.

On our way to church the next morning, I gave my family a complete report.

We hadn't been in the Midwest two months and already I could see the seasons changing right before my eyes. The leaves actually fell off the trees and it was cold outside. It wasn't long before I came face to face with the white stuff.

Christmas was quickly upon us and my cousins boarded a Winnebago and were off to Florida for the holidays.

Holidays are important to my family, especially Christmas. With our family still reeling from economic peril, my parents sounded the call, "don't expect very much this year."

My enthusiasm was tempered—if only for a moment. As the days drew closer, those words were replaced with thoughts of Santa coming through in the clutch. Despite the time when Amy let the cat out of the bag, I still believed in the guy in the red suit.

How could anyone not believe in St. Nick?

We didn't have much in the way of material things, and with Alden and Becky on the West Coast, we were apart for the first time. But our family traditions continued.

We went to a candlelight service and made Christmas cookies. My parents made sure that the Christmas spirit was alive and well.

As far as Christmases go, this one ranks at the top of the charts. Santa came through with a fire hat that had a huge red flashing light and a microphone that could reach any part of the house, a pinball game that resembled a baseball diamond, and the ever popular "Happy Days" board game.

We had our traditional Christmas nut roll for breakfast and we ate a turkey dinner in the elegance of my cousin's dining room.

There was a little snow on the ground during the holidays. However, it was nothing compared to the Blizzard of '78. I wanted snow, and I got it. The blizzard was so bad that we had to stay home from school for several days. It was great. Heidi and I kept ourselves busy playing board games. She'd win most of the time, only because she cheated.

Our family split apart again when my mother and Amy left for the warmer climate of Santa Barbara. I had always thought that the reason they left was because my mother hated the weather in Indianapolis. My parents weren't having any personal problems that I knew of, so I ruled that out.

Eighteen years later, I found out that my father had a line on a job at UC Santa Barbara. Moreover, the way he explained it, it was in the bag. So, it would appear that they were just getting a head start on the move back to California. As it turned out, the plan went belly-up and he didn't get the job.

So, the family remained separated and my father continued his work as a handyman and his search for a real job. It was at this time that we started to grow closer to each other.

It was in the spring that my father hit pay dirt. He was hired to be the Director of Plant Operations for Mercy Hospital in Benton Harbor, Michigan. Until he could get the family back together, he lived at my Grandma Studebaker's house during the week and came down to Indianapolis to be with me on the weekends. He figured he could do this until I got out of school.

It was during this time that I had to learn to do a lot of things by myself. Except for Uncle Art helping with getting a bath and having my clothes washed, I was the captain of my own ship. I even got to choose my own bed time. I enjoyed this new found independence.

I had about a month left of school when Aunt Jan dropped the Big One. She told my uncle to kick us out. Right after my thirteenth birthday party, we had to be out of their house. Moreover, she said that if he didn't, she'd kick all of us out—including him!

My father was forced to put me in a foster home where he paid fifty dollars a day to have someone take care of me. I told him that living at the Chamber's house was like staying at a hotel. During my ten day stay, they treated me like royalty.

The financial burden of having me in a foster home, keeping my mother and Amy afloat on the West Coast, plus taking care of himself, was taking its toll on my father. The money wasn't coming in fast enough.

My father arranged to have me pulled out of school with two weeks left in the semester. I went up to Dune Acres to live with Grandma Studebaker during the week, and we drove down to Naptown and stayed at one of my uncle's rental houses on 32nd Street.

The house on 32nd Street was in a mostly black neighborhood that was riddled with crime. People often used violent means to settle their differences, and there were times where my uncle had to clean up bloody messes in these houses.

As we laid on our mattresses before going to sleep, I remember my father telling me true stories about people getting stabbed, or having their house burned down in order to settle a score. He would tell of how someone would break into a house with a can of gasoline and go from room to room carefully marking a trail that went throughout the house. The trail would go outside and around the house until a match was struck. Then, poof! The small spark would turn into a fiery inferno in a matter of minutes. Hearing those stories made getting to sleep extremely difficult.

Vacation Bible school and summer camp were the summer activities that took up most of the first part of that summer. My father was rounding up the rest of the clan for the move back to the Midwest. Alden and Becky would join Amy and my mother and thus, we would be reunited.

We planted our digs in Stevensville, Michigan, a community of about four thousand people.

Amy and I went to public school and Becky went to the local community college. Alden lived about an hour from us in Kalamazoo and attended Western Michigan University.

Of all the places I lived while growing up, Stevensville was by far my favorite. I always tell people that if I had a chance to do it all over again, I wouldn't have left to come back to the West Coast.

I was probably foolish to think that I was going to be here longer than two years, but I did. I thought I was going to at least finish high school and graduate as a Lakeshore Lancer. I loved the high school experience where football games brought everyone in the town together. I liked going to the after-game dances and being involved in club activities. I was a member of both the German Club and Key Club. The Key Club gave me my first exposure to community service and doing things to help others.

I also liked going to the same school as my sister Amy. For one year, we shared some of the same teachers. I also didn't pass up the chance to be a typical little brother who occasionally drove her crazy.

Since our lockers were three doors down from each other, I had a pretty good surveillance on all the guys that said hello to her in the hallway. Don't kid yourself, I took copious notes.

On those occasions when Amy wanted me to keep a secret, like the times she used to pilfer peppermint schnapps to take to the football games, I had leverage to get almost anything I wanted. Did I take bribes from my sister? Of course I did. She was a good negotiator.

Living in a small town, it doesn't take you very long to make friends. One person who I got to be good friends with was Andy Wooley. He's the only person who could get away with calling me "shorty."

Andy was a year behind me in school. We first became friends during study hall. I introduced him to my hobby of creating sports leagues and the friendship just clicked.

Whether it be football or baseball, we spent hours as "co-commissioners" running our leagues. By the way, we also talked about girls.

I'll never forget the time Andy's family took me to Comiskey Park (the old Comiskey) to see a White Sox game. The weather was freezing cold but we made the trip to Chicago.

When we got there, it was raining and the wind was causing the temperature to drop. We watched a few innings before heading home. Normally, I would have put up a fight to see the entire game against the Rangers. We had stuck it out a pretty long time and as it turned out, we ended up watching the rest of the game at his house.

Having friends like Andy sort of embody the character of the area. Though his parents were rather stringent in his upbringing, they were very gracious people. It is this graciousness that made it very difficult for me to accept leaving the area.

Even though I was happy for him personally, I was heartbroken when I was told that my father had gotten a job with the Department of the Navy back in our old stomping grounds, the Bay Area. In my mind this move was going to be like leaving heaven for purgatory.

Our family split up again on our move back to the Bay Area. Becky went to UC Santa Barbara and later moved to Los Angeles. Alden stayed in the Midwest and went to ministerial school.

We returned to San Mateo and later moved to Belmont for my senior year of high school. After spending time away from the nest, Amy returned home and finished school at San Francisco State. Yeah, she graduated as a Gator.

The one overriding negative about living in the Bay Area was that every time I wanted to go anywhere, I had to use a car. That's not to say that I didn't have to do that when we lived in Michigan, but there's a difference between a five minute drive and a thirty or forty-minute one.

On top of that, I didn't live in the same neighborhood in which I went to school. So, I was a bit less mobile and it wasn't as easy to do things with my friends. Then, having to take a long bus ride to school with all the special ed kids every day didn't give me a sense of belonging to something special like I did when I went to Lakeshore. I felt like I was being forced into my own peer group.

Throughout much of the first two years of our stint in the Bay Area, I felt disconnected from my parents.

First, I spent a lot of time in the hospital due to a fall, rodding of my leg, and a spinal fusion that took two operations. I was away from home a lot.

With my grades taking a huge nose dive during my junior year, I spent some time in the dog house. That wasn't much fun for a guy who was experiencing his "terrible teens."

Distance became a factor when I wanted to do the fun things you do in high school. My father worked a lot trying to defend our country from the evil Soviet empire, and my mother didn't drive—period. I spent a lot of weekends at home watching television.

The summer of 1982 started with a big lecture from my parents about my grades. They came down on me pretty hard and it's just as well, I deserved it.

Soon after, we had to put Ilio to sleep. His mind and heart wanted him to live, but his legs wouldn't support his body. We threw a birthday party for him and he sang right along with us. I saw my father cry for the first time when he put Ilio in the car for his ride into the sunset. My parents did not get a replacement. How could you?

Also that summer, I had a part-time job doing clerical work at a family practice clinic. The doctor saw a lot of poor people; some of them were Hispanic and didn't speak much English. It was an eye-opening experience being on the other side.

It seemed as if things were starting to turn for better in terms of getting something meaningful out of my high school experience.

Along with school, I had a part-time job as a sportswriter for a weekly paper, the Millbrae Sun. I had to cover two high schools, my high school and our rivals Capuchino. In addition to game stories and features, I had to write an occasional news story.

Like many reporters, there are stories that you prefer to write over others. For example, I preferred to write football, baseball, and basketball stories. Minor sports, like track and soccer, didn't excite me.

When it came time to write a story about Leslie Maxie, a stand-out track athlete at my high school, I didn't exactly put forth my best effort. When I came into the office after the story came out, my boss let me have it.

"Now this is probably the most important thing you are ever going to hear. This is more important than what any journalism class is going to teach you," he said.

He spent an hour and a half picking my story apart, word by word. He impressed upon me the fact that I can't do a half-ass job on a story just because it's about a subject that doesn't interest me. I heeded his advice. It was a great learning experience.

My position at the paper was funded through the Youth Employment Program. When the money for my job ran out at the end of the year, the paper hired me on for the rest of the summer. I think they liked my work.

During basketball season, I did the announcing for all of our home games. It was fun to be behind the microphone, especially when you have a good team.

As promised, my grades did go up my senior year. I think it was in part because I got my act together and my classes were a lot of fun, especially economics and government. Our teacher, Mr. Phillips, a tall man with brown hair and horn-rimmed glasses, was pretty creative with his lesson material which made learning a lot easier. For example, for our government class, we had a mock legislature where we researched, wrote, and tried to pass bills. I was the majority whip and had to make sure everyone was in line when it came time to vote. It sure beat having to sit in class for an hour and take notes.

It seemed as if my last year at Mills went by so fast and I was having so much fun that I wanted to do it all over again—well, almost. It was good to finally get to know a group of friends. I only wish I had done it three years ago. I mean, it wasn't as if I didn't know them. It's just that there's this huge block of time that seems to have escaped me. I wish I could have it back.

My parents bent over backwards to make sure that it was a memorable year. My father drove me to parties and school functions. He drove me to work and took me to all of the football and basketball games I had to cover for the paper. I remember when he acted as another set of eyes in our game against our arch-rival, Capuchino. While we sat in a driving rain storm, he told me what was going on as I took copious notes. He was a trooper.

My grades were good enough to be accepted at Chico State University. It was time for me to enter the real world. Now, I had to take the values that my parents taught me and apply them to the life experiences that awaited me.

As I continued to grow and evolve as adult, our family kept growing and growing. Alden and Amy were having kids and Becky got married as well. Mom and Dad moved to Ventura to be closer to the grandkids. My ties to the Bay Area were severed.

The wheels that had turned the car for so long were going in a different direction. The relationships I had with my brother and sisters were changing. Then, in 1990, we had an unexpected addition to the family.

In the fall of 1990, Alden made an unexpected trip up to Chico to visit me. It was nice to see him, yet I wondered why he was coming. I told Cam about it and he said that Alden wouldn't be making the trip if he didn't have a reason. I didn't think he wanted to go to a Chico State football game.

While sitting down in front of a plate of appetizers and drinks, Alden showed me a picture.

"Can you tell me who's in that photo?" he asked.

"Yeah, it's you, Dad, and some lady."

"Do you know who that lady is?"

"Nope, never seen her before."

"That lady is our half-sister. Her name is Bonnie."

I took a closer look at the picture. I was taken aback and didn't know what to think.

Alden had known about Bonnie longer than the rest of us—except for my mother.

My father had told the rest of the family about it a few months earlier at a family get-together. I wasn't there when he broke the news.

As the story goes, about five years before my mother and father met, he had a tryst with a local woman who was about five years older than my father. One thing led to another and thus, Bonnie came into this world.

My father told my mother about it and said that Bonnie's mother wanted to raise her on her own. My parents went on with their lives and it evolved into this deep dark secret.

Alden asked me to keep things quiet, you know, within the immediate family. He said that my uncle knew her mother as well. This piqued my curiosity level just a bit.

In talking to Mom about this, I asked her how we knew Bonnie was my half-sister.

"Well, she looks like your father," she answered.

"So."

"Well, she's smart like your father."

I didn't press the issue any further.

In the beginning, there was no real pressure to circle the wagons and welcome our new addition in the family. The thought was that it might take a little time for us to make our initial contact and I agreed with that. In fact, it wasn't long before I called Bonnie on the phone to introduce myself. I figured there was nothing wrong with having a new friend.

Meanwhile, after everyone had made their introductions, it appeared to me that the welcome wagon was moving into overdrive. It was definitely too fast for me and the pressure was making me feel a bit resentful.

For a long time, I started keeping score. That didn't do me a lot of good.

A couple of years ago, Bonnie came to visit me. She was all by herself. We got to spend some real quality time together and I was able to tell her some things. She did as well.

I told her that only time and effort on both of our parts would bring us closer together. No one else could do it. She agreed.

One thing I could not agree with was her assertion that she is the oldest sibling. Alden told me this once, too. This is where I draw the line.

With all the things my family went through just since I was born, there comes a point where time and experiences take precedence over the fact that she was born first. I mean, if we had known her when we were growing up, I might be more willing to accept this notion.

However, there was a long period of time when she wasn't around to share in those experiences, both good and not so good.

Was it her fault?

No, it wasn't. If you were to ask me who was there when the chips were down, my brother was steering the ship at some of our most critical moments. He was the eldest of the four of us, and that's what it will always be to me.

Bonnie has added a lot to our family. She's sort of like a missing spice in a gourmet dish. She's got a big heart. She's quiet, yet not afraid to speak her mind. And she's smart, just like our father.

While I spent much of my childhood being closest with Amy, I have since felt closest to Becky. We stay in touch with each other a lot and she comes up to visit me in Chico on occasion.

When we talk on the phone, much of our conversation is about politics. She is probably the most liberal member of the family and she makes no apologies about it. I wouldn't call her a radical though.

If there are two qualities that I admire about her are, she cares about others, and she has a keen sense of identifying the good things about a person that will motivate them.

For example, at a point where I was feeling kind of low, I asked her the ever popular, "Why am I here?" question.

"I think you were put here to educate others," she said.

"But how?" I wondered.

"By just being yourself and doing what you are doing."

To see the two pictures, the one wheel that my parents see and the car with now five wheels, I can appreciate and begin to understand how the two are alike, and how they are different. My parents have pretty much allowed us to be ourselves and do whatever makes us happy. Each of us has gone in our own direction, charting our own course.

Still, whether it is in a phone conversation, or a family gathering, I am reminded of that wooden wheel where they are at the hub, or center. We are the spokes connected together by the rim which represents the experiences we have, and will continue to share.

What Do You Like To Be Called?

In speaking to students about people with disabilities, I know exactly what they want me to talk about. Sure, they want to know how I get dressed in the morning and how I use the bathroom. They want to know how a guy like me can play baseball or any other sport. They ask me if I sleep in my wheelchair. They also want to know what it's like when other people stare at me.

"What do you do when someone looks at you funny?" a student cautiously asked me.

"I stare back at them and say, hello," I replied with a smile.

Oddly enough, this is one of the reasons why I ventured out on to the speaking circuit. On many trips to the supermarket, kids would stare at me in wonderment. A conversation would soon follow, and go something like this:

"What's your name?" the small child's voice spoke. A mother, clutching her child's hand, offered a careful smile.

"My name is Jonathan."

"Why are you so small?"

"Well, I was born like this."

After explaining to the child in the best way I know how, this and many other conversations in the store made ordinary shopping trips both interesting and time consuming. Don't get me wrong. I love talking to people, especially children. However, if you are in a rush to get home, it can make you late for those very important dates.

Seeing a need to talk to young people, I made schools one of my primary target audiences. Students in general want to know what it's like being disabled.

In the forty or so minutes that I have with each class, I do my best to answer this for them. Sometimes it is difficult to answer this given the time constraints, and the scope of this question.

The disabled population has much in common and share similar experiences of overcoming obstacles and attitudinal barriers as with other minority groups. However, there are marked differences in the way we are viewed and treated in our society. Being disabled is not the same as being African-American, Hispanic, Native American, Jewish, or any other minority.

So, what is it like being disabled? That, my friend, is a very difficult question to answer. It is a complex question likened to asking my father about boilers, or cars. You just can't give a short answer to this one.

My own answer to this question is by no means right or wrong. It only represents how I feel. Neither should it be taken as how others feel, or should feel. Only that you should understand that I feel this way.

Like I said earlier, it is important that when talking about what it is like to be disabled, that we do justice by focusing on the many aspects of having a disability. That's what makes it so complex and interesting. By looking at these aspects in greater detail, I hope you will have some idea about how I see myself as a disabled person. These views come from living a life full of interesting experiences.

Osteogenesis Imperfecta

Being born with osteogenesis imperfecta is a part of what I am, a very small part indeed. Though it stands out as a very visible part of me on the outside, I do not see it as a part of who Jonathan Studebaker is on the inside. In fact, the only words it should communicate to others are; "When picking up, HANDLE WITH CARE." That's it!

I don't mind talking about osteogenesis imperfecta. In fact, I believe in the importance of letting others know about it. Telling others what OI is, and how having it has affected my life, will hopefully heighten people's awareness to the uniqueness of my disability in particular, and the wide range of disabilities in general.

Look, just because people see me as a small guy in a wheelchair doesn't make me a dwarf or a midget. This is a common misconception by those who see me for the first time.

Osteogenesis imperfecta affects the way I can, or can't perform physical activity.

It affects the way I type, or the way I hold a pencil. It doesn't affect the thoughts or feelings I express on the printed page. It affects the way I get things off the shelf in the store, not whether I buy a comic book or a Playboy magazine. It affects the way I boil noodles, not whether I can boil noodles. It affects the way in which I make love, not whether I can make love at all.

I do not ignore my disability or deny it; I just refuse to wear it on my chest in BIG, BOLD letters. It is not a badge of courage. And while others may see it differently, I do not go so far as to recognize it as a part of who I am—literally. It just doesn't fit.

After all, it is not a part of my personality. I am not a happy, go lucky guy because I have OI.

I believe it was Popeye who said, "I yam what I yam what I yam."

Except for when I may be in pain, it has little to do with my wants, needs, or desires. Nor should we assume that it takes away from me wanting the most out of life. The last time I checked, I can still see a human being—despite what some might think.

Never did my feelings become so clear as when I was pondering a letter written to me from a hearing impaired women. In the letter she wrote:

"...We appreciate the value of motivational-educational programs for training of people with disabilities. We will also focus on disability from a socio-cultural-political-viewpoint. Part of this entails viewing disability as a positive aspect of the self, not as a condition that necessarily needs to be overcome, medically 'fixed,' or conquered. We view it as a powerful source of group and individual identity. Focusing on social and cultural factors in the handicaps faced by people with disability, we believe, will allow disabled people to identify concrete ways to achieve social change..."

These words caused me to examine the relationship of my disability to my own self.

Though there exists a relationship between the two for some people, I don't attach a whole lot of significance to the comparison. It's not that important to me.

First of all, I do not view my disability as a positive or negative aspect of myself.

Life as a person with osteogenesis imperfecta is not a picnic in the park. Nor is it a tragedy. It's a wash.

Nor do I consider it a part of my own identity. I do not want people to think of me first and foremost as the guy with osteogenesis imperfecta. That's not me either.

To further illustrate my point here, let me give you the following situation.

While at a practice for the annual East-West Shrine Game, I was making the rounds with Robert Phillips who, at the time, was the treasurer of the OI Foundation.

Bob was an Indiana University grad, as well as a big Hoosier fan. He pulled out a pocket schedule and showed me the games he had gone to see the previous season. I was into it as my mom went to IU, and my father went to Purdue University. I played up the rivalry thing a bit, and wanted to hear more about those Hoosiers.

When he finished, we made our way amongst the scouts and coaches who were gathered in bunches across each sideline watching practice and swapping stories.

As we traveled from one group to another, Bob took the liberty of introducing me to those who were assembled. Little did he know that I knew almost all the people we came upon.

"Hello, my name is Bob Phillips. This is Jonathan Studebaker. We both have osteogenesis imperfecta," Bob exclaimed. His voice rang with pride and conviction.

When I heard this, I was shocked. I had never been introduced in that manner. I dismissed what I heard the first time, and thought, "Well, maybe he's just trying to break the ice or something."

Hearing him repeating this over and over again, while meandering through each gathering, made me increasingly upset. After all, I was planning on handing a number of these people my resume hoping to land some sort of job. I didn't want to call attention to it.

I mean, think about it. Wouldn't it bother you if you were introduced in that way?

In some cases, it's just stating the obvious. What bothered me about this particular instance was the appearance that what he was saying came from both of us.

Without knowing exactly how Bob feels about having osteogenesis imperfecta, I would surmise that he sees having OI plays a more significant role in his own identity.

Perhaps his feelings run parallel with those of the woman who wrote me the letter. With his involvement in the OI Foundation, fighting for "the cause" is probably his life. I admire and respect him for that. Also, since Bob was self-ambulatory at the practices, I don't know if he had as many fractures or suffered as much pain as I have endured. Since I've had to deal with a lot of pain associated with having OI, I am less inclined to wear it on my forehead, chest, or anywhere for that matter.

I also view osteogenesis imperfecta as something that should be cured. I hope they find a cure for it—today. I hope they find cures for other diseases like cerebral palsy, muscular dystrophy, cancer, and AIDS.

While having osteogenesis imperfecta remains a very visible part of me, I want others to view it as part of the whole package, the package with the "handle with care" sign, under which lies a human being who wants to live life to the fullest.

Walking

Rarely does anyone think about the benefits of not being able to walk. As one who hasn't taken a step without the assistance of leg braces and crutches since I was fifteen, I think about it from time to time. Primarily, I do it to amuse myself. When I am in line, sitting in my wheelchair at the grocery store, I think about how tired all those people who are standing must be feeling at that very moment. Oh, their aching feet! Time to put them in hot water and give 'em a good soaking.

While I try to make light of many things, I'm not going to pull the wool over your eyes by saying that not being able to walk is not a big deal. Sure, I would love to be able to walk, but, since I don't really know what it is like to walk, I don't know what I'm missing. So, I'll talk about the closest experience I've had to walking.

Along with the many surgeries I've had to endure, the numerous casts that were put on my body, another part of my course of treatment involved wearing braces. These aren't the ones you wear on your teeth.

Wearing braces was not fun.

First of all, I had to wake up as much as an hour early in the morning to put them on. Once I was awake and in gear, I started this process by putting on, in addition to my other clothes, an undershirt and long stockinettes. These special socks covered all of my legs.

The next step was to get into my braces. In doing this, I started by making sure the tongues of both shoes were open wide enough to fit my feet. Both shoes had metal sidings attached along both legs that went up into a corset that went around my waist.

Then, I unbuckled and opened the two sets of straps that would secure my legs, above and below each knee. Once those were unfastened, I opened the straps to the corset and fit my body into this contraption.

Sitting in bed with my braces undone, I began methodically tying the laces of my leather shoes. When I was a wee tike, they were white, but as I got older, I graduated to brown.

After my shoes were tied, I fastened the straps along both legs and up to my corset.

Back in the early days, I had to lace them up as well. It wouldn't be until the last year or two before Velcro made its appearance as part of the ensemble.

The final step of my dressing routine was putting my clothes on over my braces. At times, it was very cumbersome trying to put on the elastic fitting pants. When I was allowed to pick my own clothes, I usually chose pants that had the most give in the elastic.

Every day from kindergarten through ninth grade I wore braces. I wore braces to protect my legs from getting bumped around, thus avoiding possible fractures. They also provided added support and strength to my legs when I walked, either on crutches or parallel bars during physical therapy.

For me, walking on crutches was an accomplishment. Like a child taking his first steps, or riding a bicycle without assistance, I was proud to show everyone that I could do it. Soon after, it was determined that I had neither the stamina nor speed to make walking on crutches a viable mode of getting around. It didn't bother me though. Heck, I was thrilled just doing it!

While walking on crutches was a great thrill for me, wearing braces was very painful. I understood the reasons for which I had to wear them. However, it did not compare to the joy and excitement I had when I came home from school and took them off.

Liberating my body from the fifteen pounds of metal and leather that encased my diminutive frame was like being granted freedom! It was having the ability to control my body without having to carry its outer shell. It was being able to move my legs freely without the metal locks holding them in place. It was being able to take in a full breath without having a corset pinching on either side.

Sometime during my sophomore year of high school, the day finally came when I was rid of my braces for good. Unlike those who temporarily wear braces on their teeth, I was always under the impression that my wearing braces would be something more permanent.

That is why this day was so special for me.

It is hard for me to separate walking from wearing braces. It was such a big part of my childhood. And while I talk about the few times I walked on crutches, it doesn't include walking as the primary mode of transportation used by able-bodied individuals.

Since I don't know what it's like to walk, there is a big difference between wishing for the ability to walk versus wanting to have the means to get around.

If a genie came down and asked me if I wanted to walk, I would tell the genie, "Only if I could play football." I am dead serious! I dream about walking or running on and off a football field, and that's about it. But, in order to play football, I would need to be about three feet taller and at least a hundred pounds heavier.

Not being able to get from one place to another can be very frustrating. Since my electric wheelchair serves as "my legs," I am very sensitive to the sounds that come from it as it motors down the street. I always make sure there is enough water in the batteries, and I do my best to trouble shoot those small problems before they turn into big ones.

As with any car, my chair has had its share of blowouts. They aren't much fun.

Once, I had a motor go out on me. While some car repairs can take a few days, perhaps even a week to fix, this instance left me virtually stuck in my house without "my legs" for about four weeks. And, they didn't give me a loaner either!

Using an electric wheelchair is not a measure of convenience, it is a necessity. Not having "my legs" left me with having to depend on others to do things for me. I also found myself dwelling on what I would do if I had my electric wheelchair.

Lately, I have often felt that having your wheelchair break down is worse than being sick. For instance, as with a cold or the flu, I usually heal myself by using the usual remedies. If I don't get better quickly, I go to the doctor. Basically, I have most of the control in the healing process. When my wheelchair breaks down, I relinquish this control and sometimes have to rely on others to do things for me.

Not having the mobility to get around makes ordinary things harder to do. It makes the difficult things almost impossible. It's like putting your life on hold. That is how important my chair is to me.

Why did it take so long to get my wheelchair fixed? First, it sat in the repair shop as state Medi-Cal officials took two and half weeks to approve the repairs.

Remember, these are people who walk on two legs and drive cars.

Once the bureaucrats were finished, it took at least another week for the repairs.

These people can walk too.

While I was at the mercy of others waiting for "my legs" to arrive, I wondered if they gave a rip?! Do they understand? Or, do they know what I mean when I say, "these are my legs." I wonder what goes through their mind.

As with many issues that concern myself as a disabled person, walking means so many things. Having the means to get to anywhere I need to go is very important to me. I can't say that I miss something that I have never done. Yet, I still have my moments where I wish both legs could get up and run up and down the football field.

Poster Boy

In the last few years, the portrayal of the "poster child" by charitable organizations has come under fire. The controversy has gotten so much notoriety that charities have had to re-examine the way they use the "poster child" as a tool for fundraising.

This debate has in large part, been fueled by disabled adults. As children, they were the smiling faces with pitiful stories that television producers hoped would have viewers lighting up the phone lines with their pledges. Now, these people are unhappy with this depiction and feel that it's hurting the disabled community.

As both a child and young adult, I was asked to be a spokesperson for two organizations who were seeking donations to continue the work to help people with disabilities.

From 1975-76, I was the poster child for the Easter Seal Telethon in Honolulu, Hawaii. And from 1983-92, I was the Honorary Head Coach for the East-West Shrine Game, the annual fundraiser for the Shriners Hospitals for Crippled Children.

My experience as a "poster child" was a very positive one.

This ten-year old kid's pint-sized body was plastered on posters throughout the Aloha State. I did a few television commercials with Artie Johnson of television's "Laugh In."

That was a blast! I went to parties where other stars like Arthur Godfrey, Rose Marie, Richard Deacon, Jessica Walters, Bern Nadette Stanis, and Henry Winkler who were brought in to assist the locals with the telethon. I hosted an hour with Jessica Walters and we raised a pile of money. During the hour, I walked on crutches and the phones lit up like crazy.

My parents told me of the honor and responsibilities that went with being selected. They were also there to make sure that my head didn't swell up.

I wasn't forced to do anything against my will. They asked me if I wanted to walk on crutches for the cameras, and I said, "Sure, as long as my sister is there to help me out."

Throughout my childhood, Easter Seals played a significant part of my life. Because of Easter Seals, I went to pre-school where I had therapy every day. Also, no summer was complete without a week or two at Easter Seals Summer Camp, held at Camp Mokuleia. Summer camp was great!

When officials of the East-West Shrine Game came to my house and asked me to be the game's spokesperson, I was thrilled! Since the Shriners Hospitals have basically been responsible for keeping me together in one piece, while helping to shape me as a person, this is something I really wanted to do.

While I wouldn't trade these experiences for anything in the world, being under the spotlight under these circumstances has its drawbacks. In some instances, it caused others to view me in ways that could be construed as condescending and patronizing.

For example, while performing my duties in an official capacity at the

East-West Game, I seized this opportunity to make contacts with coaches in hopes of moving up the coaching ladder. Basically, I was looking for a— real job.

In telling NFL coaches and personnel directors about my experiences as an assistant coach at Chico State, the response was often cool and polite. There was little conversation going back and forth. I did most of the talking. Soon after I had finished, the conversation moved on to other subjects. While virtually everyone said that they would see what they could do, I knew most of them would toss my resume in the garbage can. Afterwards, I thought to myself, "Is this person listening to me?" What can I do or say to get through to these people? Am I just another pretty face? My views were confirmed not so much by what they said, but by what they didn't say.

Debunking the "poster child" image has been difficult to overcome when trying to get others to take me seriously, or value me as a person. This has affected everything from prospective job opportunities, to interpersonal relationships, and even normal everyday conversation.

I can see how this has the disabled community in an uproar. To be used like this in order to seek the almighty dollar has reinforced the negative stereotypes that disabled people like me, have been fighting for years. It strikes at the very root of who we are, and how we are valued in society.

Perhaps it is time that today's "poster child" undergo a face lift. Let's get rid of the sob stories, the guilt trips, and the pity. Replace these stories with positive images that will appeal to the other psyche that has yet to be seen.

If a child received an assistive device that has helped in his/her schoolwork, show it! If the child has received therapy or treatment for their disability, show it! If the organization provides activities such as summer camp, which show the child having a good time, show it! Showing what the organization does for people with disabilities is critical with getting their message across. It also places the child in a positive light doing some really good things.

Seeing Jerry Lewis cry on national TV every Labor Day is getting real old. These guilt trips have got to go! Replace them with stories of children with goals and aspirations. Ask the "poster child" in front of all those viewers what they want to be when they grow up. If they say they want to be a doctor, policeman, or President of the United States, praise that child.

Encourage that child! I tell you, something like that would make me want to go to the phone and call.

Some may think that this is an unrealistic portrayal for one reason or another.

The child could have a terminal or life threatening disease. So what? You could just as easily die in a car accident tomorrow. Should that stop you from aspiring to do great things? No. Look, whether you choose to see the glass as being half empty or half full, it can just as easily be said that life is eternal, or we all have a terminal illness.

Also, others may think that we're putting false expectations on a child. C'mon they can hardly feed themselves, much less worry about being President of the United States," they'd say. "You are creating some kind of dream world, or something."

Well, what if FDR had been a "poster child?" Would he have been elected President? Whether you have a disabled child or not, you should want your child to dream of being the best he or she can be. Telethons that feature the "poster child" should reflect this as a part of their depiction.

There is a natural urge to reach for the sob stories because it has been so successful in the past. But if there's a different way to reach people's emotions while achieving the ultimate goal, it would alleviate a lot of the conflict and tension that exists.

Being a "poster child" was a lot of fun, but as I got older I realized that there is a price for having a "pretty face."

Being Born With A Disability vs. Acquiring One

When I fractured my neck five years ago, I lost some feeling in my arms and legs. Though most of it came back over time, it caused me to think about something I had which had been lost. Ten years earlier, I lost most of the vision in my right eye. But, I hadn't really thought about it, since I had all the vision in my left eye.

There is a big difference between being born with a disability and acquiring one later in life. As I began to learn how to do things over again with this new found circumstance, I was once again thankful for what I do have. I have a sense for what others go through who may become disabled, either through illness or accident. Losing the ability to walk, see, or hear must be devastating.

Every so often someone will tell me about a friend who became disabled as a result of a car accident.

"Is there anything I can say to get 'em going again?" the voice would say. "I mean, I look at you. You've got such a great attitude."

I'm no psychologist when it comes to these things, but, when someone asks me for advice on something like this, I try to offer encouragement to them.

When it comes to having a disability, no two people are alike even when they have the same disability. For example no two cases of osteogenesis imperfecta are the same.

The way people deal with it is different as well. I deal with some things better than others.

In this particular instance, there is a time to grieve at the loss of a function. In a way, it's almost like losing a relative or a close friend. It is that traumatic. I generally have more empathy, for people who have lost the ability to perform a function, especially if it is something they do well. Please don't confuse the word empathy with pity.

After a period of time, it's time to get on with life. It's time to start living life again, even under new found circumstances. I know that it may be hard for some, but it can be done.

So, how does it happen? Well, in many respects, it is a renewal process. It is discovering new ways to do old things. It takes a long time. It requires an incredible amount of patience. Allowing your mind to receive and accept the flow of new ideas to perform the simple and complex tasks is essential.

But, most of all, it demands an inner strength that comes from the heart and is fueled by others. That inner strength can be just a flicker of hope. From there, it can grow into a small flame with the help of others. That is, don't be afraid to lean on people who offer you their encouragement. I always drew strength from people who came to see me at the hospital. Whether they were there to cheer me up, or just in to say hello, this was an important part of my rehabilitation.

An important part of the process of rehabilitation is adding activity to the day.

Even if it is going outside for fifteen minutes, or making a phone call to a friend, the process has to start somewhere. Then, add another activity, and another. As activities are added, one by one, the day is filled with things to do. Living life begins once again. It must!

The reason why I have such an upbeat attitude is because I try to occupy my time doing many different things. This way, I don't think about my disability as much.

It doesn't matter whether you are born with a disability, or become disabled later in life. It is interesting to look at the contrast in perspectives between the two. It is something that I think about from time to time.

Images

I often adhere to the saying, "I don't care what they say about me, just as long as they spell my name right." With a name like Jonathan Studebaker, the latter is sometimes overlooked. Some people have a heck of a time spelling my name.

Over the last few years, I think we have made significant progress in the way disabled people are portrayed in the mass media.

People with disabilities in television commercials, TV shows, and movies are pictured doing everyday things.

Do I think Hollywood and the TV industry are one hundred percent accurate in their characterization of people with disabilities? Hardly. But, as with a lot of things that have to do with Tinseltown, we're not talking about reality here.

Are audiences going to want to see a quadriplegic sitting in front of the television, waiting for his attendant to show up so he or she can be fed dinner? The attendant, who is an alcoholic, often times asks the disabled person for money, promising to pay it back.

Or, how about watching a group of developmentally disabled people in brown uniforms cutting hedges for twenty-five cents an hour?

People want to be entertained and put in their own fantasy world whether they are watching Forrest Gump, or Melrose Place.

Five years ago, I wrote a screenplay about a guy with OI who was searching for Miss Right. He receives a letter from a woman who turns out to be his newly hired boss at work. He works part-time for a medical supply company because the company can't afford the risks of keeping him on full-time.

After a rough start, the two fall in love. She tries to get him hired on full-time. Their relationship is threatened however, by the expectations of the two families.

His parents don't think he is good enough to go out with her. They suggest that he date the woman down the street with OI. Meanwhile, her parents think she is too good for him and try to set her up with one of her father's lawyer friends.

The response I received from those in the industry was positive, but no sale. It's not to be expected, but I thought I had done a decent piece of writing. Their criticism of the script was that it was too much like... Also, some felt that the main character, the guy with OI, should have been a private investigator or something else more riveting.

I took this criticism in stride, and their points were relevant. However, as with so many movies, storylines are copied from one movie to another. There are formulas that even the novice movie goer can point out.

The idea that the main character was not a private investigator was in itself, a point that I wanted to make. Like many disabled people, the main character had to live within the class system that government has put in place.

Showing how such a class system has affected the life of this person is a real life issue that I as a person with a disability am concerned about. Look at how Spike Lee tries to bring to the forefront issues of importance to African-Americans in his movies, like "Do the Right Thing." I mean, it's a lot like having a black man getting shot in a dark alley, or dealing drugs in the inner cities.

Television and screen have not yet let go of the candy-coated, super-crip movies. The general public still wants to see movies like Forrest Gump. But while these stories have a place, there's room for a more accurate portrayal. My script was an attempt to do just that.

The biggest angst I have with Hollywood is their use of able-bodied actors to play disabled actors. It really gets under my skin for a number of reasons.

Forgive me if I don't consider myself to be a big advocate of political correctness. But, I have a hard time watching a movie about a disabled character that is played by someone who is not disabled. It especially bothers me when the movie is based on a true story.

Did Daniel Day Lewis do a great job in portraying the main character that has cerebral palsy in "My Left Foot?" Yes, he did. How about Eric Stoltz and Wesley Snipes for their roles as accident victims in "The Waterdance?" And, what about Laura Dern, who played a blind girl in "Mask"? Sure, they did a great job. The point I'm trying to make is that we need to ask ourselves whether these movies would have been more realistic if a qualified disabled actor were featured in the starring role.

Let's, for a moment, look at this from another point of view. In the mini-series, "Roots," no one could fathom the idea of Arnold Schwarzenegger playing the role of Kunta Kinte, or Don Ameche play Chicken George, would they? Hell no! It doesn't make sense. You wouldn't have a white person playing the lead in the story about the history of an African-American family. Steven Spielberg wouldn't dream of having a disabled woman play the role of Tinkerbell in the movie, "Hook." Would he?

Some may argue that there aren't any qualified actors to play these roles. Well, what about Marlee Matlin? She won an Academy Award for best actress in "Children of a Lesser God."

Aside from Marlee Matlin being a fine actress, I believe she was able to show how her character viewed being deaf as not purely a disability, but as a part of her identity. I don't necessarily agree with it, but she did a great job.

Chris Burke, of television's "Life Goes On" was excellent in his role as Corky, a boy with Down syndrome. Burke was able to bring to life the triumphs and challenges of a person with Down syndrome—because he has it.

I salute those disabled actors and writers who are out there pounding the pavement in Hollywood. As they try in their own way to dispel the myths and break down the barriers, they have to earn money so they can eat too. Those who are qualified should have that chance.

I just hope Aaron Spelling will save an apartment for me on "Melrose Place."

Labels

Before giving a presentation at the U.S. Fish & Wildlife Service in Portland, Oregon, I was approached by a federal worker who was dressed in a cowboy hat and assorted garb.

"So tell me, what do you like to be called?" he said in a Cowboy Bob voice.

It seems that more and more these days, people are asking me this question. In fact, I had to incorporate this into one of my speeches because so many wanted to know.

So Jonathan, what do you like to be called? How do you want people to refer to you?

Is it disabled?

Are you physically challenged?

What about the term, handicapped?

Are you differently-able?

I love all of these "well-meaning," politically correct lexicons. I chuckle and wonder who has got the time to think of all these labels. That is what they are.

For your benefit, I will dissect these one by one.

I guess the term disabled seems to be one of the more popular labels. It doesn't bother me and I don't attach any negative connotation to it. Handicapped is okay as well.

I get a kick out of the terms physically challenged and differently-able. They are so funny, it makes me laugh. Despite the humor in all of this, labels are one of the many products of political correctness that I, as a disabled person, find insincere and inappropriate.

When people ask me if I am physically challenged, I usually say, "Only when I play tennis. Table tennis, that is." Differently-able is too long and an inaccurate term as well. It emphasizes the different rather than the able.

I know I haven't answered your question yet. This brings me to my next point.

When we label something, we tend to give it a finite classification that is one dimensional.

For example, if I buy a can of soda, it may be a Coke, Pepsi, Mountain Dew, or Sprite. The name on the can tells you what kind of soda you are buying. The ingredients on the label tell you what's in it. But, it doesn't tell you how good it tastes. You have to do that yourself.

The same can be said for the word disabled. Does it describe Jonathan Studebaker? Not totally. Does it say anything about me? No, not really. Do any of these politically correct labels accurately describe who I am? Hardly.

What about the sub-group label such as osteogenesis imperfecta? Do

I think it accurately describes who I am? While others may disagree, I say that it doesn't.

In today's politically correct society we have gotten so bogged down in the semantics of group classification that it's ridiculous. We need to be more polite and less political. Labels evolve through time. I mean, it doesn't bother me if someone refers to me as handicapped instead of disabled. We have pretty much removed outdated labels that may be inappropriate.

Throughout my life, I have been hurt by the myths and the misconceptions, the assumptive attitudes and stereotypes brought out by the word DISABLED. The stereotypes associated with this word are often the same finite classifications we apply to other labels. We read what disabled means in our textbooks or dictionaries and assume that it applies to everyone in a wheelchair, blind people, or hearing impaired individuals.

The same can be said about other minority groups as well. These assumptions have impeded their participation in today's society.

By focusing so much on the most politically correct term in reference to a person of a given minority, we focus on what we call that person, rather than who is that individual. We have far more important things to do than to put our time, money, and energies into trying to figure out what we are going to call each other.

Does that mean that African Americans should forget their heritage? Should Hispanics shelve the virtues of their nationality? Hell no! We just need to take more time in telling others about the diversity that lies within each one of us. Diversity is not limited to the color of a person's skin, or the physical differences or imperfections that have come on to the politically correct landscape. It extends to the environment and life experiences we have as individuals. Who we are on the inside is more important.

So what do I like to be called? Well, if you haven't guessed by now, it's Jonathan Studebaker. And, make sure you spell it right.

An Inferior Class

History has shown us that minorities have been thought of as inferior by the majority. In their struggle for equal status, we see that in the big picture, this fight has been for the right to participate in society.

The Civil Rights Movement of the 1960's saw blacks fight for equal access to such things as education, public places voting rights, and jobs. This was because some whites found them to be different, and yes, an inferior people. Thus, the Civil Rights Act of 1964 would be the starting point by which other pieces of legislation would follow, extending civil rights to blacks, women, Hispanics, and other minorities.

Though the Americans with Disabilities Act extends the same civil rights to people with disabilities, there still remains a culture that the disabled are an inferior class. That is, they are devalued as contributing members of society because of their differences or imperfections.

While there may be a majority of people on the outside who view disabled people as being inferior, the control or "power grab" that has existed for so long has come from within, amongst a select group of people. This control has helped to further the lives of "know it all" do-gooders, while creating and exploiting a dependent under class.

Disabled children are often shielded from success and failure by "well meaning," overprotective parents and educators. Creating the "safest" environment for the child puts into place a paternal power structure by which the disabled person sees who is in control.

As the disabled child enters adulthood, this paternalistic power shifts from parents and teachers, to social workers, counselors, attendants, therapists, bureaucrats, and other professionals involved in this power grab.

As compared to the ownership role of the white slave owner of the eighteenth and nineteenth centuries, this paternalistic power is the backbone of an inferior class within the disabled community.

The disabled have been economically repressed by parents who are wrought with guilt and shame over their child, and special ed teachers who see little or no potential in their students. There are government programs and agencies that in order to exist and flourish, must create disincentives for the disabled to work. We have a healthcare system that forces many to depend on the state.

Finally, we have work programs and sheltered workshops that devalue the work that is done by people with disabilities. This "cotton candy" slavery perpetuates the disabled underclass while making those who run and support the system feel good about what they are doing.

In order for persons with disabilities to fully participate in today's society, the attitudinal landscape must change. We can't just do it by telling the private sector to hire people with disabilities or make reasonable accommodations to their place of business.

We can't limit our efforts to convincing those on the outside. The struggle to participate in society and be viewed as contributors begins by chipping away at the paternal power structure that has existed within the disabled community for so long.

As you can see by now, answering the question, "What's it like being disabled?" isn't easy. It encompasses so many issues. While I may view an aspect such as walking in a certain way, another person may view it differently. It is important that these issues be brought out for discussion and debate by both disabled and non-disabled alike.

My Second Home

In the winter of 1987, I went to Des Moines, Iowa to speak in front of a group of about two thousand Shriners.

What is a Shriner, you ask?

You know, they're the guys who wear those funny red hats and ride around on little go carts in parades everywhere. You can't miss 'em.

What a Shriner does is a question most people have a hard time answering. In fact, the Shriners have faced many of the same charges and criticisms as other charitable organizations.

In the days leading up to my speech, I was briefed by the Public Relations Director, Mike Andrews, about how the organization as a whole was under attack because a local Shrine Club had broken the rules in dispersing funds they had collected from a public event. The newspapers had a field day with it and it became a public relations nightmare.

It just so happened that both events occurred at around the same time. My speech had been set up months in advance and was not intended to perform any sort of damage control.

Still, when there is a crisis like that, people talk.

It was an honor for me to address this group. It was the first time I ever had the chance to say, "Thank you!"

From the rust belt of the Midwest, to the sandy beaches of Hawaii, one constant remained as we moved from state to state. That is, whenever their son needed quality medical care for a disability not known to many, there was always a Shriners Hospital nearby.

How depressing it was to spend nine years or nearly half of my childhood in the hospital.

It seemed like whenever there was a holiday or special occasion, I was in the hospital. But, if it wasn't for Shriners, I wouldn't be where I am today. I don't know if I would be around to celebrate many more holidays either.

If I had to do it all over again, there is no place I would rather choose to have my body put back together than at a Shriners Hospital. Whether it is the Chicago, Honolulu, or San Francisco units, Shriners was more than just a hospital. It was a "second home."

Shortly after I was born, the medical bills started to pile up. Not long after my father had the necessary security for his family in place, the health insurance policy he had ran dry.

The Shriners came to the rescue.

Honolulu Unit

Of the three units, this is where I spent most of my time. The average stay for me was around three months. Early in my childhood, I fell just a few weeks short of spending a year in "the big house."

That's what the hospital was to me. No matter how many clowns that came by. No matter how many parties they threw. No matter how many times my family came to see me. It was still the "big house."

Since my bones were very fragile back then, doctors tried to make them stronger by putting rods in my legs. The rods were said to have offered support to the bones. Hence, I wouldn't fracture as easily.

They would take a bone and chop it into pieces and then skewer them on the rod like a shish kabob. Then, they would put the bone back in, sew you up, and put you in some sort of cast.

The rods wouldn't always stay in though. Often when the bones grew, the rod would have nowhere else to go but out. Then, I would have to go back in for another rodding.

To a very young child who didn't understand, a trip to the "big house" generally meant a very long time away from home.

It meant finding yourself unable to sit up because you were in some sort of body cast. It meant being confined to your bed with your legs in traction. When I wasn't in a prone position, I was strapped to a tilt table and cranked up to various stages of a standing position in order to strengthen my legs. At the same time, I could look at things from a different vantage point.

It meant lying on a bed with a bedpan underneath you night and day. Dealing with the discomforting remedies of enemas, milk of magnesia, and suppositories to combat endless bouts of constipation was the norm. My plumbing just didn't work right back then.

It meant having to look at your dog through the glass window. It meant having to endure the sounds and vibrations of an electric saw piercing body cast after body cast. With my voice screaming and tears running, I clenched my mother's fists and grit my teeth in hopes that it wouldn't take a hunk of skin off with it. I remember accidently biting her hand once. I told her I was sorry.

Still, amidst all the pain and unhappiness, there was love.

There was love from the nurses who treated us with the nurturing care of a parent. They cared for us as if we were one of their own children.

The Honolulu Unit made good use of the rich warm climate when it came to designing the hospital.

First, I stayed in a huge room that was the boy's ward. It was divided into numerous sections with beds clumped together into groups of four. There weren't any private rooms or any doors. If you wanted any privacy, you had to close a curtain.

Each section of beds shared a black and white television. The older kids generally got first pick. There was no cable TV, no remote controls to be found. If I didn't like the show that was on in my section, I could go to another set and see if it was on. I watched a lot of Flintstones, Gilligan's Island, and Brady Bunch episodes in those days. I was also introduced to violent Japanese super-hero shows with English sub-titles. Shows like Kikaider, Kikaider 01, Kamen Rider, Kamen Rider V3, and Rainbow Man were my favorites. Even during its time, these shows would rival the Mighty Morphin Power Rangers.

Along one side of the boy's ward were the isolation rooms. I stayed there several times when I was very sick. You couldn't go in there without a gown, and sometimes you even had to wear a mask.

Around the corner were these huge bathrooms where they could wheel in a gurney and give you a bath. It was like a mini car wash.

Unless I was sick or recovering from surgery, there wasn't a day that went by where I didn't breathe that moist tropical air. In addition to having the schoolrooms and auditorium accessible by open-air walkways, they had outdoor activities for us to do.

The hospital was situated in such a way that as you exited the ward, you went out onto a covered lanai with a cement walkway that extended out to the classrooms. There was a small courtyard with a nice grassy area. On one end of the lanai was a basketball hoop that saw plenty of use.

My sister Becky would have nightly pick-up games with one of the nurses, Mr. Pang.

We ate lunch and played games outside. We celebrated Christmases in the great outdoors. And, you even had to go outside to get to surgery. There was no escaping it.

Saturday mornings were always special at the Honolulu Unit. You see, we would all go to the auditorium and watch movies on a giant screen. Once in a while, we'd get a classic, but most of the time we would see Elvis movies. We never got tired of Elvis.

Most of the children that were treated there came from American Samoa. It wasn't very difficult to speak to them because they spoke broken or "pidgin English." I learned a few songs from their homeland.

I don't know what kind of person I would be had it not been for the loving, nurturing, environment I was in through my sometimes lengthy stays. It made it easier on my mother when I returned home.

Chicago Unit

The Chicago Unit is where you could find Dr. Edward Millar. Dr. Millar was among the few who comprised the brain trust when it came to understanding osteogenesis imperfecta.

When I was born, I saw Dr. Millar a couple of times along with his partner, Dr. Sofield. In fact, I had Sofield rods in my legs for the better part of my life.

The Chicago Shriners was unique in that for the first time, I went to a clinic specifically for children with osteogenesis imperfecta. They had us all there at one time. It was kind of weird as I felt as if I were amongst a group of Martians, myself included.

Still, I was grateful that they had such a clinic for children with OI. With Dr. Millar leading the show, I knew I was in good hands.

Whether we lived down in Indianapolis or up in southern Michigan, we always left the night before and stayed at my Cousin Laura Studebaker's house in nearby Elmhurst.

She had a little bed set up for me and we always had a big breakfast in the morning. As much as I still didn't enjoy going to the hospital, that was a highlight of the trip.

Another highlight of our trips to Chicago were the visits we made to Cock Robin, a drive-in not too far from the hospital. I always got one of their freezes that had lime sherbet, pineapple, and soda water. It was refreshing, even during the cold weather.

There were two clinic visits that stand out in my mind when I think about my experiences at the hospital in the Windy City.

On one visit I asked Dr. Millar a question about something that had been bothering me for a while. My parents had given me an answer, but I wanted to get it from the horse's mouth.

While I was staying with my Grandma Studebaker at her home in Dune Acres, Indiana, I overheard her talking to her friends on the phone in her bedroom. I was in the dining room playing with my toys and watching the Cubs game.

"Oh, he's doing fine. Of course, he's not going to be with us for very long," she said.

So, what did Grandma know that I didn't know? Did my parents tell her something I didn't know? This frightened her thirteen year-old grandson.

I became increasingly distressed. I started thinking of all the things I wanted to do before my impending demise.

One of the things I wanted to do was get a full season of games completed with my baseball board game. I was determined to play all night while watching the Jerry Lewis Labor Day Telethon.

As the hours drifted into the late night, my parents asked me when I was going to bed. I told them I was going to stay up all night and play baseball. I was very adamant about it.

My staying up all night didn't bother them as much as the way in which I told them I had to get these games in right now.

"Can't you wait until the morning and finish it then? It will still be there," Mom said.

"No, I have to play them now."

After about fifteen minutes of prodding, I finally broke down.

"Is there something you know, that I don't know?"

"What are you talking about?"

"I overheard Grandma tell one of her friends that I wasn't going to live much longer."

Dad couldn't believe it. He and my mother were beside themselves. They spent a long time trying to convince me that there was nothing to what Grandma said, except her own imagination.

They let me stay up the rest of the night with my baseball game and Jerry Lewis. I was a much happier guy, though not totally convinced.

"How long am I supposed to live?" I asked Dr. Millar.

"How long do you want to live?"

I broke out into a smile along with my parents.

"Well, what's the longest a person you know with OI has lived?"

"How does ninety-three sound?"

That settled the life expectancy question for me.

On another visit, I encountered a resident doctor who was a bit knife happy. He wanted to put rods in my arms in order for them to look good.

Dr. Millar told the resident about the risk in losing range of motion with rods in my arms. As long as I didn't have numerous fractures, he thought it was pointless for them to do it simply for cosmetic reasons.

I couldn't agree with him more.

Dr. Millar is an icon when it comes to understanding osteogenesis imperfecta.

San Francisco Unit

By 1997, the building will be empty. The operation will have moved north to a state of the art facility in Sacramento.

In the big picture, I think it's a great move. But, I can't help but feel bit of nostalgia and a sense of emptiness when I know that the brick building on 19th Avenue will no longer be a "second home."

I was a patient at the San Francisco Unit during both of my family's stints in the Bay Area. I can't say I will miss the building as much as the people and the good times I had at this particular hospital. There were many.

"Good morning, boys," said Mrs. Dawson every morning shortly after seven. The tall, lanky, African American woman was not only a hell of a nurse, she would have been our nation's first six star general in military history if she wanted to be. She could crack a whip with the best of 'em.

"You are going to come here like pussycats and leave like tigers when I get through with you!" she would often say.

She was right.

There was another side of Mrs. Dawson that was genuine. She was a pleasant woman who enjoyed her work. Under that rough exterior she had a sense of humor and an affection for us unlike any other.

Aside from her duties as a nurse, she was a friend. You could talk to her about almost anything.

She was also like a mother. When we misbehaved, she punished us. I remember one instance where we were shooting spitballs at each other as we lay in our beds during rest time. Then, we started shooting them at the ceiling. It wasn't long before she caught us and sentenced us to solitary confinement in our beds with no television.

Who could forget Mrs. Halinan? She was the main charge nurse at the time. She was an older woman who wore thick glasses and had an Irish accent. I can still hear even today.

When I was a kid, she referred to me as "Shnuckles."

Along with those mother figures, I can't forget some of the other nurses. There was Cindy, Mary, and Sharon, just to name a few. Sure, I was just a teenager, but it doesn't hurt to look.

There was a team of five doctors who oversaw my treatment while I was a patient at the San Francisco Unit. There wasn't a bad one in the bunch. You had the older doctors like Dr. Ashley, Dr. James, and Dr. Larson. Then rounding out the crew were Dr. Gilbert and Dr. Gray.

For the most part, I was in the hospital for leg roddings and a spinal fusion.

Along with osteogenesis imperfecta, I also have scoliosis, or curvature of the spine.

It is common with persons of my type of OI to have it. My spine looked like the letter "S."

Most people with scoliosis have to wear a brace for nine months.

Others who have a more severe form undergo a spinal fusion to correct the curvature. Since my bones are so fragile, the only thing they could do was to straighten my spine out a little bit, and then insert a rod to keep it from getting worse.

Of all of the scheduled operations I've had over the years, this was the biggie. This was the Super Bowl and World Series combined. I even made the ceremonial trip to Disneyland before this one. Along with the risks, they told me how painful the surgery was going to be. In order to mitigate the risks, I had the surgery done at Children's Hospital in San Francisco. Following the operation, I would return to Shriners where I was to be fitted for a turtle like, fleece-lined, plastic shell which I would have to wear for nine months.

Taking a cautious approach, the procedure was done in two stages.

I went in the first time to have the hooks which would support the rod put in my back. This would allow time for the bone grafts to heal up.

A few months later, I had the spinal fusion.

I was in some discomfort when I awoke from the operation. The pain in my back paled by comparison to what I was feeling in my ribs. They were killing me. I explained to the doctors what I was feeling and they said that they cracked a few of my ribs when they turned me over to do the operation. So, I instructed my visitors not to say anything that would make me laugh. You see, laughing causes pain, and we didn't want any of that.

The spinal fusion was a success and has turned out to be a life saver. Without it the curve would continue to progress and put pressure on other organs.

We had more than enough things to do to keep us busy. In fact, except on weekends, we didn't have much time to ourselves.

We had school in the morning and early afternoon, recreation after school and in the early evening.

On Wednesdays, we had Stamp Club meetings which were alright. I mean, I really enjoyed learning about stamps. The Shriners who ran the Stamp Club meetings were great. I just wasn't very organized when it came to my stamp collection. I always had a hard time affixing the stamps to these white sticky things that went into the album.

The Recreation Director was Tom Barisone who, like me, was a sports fanatic. We talked about everything from football to ice hockey. Through the years, Tom and I remain good friends and manage to stay in touch.

I spent most of my time in the rec-room painting Plaster of Paris molds or playing NHL Hockey with Ronnie Blankenship. We were always in the middle of a Stanley Cup final. When we were through with one, we started another. Every time we took to the table which set the little plastic men that moved with the turn of a rod, I always took the Chicago Blackhawks and he was the Boston Bruins.

The one thing the Shriners knew how to do was throw a party. Not a cocktail party, or a kegger. I'm talking about a party with clowns, magicians, cookies, ice cream, and punch. I could really tell how much these people loved and cared about us.

Once in a while, we had to break up the routine and have a party of our own.

Hospital food can get old, and we had to break the rules from time to time just to keep our sanity. So, a group of us pooled our money together to buy a pizza.

One of us would sneak down to the lobby and make a call on one of the pay phones to a local pizza joint. Then somehow, it got back to one of the nurses that we ordered a pizza. We'd get lectured about the rules as she collected the money. When the pizza arrived, the nurse met the delivery guy and brought us back our pizza. We had to share it with everyone, but that was alright.

The funniest part about our pizza parties was what happened to the snack the dietician left for us. It went untouched. So, when she saw that thirty-five peanut butter and jelly sandwiches were returned, she asked questions. We told her we weren't very hungry that night.

On May 26, 1983, less than a week after my eighteenth birthday, I made my last visit as a patient to Shriners Hospital. I have a certificate on my wall that says I graduated.

Back then, I felt that way. I felt a sense of accomplishment and appreciation for what the doctors were able to do for me. I felt that I was blessed with the love and attention the nurses gave me all those many months. They instilled a set of values that remain with me to this day. They helped make me who I am.

Today, when I have the opportunity to speak to those guys in the funny red hats about what Shriners means to me, I tell them about all the things they did to help me and my family. I tell them that even though I have sprung into adulthood, I am still one of their children. I point out that while there are those who may be receiving the same quality care they got as a child, there are those who have fallen through the cracks. No single patient at Shriners Hospital should look upon their stays as the only time they had quality healthcare. Unfortunately, there are times when I personally feel this way. Sometimes I feel like I have fallen through the cracks.

Shriners Hospital was more than just a hospital, it was a second home.

Football's Finest Hour

How could I forget about "Football's Finest Hour," the East-West Shrine Game?

It's the best football game of the year.

On my family's first stop in the San Francisco Bay Area, I was in the hospital during the annual players visit. I was so excited, I couldn't contain myself. It was a football lover's paradise.

With toys in their arms, the players meandered their way down to the boys and girls wards. They were paired off with us like a dating service. Each of us had two players we got to know before meeting everyone else.

I was paired up with Gary Green and Wendell Tyler. Not bad, eh? Gary asked me what team I wanted him to go to and I naturally told him the Chiefs. Sure enough, the defensive back from Baylor was drafted by Kansas City in the first round. I wrote him a few times and he sent me an autograph picture.

The players visit took on a sad note that year. Former Cal quarterback Joe Roth who had been diagnosed with cancer did not play in the game, yet he made the rounds with the other players.

He was a quiet guy who carried himself with class. I was able to watch him from my bed as he managed to carry on a conversation in Spanish with one of the patients from Mexico. I could tell he was having a good time.

All of us were sad to learn that Joe Roth had died.

The next time I was in the hospital for the players visit, I was paired up with Neil Lomax and Ron Coccimiglio. Lomax was a superstar quarterback out of Portland State, a Division II school while Coccimiglio was a defensive back out of Cal.

Tom Barisone was in charge of matching the players with the patients. He knew that guys like me and fellow patient Raymond Watkins followed football pretty closely, so he allowed us to have sort of a "draft" to see who we'd get.

They brought me in as an outpatient to the hospital the following year. It was one of the few times I enjoyed the trip to the hospital because I didn't have to see a doctor.

Since I had taken Neil Lomax the previous year, Raymond got the first pick.

A while back he decided that he was going to take Marcus Allen. He heard that there was a good possibility that he was coming out for the game. Tom said that they didn't have enough girls, so he asked me if I would be a girl for a day and stay on the girl's side.

I didn't mind the change. I would just go from getting a player from the West, to a player from the East. My players that year were Georgia quarterback Buck Belue, and Sal Sunseri, a linebacker from the University of Pittsburgh.

Of the four visits to the hospital, this was by far the most special.

I arrived at the hospital well before eight in the morning. Along with myself, a few other kids were brought in for the visit. My friend Steve and I headed to the lobby to see if one of our friends had made it. It was not quite an hour before the players were to arrive. They were always late anyway.

We went down a long hallway to a T-intersection which divides the boys and girls sides and takes you down another hallway passed the schoolrooms and into the front lobby.

As we approached the intersection where we'd turn to go to the lobby, I turned my head and saw a huge crowd of people coming right at us. They weren't coming very fast, there were just so many of them.

Leading the crowd of photographers, reporters, cameramen, and other dignitaries was this tall man with a houndstooth hat. I thought I had just witnessed the Second Coming.

"Hey Steve, that's the Bear," I whispered as loud as I could so he could hear me.

"The mayor?" he replied.

"No stupid, the Bear!"

His eyes looked up and saw the imposing figure walk right up to us. I thought we were going to have to pick our eyes up off the floor and put them back in their sockets.

"Hiya Bear," I said. I was in such a state of euphoria, I thought I had died and gone to heaven.

He said hello to both of us. The cameras lights were flashing at a rapid rate.

"Is there anyone who can show me around this place?" said Paul "Bear" Bryant.

I immediately volunteered to take this football giant, who at the time, was the nation's all-time winningest football coach, on a fifty-cent tour of the hospital. He offered to push me around and I gladly accepted the offer.

We went past the dining hall and he mentioned how the food must be better than what they serve at the University of Alabama. I defended his school and said he was better off eating there. Later, we went by physical therapy where he caught a glimpse of the whirlpools.

"I'd sure like to get in one of those right now."

This man was no doubt a giant, a gentle one at that.

The tour came to an end when we returned to the girl's side. Coach Bryant said he would see me later.

Sal Sunseri and Buck Belue were nice guys. Buck was not only a good football player, he played baseball too.

During that week, the Shriners had a camera crew doing a story on the hospital for CBS's "Sunday Morning" with Charles Kuralt. As it turned out, the story was not just about the hospital, it was about me.

I told millions of people things that I am glad I had said, and things I wish I could take back. You might say it was one of my most embarrassing moments.

"I love this place; it's kind of like a second home." I said in that squeaky pre-pubescent voice of mine. That wasn't so bad.

I said in an interview that the only limitations you have are the ones you put on yourself. That wasn't so bad either.

I also told everyone that I had a genital disease instead of a congenital one. Now, that was bad!

My family was beside themselves when they heard these precious words come from my mouth. My parents howled with laughter when they heard it. They couldn't believe it. Hey, I was sixteen. I didn't know the difference.

After the players visit, I spent the afternoon in the rec-room hanging out with Tom and doing some doodling. I scribbled down a play I thought was pretty good. Maybe Coach Bryant could use it. There was a camera guy hanging around and I asked him if he was going to practice, would he give my play to the "Bear." He promised me he'd do it.

Later that week, I was pleasantly surprised to learn I was invited to go to the game. Not only that, I got a sideline pass!

Becky pushed me up and down the sidelines. We decided to split time between the East and the West. We started on the East side.

I saw Coach Bryant and he called me over for a sideline conference. He asked me if it was alright to have the wide receiver run the reverse instead of the tight end.

"Our receiver runs a lot faster than our tight end." he said.

Well, who was I to argue about that? When the winningest coach in college football asks you if he can change your play just a little bit, there is nothing to say.

"Sure, I don't mind," I said.

"Now I wanna tell you, Jackie thinks your play is gonna work. But Bo, he's a little bull-headed about it."

What a lineup of coaches there was that year, especially on the East side. You had Coach Bryant from Alabama, Bo Schembechler from Michigan, and Jackie Sherrill of Pitt. The West team had a Bay Area flavor with Paul Wiggin of Stanford, Jack Elway of San Jose State, and Wayne Howard of Utah.

In the third quarter, Anthony Hancock a wide receiver out of Tennessee took the reverse and turned it into a fifteen yard gain. The East scored on the next play. I never had another play work as well as that one.

It may sound a bit strange, but I was never much of an autograph nut. I mean, I liked autographs. I just liked getting their addresses a lot more.

While I tended to write longer letters, most of the ones I got back from coaches were short, sweet, and to the point. I got plenty of souvenirs alright. But, there was nothing better than getting a letter from Coach Bryant.

I could take my letter and match it alongside his and see how he had answered every one of my questions. For instance, when I told him I was thinking about going to the University of California, he thought it was great and recalled the last time the Crimson Tide had played the Golden Bears.

Paul "Bear" Bryant retired from coaching following the Shrine Game, but he kept on writing to me. I could tell by one of the letters he wrote how he must have typed it himself. It had a January date on it when the letter was actually written in June. The last letter I received from him was a day or two before the following East-West Game.

Ten days later, Coach Bryant passed away. I cried when I heard the news.

Here was a man whose life was football—Alabama football. When he retired, he had nothing left to do. I thought he should have stayed around a little bit longer.

I was glad I got to know him.

I was to get first pick the following year and my eyes were on Stanford quarterback, John Elway.

"Jon, I can't give you Elway," Tom said.

"What? Why not? Raymond had the first pick last year and I should have first pick this year."

"I know, but they told me specifically not to let you have John Elway."

"Who's they?" I asked.

"The people over at the East-West office said not to give John Elway to you."

I was astounded. I was disappointed. This was going to be the last year I would be able to see the players and I wanted to go out with a bang. Their thought was that they wanted two separate stories and not a big one.

The powers that be prevailed and I chose Jim Jeffcoat, a defensive lineman from Arizona State and Paul Skansi, a wide-receiver from Washington.

Overall, I did pretty well with my selections. Gary Green had a good career with the Chiefs before going to several other teams. Wendell Tyler played for the Los Angeles Rams and won a Super Bowl with the San Francisco 49ers. Neil Lomax had a great run with the Cardinals and Jim Jeffcoat won two Super Bowls with the Cowboys.

Not everyone who plays in the East-West Game is guaranteed of a spot in the NFL.

But as a child, it didn't matter whether or not they did. They are all good people.

My parents told me how this would probably be the last time I would get a chance to be a part of the East-West Shrine Game. I knew that. Mentally, I prepared myself for it.

It didn't quite work out that way though.

One afternoon, I returned home from school. Mom told me we were expecting company. She wouldn't say who was coming.

Both of my parents were there to answer the door when officials of the game came over to the house. Among the people that were there were Dick Skuse, the PR director for the game, and Elmer Dohrman, the selection chair of the West squad.

After a brief introduction, Dick Skuse said the magic words.

"How would you like to be our "Honorary Head Coach?"

"Sure," I said. My face was beaming.

"Now, we're probably only going to do it for a year. We'll see how it goes."

As the Honorary Head Coach, I attended all the press lunches and the annual players visit to the hospital. I watched a few of the practices, dined at the team banquet, and wrote articles for the Associated Press and San Francisco Examiner.

The press lunches were fun. I kind of had a crush on Sally Jenkins who, at the time was working for the San Francisco Chronicle. She's a big wig now at Sports Illustrated.

It felt kind of weird going to the hospital as a member of the press corps. Seeing things from the other side made me appreciate the good times. After the visit, I went to the Examiner offices to type my story.

I did so well in my role as the spokesperson for the game than they decided to do it another year, and then another, and then another. It turned out to be a ten year ride.

The manager at the Hyatt Palo Alto, Sharon Crawford, saw that the trips up and down to all of the events were taking a toll on my father. So one day, she invited me to stay a night or two, and then it later turned into a week. For me, it was like one big Christmas holiday.

Of course, everybody knew Sharon. You couldn't check in without seeing her. To me, she was both a mother and a guardian angel. She made sure I was taken care of by all of the staff.

If I needed a push somewhere, she made sure I had someone. If I didn't have a ride to practice, she made sure I had one or she'd drive me herself.

She made sure I had an invitation to her NFL party which was held in one of the ballrooms. It was first-class.

Surrounding the huge tables of hot and cold foods was a large ice sculpture that had some sort of NFL theme. One year, she had a sculpture of a Super Bowl Trophy.

Along the walls were the pennants of the all the teams. In lieu of background music, she had televisions set up around the room with old NFL highlights. What really made the parties so much fun were the people.

One time, I was sitting at a table talking with a man who was probably my grandfather's age. You knew he was an old timer. I asked him what his name was and who he worked for.

His name was Tommy O'Boyle, and he worked for the Kansas City Chiefs. He was big when the Chiefs were in their hay day in the late sixties and early seventies. It seemed like I had stayed there for hours listening to him talk about the Chiefs and their glory years. It was a real treat.

Yes, I got to meet a lot of NFL scouts and coaches. Being around them heightened my interest in the game and my desire to pursue a career in football.

Along with my duties as the Honorary Head Coach, there were a number activities apart from the game which developed into traditions over the years.

First, I had my yearly chat with Sherman Lewis who was an assistant with the Niners. We sat in the lounge with a few cold ones and some pretzels, and caught up on what each were doing.

No East-West Game was complete without having two pre-game breakfasts. First, I ate with the players and coaches in one of the meeting rooms. Then, I would go to the coffee shop and meet George Boone and his wife Dee. No wonder I got so big.

George Boone was the Player Personnel Director for the Cardinals. I always enjoyed the way he talked. He had that blue grass Kentucky drawl that was distinctive, especially to a guy from California. He was a big guy too, and could almost always be seen wearing his orange down vest that made him look like he belonged to some Harley Davidson club. No one was gonna mess with George. More than anything else, I enjoyed his constant ribbing.

"Now you go to Chic-o State. Where in the hell is Chic-o State?" he said. I could see the poker-faced expression behind the words.

"You got any players for us?" he'd continue on like this forever if I let him.

My proudest moment during my tenure as Honorary Head Coach was in 1988 when Chris Verhulst was selected to play in the game. He was a tight end from my alma mater, Chico State.

He was a big guy who broke numerous receiving records for us. He was our go-to guy when the chips were down. Unfortunately, when they gave him the ball on a reverse I designed, he fumbled away the pigskin. Chris was drafted by the Houston Oilers and played a few years in the NFL.

As much as I enjoyed myself during the week, I was constantly thinking of ways to parlay this into something bigger. I tried to talk to coaches about doing some front office work for them. You know, fill that niche.

I also made it clear to Shrine officials that I was willing to be something more than just a poster boy. I volunteered to call players and coaches that may have been leaning toward other games. I thought that as a former patient, I would be the best person that could sell the game.

I tried to position myself into being something more than a poster boy and still, nothing seemed to register. If they felt otherwise, they didn't give me their reasons.

In thanking the players at the team banquet, I never forgot to tell them to encourage their fellow underclassman to play in the East-West Shrine Game. I always mentioned how they would have other opportunities to go to Hawaii and play in other All-Star Games, like the Pro Bowl.

I came home from the 1991 East-West Game not knowing it would be my last as Honorary Head Coach. I should have expected it. After all, that year they got a hold of me kind of late and I only stayed down there for three days. My mother told me it wasn't going to last forever. I guess I just didn't prepare myself for it this time.

Before the '92 game, I made my customary October call to the East-West office to see if there was anything extra they wanted me to do. I still wanted to somehow make an additional contribution. I was fighting to the end. They said they didn't need anything and told me they would be in touch.

December came and I still hadn't heard anything. I put in a couple of calls and left a couple of messages for the Managing Director of the game, Don Johnson. He had replaced Emerson Clark who I got along with very well.

I called the office once again in late December and the secretary very politely told me to hold. While I was on hold, I could hear her tell him that I was on the line.

"I don't want to talk to him. Tell him I can't talk to him," he said.

Pretending that I hadn't heard what he said, I asked him if he wanted me to come down for the game.

"No, we don't need you!" His voice was short and curt.

I hung up the phone and looked at Cam. I told him it was over. I told him what happened on the phone. He couldn't believe it. We got in his car and went to the Cozy Diner for a bite to eat.

I was beside myself as I constantly replayed the conversation aloud over lunch.

"I don't want to talk to him. Tell him I can't talk to him," I kept saying these words over and over again. My voice grew with emotion. I was pissed. I couldn't believe how this guy was treating me. He had no right to act that way. All he had to do was use a little tact and let me know that I wasn't in their plans. And, he could have done it in a nice way.

In my mind I knew it was not going to last forever. After all, I wanted more. I wanted something to come out of it. I was hoping for something tangible. When it did end, I probably would have wanted to know a year ahead of time in order that I could savor the memories one last time. In my mind it would be sort of like a farewell tour. That would only happen in a perfect world.

As one who studied public relations, this guy didn't have any. I was constantly asking myself why such a good thing like this could have such a miserable ending.

I spent the weekend of the game in Ames, Iowa interviewing for a coaching internship at Iowa State. I didn't pay much attention to the game. There was still some bitterness inside. I felt like a part of me had died.

Recently, I went to the Shrine Headquarters in Tampa, Florida for a speech to their football committee. Don Johnson was there. I gave my speech and emphasized my voice when I spoke about the East-West Shrine Football Classic. I relived the memories all over again.

Afterwards, everyone came up to shake my hand. Everyone, except Don Johnson. There was no burying of the hatchet, no peace accord. That will have to come another time.

The good times I had, both as a patient and as a spokesperson, are etched in my heart and mind forever. The Shriners saw to it that I was not only a whole person, but a happy one as well. I am truly grateful to them.

The East-West Shrine Game is the best game of the year. It is most definitely "football's finest hour."

Educating Jonathan

Throughout my tenure on the speaking circuit, I have spoken to groups of people with diverse backgrounds.

I've talked to college students as well as kindergartners. I've given presentations to federal government workers and used car salespeople. I've spoken to disabled and non-disabled audiences.

While the make-up of each audience may differ, and the content of each speech may vary, the goal remains the same. That is, I want to educate and motivate people.

School teachers are often faced with the same set of circumstances. They have students that come from all different walks of life. Their classrooms span the colors of the rainbow.

While the make-up of their audience may change, their underlying goals remain. They want to educate and prepare their students for the real world. They want to motivate them to be the best they can be.

What happens when a teacher has a student with cerebral palsy, Down syndrome, or muscular dystrophy? What does a teacher do when they have a student with osteogenesis imperfecta or spina bifida?

What happens to those goals? Do they change? I would agree emphatically with those who say they don't change. Some say they do. Others just don't discuss it. Their actions speak louder than words.

I have experienced the gamut of attitudes and philosophies throughout my educational experience. While I think I came out alright in the end, it is important to articulate these experiences so that parents and others may learn, and can avoid the trappings of those who want to hinder their child's educational experience.

Finally, there are changes that need to be made when it comes to educating students with disabilities. I have a few suggestions.

Jefferson School

Back in the early 1970's, when our family lived in Hawaii, I attended the newly built, Jefferson Orthopedic School. It was right next door to Jefferson Elementary. That's where the other students went to school. We never saw them.

Jefferson School was staffed by special-ed teachers, aides, and both physical and occupational therapists. The age of the students went from kindergarten to high school. We were put into classrooms based on our age. There were no grade levels at Jefferson School. They didn't believe in them.

When I went to the local library with my sister Amy to renew my library card, I would always ask her what grade I should put on my card. She told me what to write.

My parents called Jefferson School a "glorified babysitting service." The teachers didn't push us very hard and the school was right next door to the zoo. We made so many trips to see the gorillas, I practically got to know them by name.

School By The Bay

We moved to the San Francisco Bay Area in the summer of 1976. It was here that I began to notice all of the red tape my parents had to go through in order to get me in the school system. I didn't get into school until the middle of the fall because my family had to jump through so many hoops. While sitting at home watching daytime television, my parents went to meetings where a bunch of people sat around a table and talked about me. I remember going to one of them.

El Portal Del Sol was a lot like Jefferson School. Again, there were no grades and they seemed to be more concerned about teaching us how to brush our hair than learning our ABC's. With my hair the way it is now, I think I would have been better off learning the three R's.

After spending less than a year at the school, I was put in a mainstreaming program at Brittan Acres, an elementary school in San Carlos. This program featured a special ed teacher supervising a classroom of disabled students. The setting functioned as a homeroom where much of our learning took place.

On occasion, I would venture outside the homeroom and have a class with a regular teacher and students from outside the special ed program.

Along with taking classes outside the homeroom, we had recess and lunch with the other students. I remember having the hots for a fifth grader named Ginger. The following year, the program moved to Cipriani School in Belmont.

A Big Step Forward

I didn't get a chance to experience what would have been my year in fifth grade because my family moved to Indianapolis where things changed radically.

After looking over their options, my parents had an interesting decision to make. They could either put me in an orthopedic school which some in the system had referred to as a "warehouse," or they could take their chances and see if I could survive a year at the local junior high down the street from my cousins' house where we were staying.

The school board strongly recommended that I go to the orthopedic school. My parents felt otherwise. They didn't want their son to wither away at the "warehouse." They wanted me to get an education.

Against the wishes of the school board, Henry and Cynthia stuck with their decision for me to go to Eastwood Junior High and enter the seventh grade.

Academically, I had a very rocky time as a seventh-grader. I had great difficulty with classes that required a great deal of reading and memorization. Subjects like health and social studies were a nightmare. I hadn't really developed any study skills and organization was never one of my strong suits. It never will be either. I have a terrible time keeping track of my papers.

My resource teacher at Eastwood was Mrs. Erxleben. She never taught me anything that had a lasting impact though, unlike my other special ed teachers; she gave me credit for having a brain. It was refreshing.

Even though I floundered at times in the classroom, I adjusted well to being the only physically disabled person in the student body. Sure, there were a couple of instances where I had to deal with getting teased by a classmate, but overall, I had no problems getting along with the other students.

Once, I was cornered in the hallway by a student who called me a bunch of names, mainly dealing with my size. He did it for several days at a time. When I told my other friends about this, they immediately confronted the guy and threatened to duke it out with him. The short remarks soon came to a stop.

On my way to lunch, I had to go down a ramp to get to the cafeteria. The ramp was just outside the classroom at the end of a long hallway. At the foot of the ramp were two double-doors that led to an area where students hung out.

I could count on the doors being held open by students who were finishing their lunch. They would see me come down the ramp and have the door open by the time I came down.

There was one time where as I came down the ramp, the doors that had stayed open before, didn't. By the time I could see that they had pulled a fast one, it was too late. A crash was heard down the long hallway, and practically every teacher peered out of their room to see what had happened.

Except for having my books and papers scattered about the threshold, I was not injured. I shrugged it off and everyone had a good laugh. The doors never closed on me again for the remainder of the year.

I loved being the only disabled guy in the school. It was great. I made many friends and participated in a lot of activities.

I was the campaign manager for David Thompson who was running for student body Vice-President. I would go over to his house and make campaign signs and buttons. "D.T. for V.P." was what most of them would read. I believe it was my first campaign victory. Not bad for a seventh-grader.

Yeah, I kind of had a love interest that year. Debbie Streeter was her name. She was kind of short with brown hair and glasses. And, she was very cute, if I might add. It was nothing big though.

I survived seventh-grade at Eastwood Junior High. The lowest grade I received was a C, despite my lack of good study skills.

Of all the decisions my parents had to make regarding my education, this was probably the most important one. To have their son go from a well-supervised, structured environment to one with very little was a very big step for them to take. A lot of soul searching must've gone into this one. In the end, I think they had faith in me and it proved to be the right call.

The Best Of Times

The road seemed to get a bit easier when we headed north to Michigan. Seeing how I had a positive track record at Eastwood, school officials had little problem with me going to Lakeshore Junior High as an eighth-grader, and later as a freshman at Lakeshore High School. Once again, I had a very positive experience. Some of my fondest memories of high school took place here.

For starters, the Vice-Principal of the school made me one of his projects and assumed the role of mentor and surrogate father. David Clark is a person I revere as one of the few people aside from my parents, who had a lasting impact on my education. He praised me when I did something good, and he let me know when I screwed up. More than that though, his concern for me went beyond that of a student. He cared about me as a person and as a friend.

He took me to athletic events and dances when I needed a ride. Sometimes the trips to the games took well over an hour, just one way. He also took an interest in my love life. That is, he asked me which girls I was interested in, gave me advice when I needed it, and supported me through the peaks and valleys. If I thought I could count on Mr. Clark for any "intelligence information" when it came to this subject, I was proven wrong.

I asked him to get me the locker number of a girl I had an eye on. I wanted to give this girl a rose and I thought the best way I could do it was to somehow sneak it inside her locker. It was the old "secret admirer" trick.

Mr. Clark gave me the number and even put the rose in the locker. But as it turned out, she switched lockers and the rose ended up in a locker shared by two guys. The rose did find its way to her, but it took a lot more effort than we thought, and I wasn't spared the embarrassment of the faux pas. Still, all we could do was laugh about it and go on.

Mr. Clark's better half also played a role in my educational experience at Lakeshore. I had several sessions of speech therapy to try and correct the shrill and volume in my voice. Unlike most of us who reach puberty, my voice did not change while I was in high school. Mr. Clark's wife, Dawn, tried to help me with this problem.

As a student with a disability, I think a person like Mr. Clark would be the perfect resource specialist for anyone. He followed my progress and nudged me when I was slipping. He praised me when I was doing well. His presence was more like a guiding light than a spotlight. I wish he had been there throughout my high school years. I know I would have been a better student.

I did pretty well as a freshman at Lakeshore. Except for my senior year, it was probably my best year in the classroom. Oh yeah, I got a lot of C's and stumbled around a bit, but I also earned a couple of A's and B's as well.

The teachers at Lakeshore were pretty good. I didn't receive any special treatment or anything. I got along with all of them, even my World History teacher, Mr. Greendonner. He also had Amy in his yearbook class.

Mr. Greendonner reminded me a lot of Professor Kingsfield of the "Paper Chase." His tall imposing figure, combined with the fact that he looked down at me when I talked, gave me the willies every time I wanted to say something, or ask a question.

I knew he thought I wasn't very bright. I also thought he picked on me a lot. He was a very hard teacher, but he was fair. I think he picked on me more because I was Amy's little brother, not because I was disabled. His son went on a date with her, but nothing came of it. So, maybe he got his kicks giving me a hard time.

Mr. Greendonner's World History class basically served as a cover for him to talk about the evils of communism and the Soviet Union. He spent nearly all of the time espousing how we had to contain the evil Soviets and their sphere of influence around the world. I could tell he wasn't a big Jimmy Carter fan. He probably hailed the day Reagan was sworn into office.

Fifteen years later, I returned to Lakeshore. One of the people who I wanted to see was Mr. Greendonner. I was hoping that he could see that I was a guy who is trying to amount to something. Maybe I was looking for his approval.

Fifteen years later, it seemed as if nothing had changed. Even though I was a bit more confident, I still got the willies when I saw him. I think I did make an impression. I don't know if I got his approval. In sort of a weird way, I liked Mr. Greendonner. The way he put the fear of God into me, gave me the impetus to prove myself to him.

Like my previous experiences as the only disabled student in the school, I had no trouble assimilating into the student body. You could say that I had the best of both worlds. On one hand, I was treated kind of special. Yet, I was treated like everyone else.

They made a fuss over me at times, though they never gave me any special treatment. I left Lakeshore High School after my freshman year. No one asked me if I wanted to go, and I didn't volunteer to leave. When you're the low guy on the totem pole, you don't have a choice. Dad tells you when to pack, and when to unpack.

What I left behind when we returned to Northern California was a small town in the Midwest that had a spirit I had never seen. When the Lancers played, everybody went to the game. It didn't matter how well the team was doing. I left behind a community where everyone knew each other. Everyone cared about each other. It seemed as if I was growing to be a big fish in small town. After all, this is a town where everyone is a big fish at one time or another. I can only wonder how big a fish I would have been. I know it would have been a lot of fun. I wish I could have stayed a Lakeshore Lancer.

ABC's In The Hospital

You'd think that spending nearly half of my childhood in the hospital would set me back by one, two, three, or even four years with respect to my education. Don't you? Well, not while I was a patient at Shriners Hospital.

At Shriners, all of the patients had to go to school. It didn't matter if I was in bed with my legs in traction. They just pushed my bed to the schoolroom where I stayed until the bell rang. The only way you could get out of going to school was if you were in surgery, or sick enough to be put in isolation.

The school was staffed by regular public school district teachers. While I don't believe any of them had any special ed credentials, it was probably better that way. The teachers made sure that when you left the hospital, you were caught up on your assignments. When you accomplished that, they just gave you more work to do.

We only went to school for about four hours a day. Sometimes it seemed as if the time didn't go by fast enough. If we were caught daydreaming or goofing off, the teacher sent you back to the ward with some homework that was due the following day.

Shriners played a key part of my education while growing up. In fact, if it weren't for Shriners, I don't think I would have been able to graduate from high school on time.

Not So "Special" Education

Even though my family returned to California about half-way through the summer, I didn't get into school until the middle of the fall semester. My parents wanted me to go to the school down the road a bit from our house. It didn't have a special ed program. However, because of my father's job, my parents had no way of providing transportation for me to and from school. Since there was no other way to meet my transportation needs, their only choice was to put me back in the same system I had known just a short time ago.

In order for me to start attending classes at Mills High School, I had to be accepted into the county's special education program. For that to happen, I had to take a battery of "know nothing, red tape running, keep a bureaucrat happy," psychological tests that never seemed to end. It was incredible!

I had to arrange blocks. I had to tell what pictures meant. I had to do everything the county shrink wanted me to do.

Apparently, my transcripts weren't good enough for them.

After all of those tests, we went through another round of meetings. These were the same kind of meets I had when we first moved in '76. The only difference was we now knew everyone at the table. It still took us forever and a day to get accepted into the program. This is one of the few times I wished I could ride a bike. It would have made it a hell of a lot easier to get to school.

The county's mainstream program at Mills High School was about a twenty-minute ride by bus, a much greater distance than Lakeshore was from our house.

"Hey shrimp," the voice said as I entered Room 108 for the first time.

The voice belonged to Jeff Marinello, a freshman. I knew Jeff from my earlier days in elementary school.

From that moment, I knew things would not be as good as they were at Lakeshore. I knew what I was missing and I wasn't happy to be here.

As a student in the program, I had to play by a certain set of rules. The county required that I spend a certain amount of time in the homeroom taking classes from my special-ed teacher, Mr. Krauss.

Mr. Krauss was a short guy with brown hair and glasses. He had the right credentials and basically did what the county told him to do. He was a nice guy, even a big football fan, but I wouldn't call him innovative by any means.

Most of us had a study hall period in our homeroom as well as Adaptive PE, or gym. I loved going to gym class a lot more than my parents did. They were afraid that I would get hurt. After a year, they got my doctor to write a letter saying that gym class would pose a risk to my health. Instead of having fun playing wheelchair football and baseball, I had to take choir. I didn't agree with the folks on this one.

Mr. Krauss seemed to have a talent for painting. He liked teaching art. As a substitute for study hall, Mr. Krauss made me take his painting class. I can only guess that he thought I was going to be another amongst a long line of star pupils who could do magic with a brush and canvas. I proved him wrong.

I was terrible as a painter. It wasn't because I didn't try. I just wasn't good at it. As much as I was a lousy artist, he's got to take some of the responsibility for not being a good teacher.

Here is a guy who had a room full of students who were all doing different things. Some were goofing around at the computer. Others were "studying." While all of this was going on, he was teaching as many as two or three different subjects to three different kids. You'd have to be an octopus with as many brains as you had legs.

When he finally got to my table, he briefly explained my assignment to me. He quickly showed me a couple of techniques. Then, he left me alone. That was my art lesson every day. It lasted no more than twelve minutes.

Mr Krauss did not like my artwork. He didn't think it was very good. In fact, he thought it was poor compared to all of the other students who had his class. He was poised to give me a failing grade.

When I came home from school with one of my "works of art," my parents complimented what I had done. Even though I put my paintings up on the family bulletin board for everyone to see, I didn't have to be a rocket scientist to know how they really felt. I knew they were complimenting the effort more than anything else.

My parents were livid when it came down that I was going to fail my painting class. They rushed down for a meeting with Mr. Krauss and laid down the law. They explained that my ability as a painter was not that important when it came to the big picture. My parents wanted me to go on to college, and they didn't think that a painting class was that important. They were more interested in my overall grade point average than anything else.

After one of those parent-teacher conferences, my parents got Mr. Krauss to switch my grade from a straight letter grade to that of pass/fail. I ended up getting a P in painting.

While I did alright as a sophomore, my junior year was one I would rather forget. It was a year that started with me recovering from an accident where I lost most of the vision in my right eye. Then, I underwent a series of major operations on my back. I spent a lot of time in the hospital that year and I didn't apply myself.

My parents gave me the push that no other special ed teacher would ever consider doing back when I went to school. You see, the teacher's goals were different than my parents'. They expected me to go to college just as my brother and sisters had done. Even though Dad may have alluded to it at times, they knew I didn't have horse manure for brains. They didn't set any goals for me to reach. Their main concern for me was that I give the best possible effort when it came to my studies. Good grades would come if I applied myself.

I rediscovered how much fun high school was during my senior year. I brought my grades up and my GPA was just over average. This made the folks quite happy.

In stark contrast to my sophomore and junior years, I was actively involved as a member of the student body. I was a member of student government as Assemblies and Elections Commissioner. During my semester as Assemblies Commissioner, I worked my butt off trying to get us a decent program. Joe Montana wouldn't come, but he sent me a nice picture. So, I didn't get an A from Mr. Faulkner. On the other hand, I did practically nothing as Elections Commissioner, and I got an A in the class.

I learned that doing more work doesn't always get you a better grade. That's politics for you.

I also read the news over the public address system. We had our own campus "radio station." I would always end every newscast by wishing everyone a "very pleasant day." It was my own signature.

Having a homeroom with a locker in it, and an aide to go to the cafeteria and get your lunch for you was great as far as convenience goes, but it did little in the way of improving my social skills.

Instead of eating in the cafeteria or outside with all of the other students, I spent most of my sophomore and junior years eating my lunch in the safe, friendly confines of Room 108. It became a force of habit.

In stark contrast to spending most of my free time in the homeroom with my disabled classmates, I spent my senior year discovering a new group of friends, my classmates. I was also voted "Most Inspirational Student" by the senior class.

Like many seniors, I was thinking about life after Mills High School. What was I going to do?

As part of my classroom requirement, I took an independent living skills class taught by two people from our local Independent Living Center. The class was supposed to equip us for life after high school.

While I learned a number of things such as how to cook, shop, and a little bit of sex ed, the class was largely a disappointment. Yes, I did learn what the real world is like for many people with disabilities who took the class. This world is largely a world of bureaucrats and social engineers working for a class of people who have become dependent on them.

For example, they spent a day telling us the difference between a green SSI check and a gold one. Personally, I didn't care what color the check was, as long as it had the right numbers on it and it didn't bounce. When I got direct deposit, I never had to mess with getting a check in the mail.

The teachers told us about all of the services that we could get through their agency. As they were trying to "sell" their services, the intent was to prepare us for a new group of people who would take over from where Mr. Krauss and all of those folks left off.

From my standpoint, I was facing a different world after high school. I had been accepted to Chico State University and I was getting ready to go off to college. I asked my teachers to tell me about college and that whole way of life. I mean, they had both gone to college. Why not?

Well, since I was the only student who was going away to school, my teachers didn't spend any time on this topic. In fact, they ignored my questions and I felt as if I were being shunned for bringing it up.

Our final class project was to spend a week in an accessible house and live independently. We would apply everything we learned throughout the year and see if we could make a go of it.

They had a two-bedroom apartment set up for us near a small shopping center. I was to share the apartment with an older gentleman who had multiple sclerosis, and his provider. He was basically a vegetable and required 24-hour care. I wondered what he was going to get out of the experience.

Before moving in, I made arrangements with the gentlemen's attendant to help me with some of my personal care needs. I paid him upfront and felt pretty comfortable about how things were going to run. I explained to my teachers that I could do many of the household things by myself and I didn't need a lot of assistance.

The three of us went shopping and bought what we needed for the week. I cooked dinner and did the dishes afterwards. I slept very well that night. I woke up the next morning and made my way to the kitchen. The two of them asked me what was for breakfast. I checked the menu and went right to work.

As soon as I was through making breakfast, I had to do the dishes. By the time the dishes were done, it was lunch time. I stayed and made lunch. Then, I did the dishes. After catching my breath, it was time for me to have a beer.

"So, what's for dinner?" the attendant asked me.

I checked the menu and started working on dinner. While I was washing the dishes for the fourth meal in a row, it suddenly dawned on me that I was doing all the work. Gee, what an idiot!

My girlfriend, Loretta, was supposed to come and visit me in the apartment so we could have some fun. Yeah right, this was more like boot camp and I was doing all the work in the mess hall.

My teachers came by to see how things were going. I gave them an ear-full.

"But you told us you could do almost everything by yourself."

"Of course I could do a lot of things by myself, but this guy has been sitting around all day waiting for me to bring him something to eat. No one is sharing in the housework!" I said.

Living in a kitchen for almost two days gave me a greater appreciation for all those things Mom did for me. It is a full-time job.

With my high school education complete and college just around the corner, I knew things weren't going to be any easier. I don't think I was prepared for what was to come.

Perhaps if I had stayed in the Midwest things would have been different. I would have been more studious. I would have had more fun.

Again, it is something I think about.

Chico State University

For one reason or another, some disabled students have problems with their professors. Perhaps they have to deal with attitudinal barriers that are as thick as cement. Maybe their expectations of the teacher are radically different than mine. Or, as with non-disabled students, they just might be a constant pain in the ass. You know, you don't have to be disabled to be a pain in the ass.

While attending Chico State University, I basically got along with all of my professors. Does this mean I had it easy? No, not if you took Dr. Milo's public relations internship class. If you had one mistake on your paper, whether it was a misspelled word or style error, you got a big fat zero. There were no exceptions.

I couldn't go and lay the typical "woe is me" crap on her. I didn't even bother to try. She expected excellence from all of her students, including me.

I got one zero on a paper and that was it.

As it said in the course catalog, my teachers paid special attention to me, just like all the other students at Chico State.

To prove to myself that I had some artistic talent, I took an art class that had a lab. In the lab, we got to do different kinds of art, including painting. This time, I got real instruction, and a better grade.

Going into CSUC, I knew my major was going to be communications. With that in mind, I had to decide between public relations and journalism.

I took a bunch of my clips from an internship I had completed at a weekly paper to the advisor of the school newspaper, *The Orion*, and asked him if I could submit a few stories even though I wasn't on staff.

He asked if I had taken his newswriting and copy editing classes. I said I was a freshman and I hadn't done so. I explained all the experience I had at the paper and how it provided me with some much needed skills.

Instead of saying that he would take a look at my work, he got on his pompous, self-aggrandizing soap box and said that I needed to take his classes. Well, la-di-da!

I told my undergrad advisor, Dr. Sutthoff, that I was leaning toward PR. I wanted to minor in PE but I didn't want to take all of the science classes. Now, you're probably thinking I was trying to take the easy way out, but personally, I had no need for anatomy, physiology or kinesiology.

He suggested that I put together a minor from a couple of areas. So, I chose speech to go along with PE. It was a perfect match. I officially declared myself a PR major after my first semester. I went to the journalism advisor's office and told the egomaniac the good news.

I explained that I had just written two articles for the Associated Press and San Francisco Examiner during the semester break, and that I didn't need to be a journalism major if I wanted to write.

I opted to take the newswriting class for PR majors instead. The reason why I chose public relations over journalism was simple. For myself, I felt that I would learn a broader range of skills that could be applied to almost every profession. Journalism seemed too limiting for me.

I learned how to write news releases and feature stories. I learned how to make a brochure and put together a presentation. I learned what works, and what doesn't work.

Once I had chosen PR as my emphasis, I was given an advisor. Bob Vivian was just my kind of guy. He was a big sports fan like me. He liked the Miami Dolphins and Syracuse Orangemen. That was his alma-mater.

Even though he wore a tie, Bob was by no means flashy. When it came to public relations, Bob was a nuts and bolts person. I almost want to call him blue collar.

We got along very well. He understood how I wanted to use my major. We talked about my going to another school and finding a position in their football program where I could coach part of the time, and spend the other time working on things like recruiting or fundraising. My skills would be perfect for that kind of job.

Aside from having Bob Vivian as an advisor, he was one of my favorite professors. I had him for several classes. I'll never forget the time when I showed up to class dressed like Santa Claus.

Whenever I see Bob around town, he would tell me how he shares what happened that day with his students. It was a memorable experience.

There were a few instances where I needed special accommodations. My professors were very helpful. After I broke my arm and leg in a car accident, it was difficult for me to write and I had to take my final exams. I brought this to the attention of one of my professors, Chuck Harvey. He taught U.S. History.

He said, "No problem, you can take the exam orally."

We went outside and he asked the questions, for which I managed to have a few answers. As difficult as it was to take an oral exam, I actually enjoyed it. The test ended up being more like a discussion than a test.

I also had professors who came to visit me while I was in the hospital. I'll never forget the time I was in the hospital due to one of my falls off a curb because I had too much to drink.

One of my teachers, Dr. Main, came to see me and gave me some advice about drinking. What he said didn't leave as big an impression on me as much as his mere presence. This was a man who cared about me as a person so much so, that he took time out to come to the hospital.

Did I ever use my disability to get something out of a professor? Yes, but only once.

During my first semester, I was supposed to head down to the Bay Area to go to the Stanford-Cal game on the weekend before Thanksgiving. Unlike it is now, school was in session for part of the week and teachers always scheduled tests and papers so that no one would go home early. My math teacher, Dr. BeMiller was a really nice guy. There wasn't a mean bone in his body.

Not to my surprise, he gave us an assignment that was due on the Tuesday of Thanksgiving Week. We could only turn it in that day, or we would be penalized for turning it in late. He was very adamant about it and wouldn't even accept early papers. He wanted you in class on Tuesday.

As he was doing a problem on the board, my mind was busy trying to figure out a way I was going to go to the game and attend my math class. I had arranged a ride home the Friday before Thanksgiving and I was going to spend a long week with the folks. My mind was racing. Class was almost over. I started to look down and saw the long-leg cast on my leg. All of a sudden, a light went on. BINGO!

I went up to him after class and said I had to go to San Francisco to see my orthopedic specialist about my leg. I volunteered to turn the paper in early.

Not only did he buy it hook, line, and sinker, he gave me until the following Tuesday to turn in my assignment. Whoopee!

Normally, I wouldn't have done It., but in this case, I had to go to the game. I had my priorities, you know.

Just before graduation, I went to Dr. Milo's office to hear her words of wisdom before checking out. Even though she was a stickler for perfection, I had grown to like her over the course of the semester.

She said that there was a place for me out there. She said that I had a niche to fill, and I would find it someday.

Well, I'm still looking to find that niche.

From the time I was segregated from the regular students at Jefferson School to the moment I exited the halls of my alma mater, Chico State University, I think as a whole I received a pretty good formal education. There are some things that worked very well for me. And if I could turn the clock back, I would do some things differently. Perhaps I could have studied a little harder. But heck, we can all say that.

Of course, no one can turn back the hands of time. However, I think it's important to relate these experiences and make some suggestions as to how I think the system can work for future generations to come.

Goals...Then and Now

It is my belief that while I was a student in the special ed program at Mills High School, the goals of the bureaucrats and social engineers were radically different than my parents'.

I think the custodians of the program in San Mateo County felt their job was to treat us like lab rats while we were there, and then ship us off to another group of people who would take care of us for the rest of our lives. They didn't even think about turning out students who would become productive members of society. Their idea was to send us off on a wing and a prayer. This may be hard for some to take, but there is a lot of truth to it.

In my special ed class, we had five or six of us who graduated in my class. Of the five, I was the only one who went to a four-year school. I believe my friend Andy went to a computer school in the East Bay. Meanwhile, the rest stayed home and got to look at their green or gold checks.

Here's another thing to think about. If you are required to spend time in a classroom with a certain group of people, how are you going to get along with the rest of society? Heck, I didn't really get to know the people in my senior class until it was practically too late.

Sure, to a degree this was my fault. But if a rat is kept in a cage with a bunch of other rats, he's got nowhere else to go.

During my freshman year at Lakeshore High School, I took a careers class. In that class, we took tests to see what we were interested in doing. When I got to the county program, the only tests I took were IQ and other psychological tests.

So tell me, what does this have to do with me when I leave? How is a battery of psychological tests going to help me cope with the real world? Well, if I'm not going to the looney bin, it does absolutely nothing. It doesn't put money in my pocket. It doesn't put food on anyone's table—but theirs.

I didn't really learn how to read or outline a chapter until I went to Chico State. God, if I had learned it in high school, life would have been a hell of a lot easier.

Basically, while I was going to school, the folks in special ed thought that our physical disabilities extended to our brains. They thought this way, and they believed it.

If we as a society want to make the disabled givers, and not takers, attitudes must change. The goal of educators should be to produce productive members of society. This applies to everyone who crosses the classroom threshold.

Some may think this is unrealistic. I disagree.

Let's take for example two friends of mine who went through the same program I did. Their names are Frank and Ted.

I was at home on semester break when the telephone rang. It was for me.

"Hey Jonathan, this is Frank." I was surprised to hear his voice.

"What's going on?" he asked.

I told Frank about all the fun I was having up in Chico. I talked about all the babes and the parties. Oh yeah, I briefly mentioned school.

"What are you doing, Frank?"

"Oh, not much, I'm living at home with my parents." There was a pause.

"I got a color TV" he said.

"Uh-huh."

"I got a telephone. I'm talking to you on it right now. The people at Independent Living helped me get it."

"So, what else are you doing?"

"Oh, I worked for a while at Easter Seals, but I quit."

"Yeah, well are you doing anything now?"

"No."

I went back to watch the second half of the game.

I felt really bad for Frank. I mean, here he was sitting at home and the only thing he could tell me was that he had a new phone and a color television.

Frank was no genius, but he wasn't stupid either.

About three years ago, I got another phone call. This time it was Ted. Ted was a sophomore when I was a senior.

I asked Ted what he was up to, and what he said was disheartening. Ted lived at home with his parents and went to a community college after high school.

Shortly thereafter, his mother passed away. His father couldn't take care of him and thought the best thing to do for Ted was to put him in a nursing home."

I thought, "What's up with that?"

Ted said that he had recently gotten out of the nursing home and he was living independently in Sacramento.

I asked Ted if he had any skills. He told me he was good at playing craps.

Better send him to Vegas.

Though I don't know everything about their situations, I could only venture to speculate that someone dropped the ball along the way.

What we have here are two people who, in their own way, could make a positive contribution to society. By not having the motivation, and knowing only a world of dependency, it is understandable that they are in that situation.

Are teachers going to make rocket scientists and lawyers out of every student? Of course, not. But it has been my experience that when it comes to special education, teachers have viewed the cup that holds the mind as being totally empty instead of at least, half full.

We need to think of every student as possessing the ability to learn and achieve. This is a must! Educators should be as equally concerned with figuring out a way for a student to learn as they are when trying to figure out why a student cannot learn. The challenge is finding the key that will unlock that potential.

The first step toward making disabled people a contributing part of our society is by educating them to be the best. There must be a comprehensive shift in attitudes.

If the old attitudes remain in place, we will have perpetuated a cycle of dependency, and we will have done a great disservice to a segment of society.

Changing The System

As we think about ways we can tailor our resources so that we can better meet those needs, the same holds true for special education. It's time for us to sit down and rethink how we can retool the system, and make special education really mean something. It needs a complete overhaul.

We need to downsize a bureaucracy that is loaded with therapists, shrinks, and social engineers who are feeding off the public trough. If a student needs a psychologist or therapist, then it should be done on a contract basis. Let's not assume that every kid needs a shrink.

It is high time that we greatly reduce the number of special schools and put those resources into mainstreaming and inclusion. Overall, I am an advocate of inclusion because of my experiences outside the system.

We can start by increasing the number of students with disabilities in elementary schools.

There needs to be a significant reduction in the amount of paperwork so that teachers can spend more time on educating the students, rather than filling out a bunch of forms that are supposed to make everyone feel good. If laws need to be changed in order to make this happen, let's do it—now!

The IEP (Individual Educational Plan) process needs a lot of H-E-L-P!

Personally, I would scrap the whole thing in lieu of just having a parent/teacher conference. You can accomplish the same thing.

Another reason why I didn't like going through the IEP process was because I felt it was demeaning.

At a meeting, you have fifteen or so people sitting around a huge table because law required them to get together twice a year to talk about you.

You've got the program coordinator, psychologist, special ed teacher, and a social worker, just to name a few. They get paid big bucks to go to meetings about every student in special ed, whether their presence is needed or not.

When I did choose to go to some of these meetings, I saw these folks talk about me as if I wasn't even there. They barely acknowledged my parents.

Would you put up with these meetings, the way I described them to you? Probably not.

With all of the meetings and paperwork, I dare to ask, what we do have to show for our efforts?

The system has got to change—now!

In order for the system to change, we need to look at the big picture. Whether it is a student with poor eyesight, a physical or developmental disability, or other impairment, we need to think of each student having special needs. When it comes to securing books, facilities, or other learning devices, teachers become "specialists" in dealing with the needs of their students. They become advocates in seeing that those needs are met.

As our nation moves into the next century, we will see dramatic changes in the way we educate our children. With teachers acting as pioneers, catalysts, and innovators, the challenge still remains, that of tapping the most precious resource we have—people.

Finally, a Word to Parents

I could go on and on about what would have happened if I had stayed in the Midwest. I could talk and talk about where I thought things went wrong, and how the system needs to change to meet the needs of today's student.

But, I would be remiss if I didn't have a word or two of advice for parents of special needs children, or anyone's children for that matter. This advice is largely based on the observations of my parents, and how they were able to do what they thought was best for me.

Though at times I am critical of the system, my parents would be a little bit nicer and say these folks were just doing what they thought was best for me. They never spoke ill of anyone, and were very complimentary to people whenever they had the chance.

My parents knew that even though I had many gaps in my education, they viewed it as ignorance rather than stupidity. They knew I wasn't a genius, just an average student who, with a little motivation, could do above average work in the classroom.

With that knowledge, they took the less conservative, less protective route, and tried their hand at sending me to a regular public school with no county special ed program. Their gamble paid off.

Then, when they realized that they had to play by some set of rules, they didn't lose focus on getting me the proper education that would help me get into Chico State.

The school psychologist told them that I didn't have the IQ to go on to college. Instead of standing up and telling the guy that he himself was an idiot, they just smiled and nodded their heads.

There are many parents who bought everything the shrinks and social engineers were telling 'em, and then some. My parents didn't. Henry and Cynthia just sat there and took it all in. They talked about it, and then moved on with their game plan.

If I were to give advice to a parent, I would start by saying that your son or daughter has the potential to make some sort of contribution to society. They have something to offer. They may not become a chemist or an engineer. They may not become a football player or astronaut. But, look around and see all of the things they can do. There is a place for them in our society that involves making some contribution to the common good.

Besides being your pride and joy, there is a reason why they were put on this earth.

So, let's start with the understanding that you will not underestimate the potential of your child. You will start at the very top without ever letting your child sink to the very bottom. Most parents with disabled children start at the bottom, and stay there because some "all knowing" bureaucrat told them that's where they had to be.

What you have to understand here is that your child is a student, not a lab rat. No matter how many people tell you that your son or daughter is stupid and can't do a thing for themselves or society, you don't have to buy that nonsense. Quietly, you can tell them they're full of it, and then move on. That's what my parents did.

For too long, parents have been nodding their heads "yes" like little children when they are being preached to by those in special education. It's time that parents and teachers expect the best from their children, no matter what their disability may be.

Are we going to lose some? Sure. But if we start at the top and end somewhere in the middle, there won't be as many students sinking to the bottom. Remember, no one knows your child better than you.

I Feel My Pain

So, how does it feel to break a bone? How does it feel to break your leg? Your arm? Your ribs? Your nose? Your neck—twice?

Well, if I told you that it felt good, I would be lying. If I said it didn't feel that bad, I would be lying again. If I said it hurts, it would suffice as an answer. But, if I told you that it hurts like hell, that would be an honest response. Harsh, but honest.

Do you want to take a guess at how many bones I have broken in my life? Ten? Twenty? Fifty?

My guess would be better than yours, but I can't give you the exact number of fractures this body has seen, heard, and felt. My parents stopped counting after twenty. I have likely broken over a hundred bones in my life. Each one having a time and a place. Each one with a story to tell.

When I was a child, I once broke both of my legs in one day. It wouldn't be the first time either.

One morning, I broke my left leg playing football in bed with my teddy bear. I went to tackle my teddy, and he fell on my leg. I don't know if he scored on the play, but after a trip to the hospital, I came home with a cast.

When we arrived home, I was all excited to see our dog, Ilio. Dad opened the door of the car where I was sitting. I called the dog to come in the car to give me a kiss. For the first time in my life I got more than just a kiss. As he jumped into the back seat of the car to greet me, the eighty-five pound German Shepherd's paw landed squarely on my leg and—snap!

Dad, understandably tired from spending the day at the hospital, brought Dr. Max from across the street, and he told my dad to wrap my leg in a comic book until we made a return trip to the hospital.

As a child, I was also in a number of bus accidents which often resulted in my breaking one or both hips. On one occasion, I even fractured my pelvis.

Back in those days, the mini buses we rode had the engines placed in the front between the driver and the front passenger seats. As the bus approached the driveway into my house, I yelled to the driver, "The Belt!! The Belt!! It's squishing me!"

He looked around the bus with a puzzled gaze.

I continued to yell at the top of my lungs. I felt the bones of my midsection being crushed under the pressure. By the time I took off the seatbelt, my eyes welled with tears. I was screaming in pain as the bus came to a stop. Mom was standing in the driveway, waiting to pick me up. It didn't take her very long to figure out that something was wrong. In this instance, the seatbelt had gotten caught in the fan belt. I was soon not a fan of seatbelts or fan belts.

There are instances when my bones fractured simply by laughing or sneezing too hard, or break spontaneously, like a twig. Cold and flu season is commonly known as rib fracture season. There's really nothing you can do about that. Other times, I would break something by falling out of my wheelchair.

On a warm summer night in July of 1981, I went for a late night walk with my father and Ilio. On our excursion, we went around the rec center which was next door to our house. Adjacent to the rec center was a medium sized hill which I had gone down many times. I pretended I was Mario Andretti at the Indy 500.

Unfortunately, on this particular try, my wheelchair hit a rock and tumbled on its side. As I anguished in pain, the momentum of the fall caused my chair to slide about thirty feet down the asphalt. My father was close, but too far behind. He picked up what would be another broken body. Only this time, my face was covered with blood—lots of blood. Dad tried to humor me by saying that it looked like I'd been hit in the face with a cherry pie.

While doing his best to clean me up, Dad was concerned about the blood left on the hill outside the rec center. It looked like a stabbing had taken place.

The pain was so bad, I fell into shock. We went to the emergency room where the doctor on call said I had suffered a concussion, along with six fractures in my legs.

After much discussion, the two thought it would be appropriate for me to get my broken legs set at Shriners Hospital in the morning.

The doctor gave me a pain shot before Dad packed me up for the short ride home.

Soon after Dad had prepared a makeshift bed on the floor of the living room, I would escape the pain of this terrible nightmare and begin a journey into another world.

The next morning, my father took me to Shriners get my legs set. I was not responding to anyone. He thought I was just groggy from the pain killers. The nurse immediately summoned a doctor. After taking one look at me, Dr. Sampson requested an ambulance to take me to Children's Hospital in San Francisco. I had slipped into a coma.

After undergoing a cat-scan, the neurologist, Dr. Palmer, informed my father and Dr. Sampson that I had suffered a subdural hematoma. I had two blood clots in my head.

He said I didn't have a prayer, and at best, I would probably end up a vegetable. He strongly urged they let me go peacefully.

Dr. Sampson asked Dr. Palmer to do what he could to save me. He wouldn't make any guarantees. They would have to perform emergency surgery.

Soon after the first cut had been made, blood spewed from the top of my head like a Texas oil well. My heart stopped beating. For four minutes, doctors worked frantically to bring me back. Once I had stabilized, the surgery to remove the blood from my head resumed. I would later return to surgery to drain more blood from another clot that had formed.

So, what was it like being dead for four minutes? Did you see Jesus? Did you go to heaven? Were there angels waiting for you at the pearly gates?

What I experienced during this journey was more feeling rather than seeing. It was the feeling of being in a very peaceful state. I felt as if I were immersed in a bright white light. It was very comfortable. I can barely recall a period of darkness; it was more like going through a tunnel, before entering this comfort zone.

While all of this was going on, I was beginning my journey into the unknown. Scientifically speaking, I was in a deep coma. While I was unable to communicate with anyone in this state of being, I can recall many things that were going on around me. I felt like the boy in the plastic bubble.

I heard the nurses talking to me as if I was awake and coherent. I could see my special ed teacher as he came to visit me. He appeared very distraught. I recall hearing my sisters read me articles out of *The Sporting News*. Due to a major league players strike, the only game stories they read to me came from minor league baseball. So, they kept me up to date on the games going on in the Pacific Coast League.

The most important image I can recall during my deep sleep is one that would later save me from being taken off life support. Whenever my father came to visit me, he would gently place his finger in the palm of my hand. He then asked me to squeeze his hand. I did. In fact, I squeezed it on command. He knew there was something going on in the back of my head. He knew I was there. Then he told the doctors that if anyone was going to pull the plug, it would be him. This was the only form of communication I would have with anyone.

Two weeks after my accident, I returned from my journey. The first two people I saw were my mother and the nurse on duty.

"What the hell am I doing here!?"

She told me I had fallen and that I was going to be alright. She then asked me if I had remembered dying in surgery. I told her I could not pinpoint when I actually experienced this peaceful feeling, but I did let her know that something happened.

The next few days were touch and go. I wasn't breathing very well and the doctors thought they were going to have to do a tracheotomy. Fortunately, it didn't happen.

While my head and legs have healed from the fall down the hill, I suffered nerve damage to one of my eyes that is irreparable.

The neurologist who didn't give me a chance to live was beside himself. "This has been a most unusual case," were his parting words to my father.

You can say that again! We can all thank Dr. Sampson as well.

Following the accident, I slowed down quite a bit. I began to have a new appreciation for life. I looked at things a lot differently than other students my age. To this day, the experience of that night proved to me that there is something here for me to do.

Growing up, I viewed the physical pain that came with each fracture as being temporary. Even after taking a tumble that fateful summer night, my body managed to heal itself quite well.

As an adult, the pain that follows the snap, crack, or pop of a bone still lingers. Lately, I've been able to express my feelings about my pain.

Following my last two fractures, one of my legs, the other my neck, my views toward pain have changed. It has caused me to think about the quality of my life and what we are doing to improve the quality of life for all people who suffer with pain.

If I had to determine which fracture hurt the worst, I have to say that it was when I broke my neck the second time, in the winter of 1991. It would rank as one of the worst experiences I've ever had as a patient in the hospital.

Unlike some of my previous falls, the way I broke my neck this time was as a result of a freak accident. It was almost like being hit by lightning.

I was going to visit a friend down the street from my house. The weather was cold and I was traveling in between rainstorms. I thought it might rain again before I got to my destination, so I put on my Kansas City Chiefs poncho Dad had bought me for Christmas.

It would be the first time I would don the red and gold cover. I was going at a pretty good clip down Orient as I crossed Seventh Street. His office was on the other side of Eighth. As I approached the sidewalk threshold, I felt a quick, hard pull on the front of my poncho. Thinking I wasn't safely across the street, I kept my finger on the joystick; the chair continued moving at a high rate of speed. In doing so, the poncho wrapped itself in the wheel and ejected me out of my chair. I fell to the ground and a sharp pain shot through the base of my neck. The left side of my body went numb.

A woman ran over to where I lay motionless, but conscious. I told her I was hurting, and that I couldn't feel my hands. I fell into a state of shock. She told me help was on the way.

The ambulance arrived shortly thereafter. After checking my vitals and asking me countless questions, I was placed on a board, and strapped from head to toe. I did not move.

As the ambulance sped from the scene, I was asked by one of the paramedics which hospital I wanted to go to.

"Do I have a choice?" I replied.

I told them I wanted to go to the closest hospital, of course. What a stupid question.

Even though the trip was probably less than two miles long, it seemed like we were on the road forever. Perhaps we were taking the scenic route. Or, maybe they stopped at McDonald's, and I didn't know it. Anyway, my mind was racing. My body was trying to deal with this latest trauma. The pain was increasing by the moment.

While in the emergency room, all I could think about was the pain.

"Please, give me something for the pain," I pleaded. I was given a shot of Demerol.

After taking X-rays, it was discovered I broken the third cervical vertebrae in my neck. Doctors decided the best way to treat this was to put me in a collar, or neck brace, and let nature take its course. The fracture wasn't bad enough to warrant surgery.

I would spend ten days in the hospital before being moved to a rehab unit at an adjacent hospital. So, I ended up spending time in both hospitals.

From this latest stint in the "big house," I experienced the best, and the worst of hospital care. In the end, the bad outweighed the good, and it is hard to forget.

The first two days of this nightmare were one big blur. I was basically strung out on drugs I was taking for the pain. The drugs were as incredible as the pain. They put me on a machine which gave me a small dose of morphine every time I hit a button. I was able to activate the supply every ten minutes. I swear I could hit that button in my deepest sleep.

I vaguely remember having to leave the hospital to go next door to have an MRI done on my neck. I was placed on a gurney that put me in a van, only to be driven about twenty yards to get pictures taken of my neck. This was not fun.

While in this trance, I still had many visitors. My parents drove up from Ventura to see their listless son. They brought my nephew, Michael, and my sister, Becky, from Santa Cruz. Dad felt really bad about the poncho. I told him it was an accident.

On about the third day, doctors decided to take me off the "happy machine." I was told I could have a pain shot about every two hours. I requested a pain shot every two and a half hours, or so. Don't hold me to it.

The first nurse I had was great when it came to giving me my medicine. She told me to let her know when it hurt, and she would bring me a shot, no questions asked. When I hit the call button to ask for my last shot while she was on shift, she was en route to my room, armed with needle and swab.

In this initial state of consciousness, I wished I was on the "happy machine" just a little bit longer. My body felt like a pretzel and I felt as if my back had been slashed with a thin knife, like someone had drawn a football field with a thin razor blade. With this discomfort, I mentioned it to the nurses who had come aboard for the evening shift. They discovered sores on my back and it was determined that I had a yeast infection.

To treat this infection, I was turned from side to side every two hours and they applied white powder to the infected areas. I was not happy.

After asking for a pain shot, the evening nurse made some sort of comment regarding the frequency for which I was asking for medication. It was difficult to get any sleep before I would have to be turned, again. This would turn out to be my worst night in a hospital ever!

I felt a lot of pain being turned from side to side. I couldn't get back to sleep as the sharp pain shot from my neck to my shoulder and back again. I asked the nurse for another pain shot. In turn, she asked me a number of questions. I was willing to cooperate.

"At what level is your pain at right now? she asked.

"It depends which pain you're talking about. If you're talking about the pain in my neck, it's a solid seven or eight. The pain in my back is a ten," I replied. To me that adds up to seventeen or eighteen.

"When we give you a shot, at what level does it go down to?"

"About a two or a one."

"For how long?"

"I'd say between two, and two and a half hours."

"Well, maybe we need to give you a shot in your muscle, or some other place so you can feel more relief. I'll call the doctor."

What she said sounded alright to me. I didn't care where they stuck that needle. They could shoot me in the head if they wanted to. That's with a needle, of course.

She returned to my room with what would be my last pain shot.

"I talked to the doctor and he told me that you can have one more shot. After that, it's pills from here on out."

The doctor she was referring to was my orthopedist, a Stanford grad who knows his bones, but doesn't quite cut it when it comes to bedside manners. Though I continue to see him, his best work on me has been done while I've been unconscious.

After hearing what she had told me, I became very upset. I believed that she told my doctor that I was turning into a drug addict. I didn't know what the hell she was doing, but it was obvious that she wasn't interested in my well-being.

When it came time for my medication, it was "down the hatch we go." I would have to be turned once again. Soon after, the pain reared its ugly head once again. The pills weren't doing the trick. After I couldn't take it anymore, I started to cry for the first time in nearly ten years. The tears were flowing from my eyes into my Kleenex as I cried for my Mom and Dad to help me. No one was there. I cried for somebody, anybody.

There was no answer.

I was angry, frustrated, and rendered helpless in my hospital bed. I couldn't believe decisions were being made about me without my involvement or consent. My doctor never checked on me, or even bothered to talk to me on the telephone. I felt the nurse had overstepped her bounds and was trying to play doctor.

As my first round of crying slowed to a soft whimper, she returned.

"Is there something wrong? Something I can do to make you feel better," she asked.

"No! Get out! Get the hell out of here! There's nothing you can do to make me feel better!"

It was the first time I have ever uttered words like that to a nurse. In this case, I could have said a whole lot more.

When she left the room, I cried myself to sleep. I wondered when this nightmare was going to end.

The next morning saw much joy and happiness...not! A social worker came to tell me that if I wasn't able to transfer myself into my wheelchair according to their timetable, I would find myself in a convalescent home. What joy!

"Would you be telling me this if I had private insurance? I asked. My voice was strong, yet soft spoken.

She said it didn't matter, but she didn't sound very convincing.

I was astounded by everything that was going on around me. Here I lay on a hospital bed with a broken neck and knotted pustules on my back, and they expect me to do cartwheels less than a week after the worst accident of my life.

Later that day, the neurologist stuck his finger up my ass. I asked myself, "What did I do to deserve this?"

My stay at "the hospital of my choice" came to a close when I was transferred to another hospital with a rehabilitation unit. I was going to be treated by a female doctor who had recently moved into the area. I thought it would be interesting to have a female doctor. Maybe she would be a bit more understanding and empathetic about how I was feeling. Perhaps she could make me feel like I was being treated by a competent physician. I wasn't impressed by the rehab doctor who saw me after I broke my neck the first time. He didn't earn the money the state was paying him to treat me.

Unfortunately, the way my luck was running, I was going to take it in the shorts. I found myself at the mercy of the same blowhard, incompetent, phony Dr. Seuss once again.

Every time I had a question or concern about my treatment, he would respond with some version of "I don't know." It was followed by a shallow, disingenuous look of concern.

Then, he would say, "I'll see you tomorrow." This would play over and over again like a broken record.

Soon after, I returned home from the hospital. I was able to transfer myself in and out of my wheelchair.

The pain was still there, shooting its way up and down, between my neck and shoulder. It was sharp and relentless. I also was having to adjust to the lack of sensation in my fingers and my left arm. The tips of my fingers felt numb, as if they had gotten caught in a door jam. I could not feel certain areas of my left arm. This would be a problem for me while in the kitchen because I am not aware of the heat of various pots and pans.

I continued my treatment on an outpatient basis, receiving therapy until the well ran dry. That is, until the money ran out. My left arm was still in pain, but it didn't seem to matter. I was healed according to them and that's all that was important.

While the tears have long since dried, they often return after another fall. Though the whimpers soften to an occasional grimace, the pain still remains—and it is real. It burns, aches, throbs, pinches, at varying degrees.

As each day passes, I become less hopeful that there lies a "pain free" day in my future.

This experience caused me to think a lot about the pain I feel. It makes me wonder about how much control I have over the quality of my life, and how much control we all have over the quality of our lives.

When I think about the quality of life for those who suffer from chronic pain, it astounds me to think that a country that put a man on the moon, manufactures the most sophisticated weapons that can destroy the world many times over, can't spend more time and money finding cures and remedies for what ails us. Hey, if you can't cure what I've got, at least do what you can to make me feel better.

Why is it that we live in a country that guarantees an attorney to those who are charged with a crime, yet doesn't guarantee healthcare to its own citizens? Think about it.

If you are charged with committing a crime, the state will provide you with someone who will try to get you out of the slammer. If you are in the slammer, you have healthcare. But, if you need to see a doctor and you aren't in prison, that's another story.

How does it relate to pain? It's simple. If you hurt, you should be able to see any doctor who can make you get well, no matter whom you are. You should have access to those medicines that will make you feel better, no matter how much it costs. This should be a right of every American citizen.

How often do we hear horror stories of people making choices between prescription drugs and food or heating for their house? Or, how about the time you may have put off a visit to the doctor or dentist until the very last minute only to find that the problem has gotten worse?

What about those who choose between life and death?

Right now, the debate in our country has escalated over doctor assisted suicide, or euthanasia. The debate has been made famous by pathologist, Dr. Jack Kevorkian, who has assisted a number of people in ending their lives.

While I oppose a number of the suicides this doctor has helped to facilitate, it is important the debate continue. This discussion should not solely focus on ending the suffering of people by helping them die. But rather, it should focus more on how we can improve the quality of life for those who suffer from pain. Choosing death by whatever means should be a last resort, not a first or second option.

The biggest problem I have about doctor assisted suicide is the adverse way it could be used as a solution to ending life for people with disabilities who suffer from pain.

A number of Dr. Kevorkian's victims have been people with disabilities, and that concerns me.

A woman with multiple sclerosis chose to end her life because she couldn't live with the pain any longer. Though I don't know anything of this woman's particular case, it prompts me to ask one question. Are we doing enough to help her and many others with pain to ease their suffering?

With my experience in dealing with the pain associated with countless traumas I have endured, my answer is NO! On a visit to my orthopedist, I explained how the pain in my left arm was racing up and down like rush hour traffic on an L.A. freeway. He told me to go home and make a list of the times when it REALLY hurt.

When it REALLY hurts? What's that supposed to mean? What is a person to do when the government insurance runs out, and the healthcare providers say you're all better, even when you're not?

As a person who suffers from pain, I am frustrated by the appearance of a lack of effort by healthcare practitioners, or our present healthcare system, that features little "care" in it.

Jeff Trimmer, a good friend of mine, once wrote a paper on why he wanted to be a doctor. He explained the pain his mother feels with her many respiratory ailments. He explained her constant suffering and that he wanted to be a doctor so that he could do whatever it took to make her and other people feel better. Along the way, he would tell his patients how much he cared, and that he understood what they were going through.

I'm sure there are doctors who care about their patients and do whatever they can to make their patients comfortable. But, in the case of the woman with multiple sclerosis, and many people who suffer with pain, I have to ask this question again, and again, and again.

Are we doing enough to help people so they don't consider death as an alternative?

Let's look at people who suffer from cancer or AIDS. Some patients get relief after smoking marijuana. Yet because marijuana is illegal, it is nearly impossible for them to use it as part of their treatment.

Is this the way we should be taking care of people who are sick? Are we a society that says if a person is in constant pain, or is terminally ill, they should be denied the right to smoke a joint just because the substance is illegal? In this case, marijuana should be considered along with all other narcotics available by prescription.

Have I ever thought about committing suicide? In times of great despair and confusion, I have thought about it. When I have felt alone with nowhere else to go, the notion rears its ugly head.

When I was lying in my hospital bed crying in my box of Kleenex, I didn't know what to think. Perhaps I should have thought about it then.

While I deal with pain on a day to day basis, suicide has not been a part of my thought process, yet. There are two factors that have kept me from thinking about it.

First, because I don't think an honest effort has been made in relieving the pain I have, there is cause for me to hope that one is on the way—someday. Unlike others who have considered suicide, my pain has not pushed me to the brink of considering the thought of ending my life.

If a conscious effort was made to ease the suffering of those who have a terminal illness or chronic pain from disease or injury, maybe we would have less people seeking those like Dr. Kevorkian.

The one main concern I have about euthanasia is the danger it presents if used for the wrong reasons. For elderly people and people with disabilities who live in institutions, hospitals, and other care facilities, the "magic needle" appears to be too readily accessible and considered as the only option. This option is made easier if the person cannot speak for themselves, or do not have a relative or person to advocate for them.

What if our country plunged into an economic crisis, the likes of the Great Depression, or even worse, that we too would consider reducing the surplus population?

Is this abhorrent? Sure it is. Is it possible? I think so. In fact, it may be going on even as we speak. We just don't know about it.

It would be good for us to debate the issue of euthanasia, or doctor assisted suicide.

Where do I stand on this issue?

Well, if a person has the right to life, liberty, and the pursuit of happiness as dictated by the Constitution, then if ending life finds them happiness, and they are competent in making that decision when all other options have failed, then so be it. They should be able to end their life.

If we choose to allow people to have this option, it should be heavily regulated, monitored, and reviewed so that abuse does not occur.

As for the current debate going on right now, it is time for others to step up to the plate and begin the process of constructive dialogue.

When it comes to the issue of having a child with osteogenesis imperfecta, pain is the primary factor in making this decision. As a person with OI, the chances of me passing the disease to my offspring is fifty-fifty with someone who doesn't have it. With someone who has OI, the chances are almost certain.

There is the opinion of some with OI, that the risk is no big deal. For them, having a child with the disease is alright because as parents who've had it, they can help the child deal with the ups and downs of having OI.

I agree that a person with OI may be better equipped to understand the pain and trauma that comes with the disease. However, I think the risk in having a child with OI is a BIG deal and shouldn't be taken lightly. Bringing a child into the world is certainly a blessing. Having a child who could suffer pain as the result of a sneeze is a different story.

When I think about all of my stays at Shriners Hospital, all the times I spent under the knife, all of the casts that sometimes covered most of my body, I wonder how I was able to handle it.

When I think of all the times my arm or leg would snap, just by sitting at a table playing cards, I would always ask why? Why is this happening?

It seemed that just when life was getting good, it would be interrupted by yet another fracture.

Having had many fractures associated with this disease, it would be extremely difficult for me to take that risk knowing what might lie ahead. If it were my choice and no one else's, I would not want to have a son or daughter with osteogenesis imperfecta. It's that simple. I would not want to watch my child suffer in pain as I have done. If the system can't help me cope with what's ailing me now, how is it going to be for my son or daughter as an adult?

Don't misunderstand what I am saying. I am happy with who I am. I am grateful to my parents for going through the trials and tribulations of having a son with OI. They deserve a thousand gold medals. But, if they knew then what they know now, and were asked to take the same risk, they would probably feel the same way. And, that's alright with me. If I were in their shoes, I would still love my child in the same way they love me. I would love my child no matter what imperfections they might have. There is a fine line between knowing the risks, and not knowing the risks.

A number of people have said to me that having kids would be natural for an upbeat guy like me.

"Really? What makes you think so?"

"Why you have such a great attitude about everything. You don't seem to let things get you down. Your kids would probably have the same attitude as you do."

This is complete nonsense! Look, no matter how positive my attitude may be regarding my own life, it doesn't mean that it will transfer to my offspring. Attitudes are shaped by so many things. Sure, as a parent, I would try to instill the best in my children, just as my parents did with me. But, the circumstances here are quite different.

Just as there is a risk with having sex—period, the only way that I would even consider having a child with OI is if it were a mistake to begin with, and my wife or significant other was dead set against having an abortion. Though I think I could handle it, if the unfortunate thing happened, I know there are better ways to bring children into the world.

By now, you have probably guessed that I am pro-choice when it comes to abortion.

Let me make it clear that I am not "pro-abortion." I am pro-choice.

So, do you approve of abortion being used as a form of birth control? Do you condone women who have more than one, or even two abortions?

No, I am against abortion as a form of birth control. Women who have even one abortion should seek counseling.

Don't you value the rights of the unborn? Shouldn't they be protected as well?

Yes, I value the rights of the unborn. But shouldn't these rights extend to include the quality of life of the unborn as well? The quality of life should be valued as much as life itself.

Again, that four letter word comes up when I think about abortion. I would want to have the option of making the choice of bringing a child into the world. I would want anyone to have that option.

While pain remains a facet of my life, it does not consume it—yet. The hours I spent venting my anger, frustration, and desperation, crying myself to sleep five years ago, are replaced by discussing it with my close friends, family members, and professionals who might be able to help.

Though I may be uncomfortable some of the time, my happy go lucky, cheerful, attitude is not a facade.

Look, whether you are a person with osteogenesis imperfecta or cancer, whether you have multiple sclerosis or arthritis, if you have a physical or mental illness, do not hesitate to let others know when you are hurting.

If it helps to discuss it with a relative or close friend, don't be afraid to let them know how you are feeling.

If someone asks, "How are you?" tell them. Tell them exactly what ails you. Lately, as I have been more open about discussing my pain, I've discovered positive results without being labeled a complainer.

What do I mean by positive results?

First, it makes me feel better to bend another's ear. It's just like telling someone your personal problems.

While spending time at my Grandma Studebaker's house in the Indiana Dunes, I remember sitting in her dining room watching the Cubs play on WGN while she was on the phone with her friends explaining her aches and pains from head to toe.

Years later, on a train ride from Chico to Ventura, I was sitting in a row in front of two senior citizens who were doing the exact same thing. The discussion was interrupted by one of them who had bouts of coughing spells. A few of the spells were so bad, the man had to leave the car to cough in the hallway because it was late at night and the rest of us were trying to sleep. Still, when he returned, the conversation continued until each symptom was fully scrutinized. Even though it was depressing to hear these stories then, I have since been on both ends of this discussion and have found it to be very helpful in communicating these thoughts to others now.

For example, there have been times when my attendants will come over to get me ready for the evening and when he asks me how I am doing. Sometimes I will say, "Great, how are you?"

Other times, I respond with, "I think I cracked a rib,"or, "My arm hurts."

In doing this, I have found some intrinsic value in telling it to a friend. To hear them say, "That's too bad," or "That sucks" does make me feel better, even if only for a moment or two. It's better than some of the responses I have gotten from my doctors. Hey, if it was good enough for Grandma Studebaker, it's good enough for me.

Once, I told a friend about the pain in my left arm. After hearing this, she referred me to a rehab doctor who she had heard good things about. I went to see him. Though he wasn't the miracle worker I had been looking for, he was head over heels above the doc I had seen while in the hospital.

On another occasion, a fellow Chicoan who had a milder form of OI asked me where to go for help. I was able to direct him to the right people.

Another benefit of discussing your health challenges with people you trust is the way in which they can be a resource. They may know of a particular doctor or health professional that may be able to help you.

If you don't have a relative or friend nearby, another person you can go to is a minister—any minister. Also, there are local government agencies that may help you as well.

I have a social worker who calls me once in a while and asks how I am doing. I've looked to her for help as well. Part of these people's jobs is to help those in distress. They may not carry a magic pill in their pocket, but they can certainly refer you to someone who can help.

Part of the reason why people contemplate taking drastic measures like ending their lives to end their pain is because they don't like their doctor. They have lost hope. They say that their doctor isn't helping them.

If you aren't satisfied with your doctor, go until you find the one best suited for you. Instead of being rendered helpless in your bed as I was three years ago, find that last bit of strength and demand a new doctor. Also, make sure that if you have chest pains or heart problems, don't see a podiatrist or dermatologist. Go to the right doctor or health professional.

While you may not find a doctor who can alleviate all of your aches and pains, you deserve to have someone who is compassionate and willing to give an honest effort in treating you. Only you can be the judge of that.

On the other hand, I bet there are some doctors who feel that it is the patient's fault. I mean, what's a doctor to do if a patient doesn't adhere to their prescribed course of treatment? As a recipient of services, you should be cooperative in following doctor's orders. If your doctor tells you that your liver is in bad shape and it's time to stop drinking, I think he or she is telling you something. Should a doctor give you medicine designed to make you feel better, give it a try. If it works, great!! If not, then call your physician and say that your medicine isn't working.

Making an effort in treating what ails you is a two-way street. As a patient, you must take an active role in your treatment. You also carry the responsibility in taking care of yourself. You are in charge!

Finally, I have found that I pay attention more to my pain when I am not active. Having a day full of activity is by no means a cure all, but having something else to do takes my mind off of what ails me, at least temporarily. Yes, it does make a difference.

The issue of pain extends to include issues that our society is focused on right now. In some ways it energizes me when I speak or write about it.

Pain is something that confronts all of us. It starts from the day we are born until the day we die. While others can empathize and say they feel our pain, no one else can feel it for us, nor can they tell you how you feel.

Mirror, Mirror, On the Wall

Most relationships evolve once you cross the threshold of adulthood, and such was the case with my relationship with Grandma Elster. On her last visit to my parents' house during the Christmas holiday several years ago, we ate lunch together and spent some good quality time talking to one another. Our conversation was that of two good friends talking about what each other was doing.

I think I got my writing genes from Grandma Elster. While she was more of an artist, painting pictures with her storytelling and poetry writing, I want people to react to both my writing and speaking. Ironically, I soon discovered the importance of writing letters when you are trying to drum up business. I think Grandma Elster would be proud of the fact that I am keeping the post office busy.

What really makes Grandma Elster special was her unconditional acceptance of being happy with whatever I was doing. When I decided not to move away to Iowa and instead become a public speaker, I asked her if I could use the money she had loaned me to move to the Midwest to start Project Speak Out. She said that I could use it to start anything I wanted to, as long as I was happy doing it.

Grandma Elster's encouragement came just at the right time. And from that time on, until she passed away, her support was always there. Today, she still remains a shining light.

C.W. Nevius

To readers of the *San Francisco Chronicle*, C.W. Nevius is just another sports columnist. To my family, they know him simply as Chuck. To me, whether it be C.W. or Chuck, he is a friend who is always concerned with everything that is going on with me—literally.

No, he is not a doting sort of guy who's got nothing better to do. He's got a wife and family of his own. He's just been the kind of friend who asks about anything from how are you doing, to have you met any women lately?

I first became acquainted with Chuck on a personal basis in the summer before my senior year of high school, the summer of '82. While I was going through the Youth Employment Program, my counselor asked me if there was someone I wanted to meet in the professional world. Since I wanted to be a sportswriter at the time, that's what I told her. She arranged for me to have lunch with Chuck during my break at work. I was a clerk for a family practice doctor at a local hospital.

Meeting and talking with Chuck was not the same as seeing Len Dawson or Otis Taylor, but it was pretty special. When I first saw him, he looked kind of familiar.

Chuck talked about his job at the *Chronicle* and gave me some tips about sports writing. I told him I wanted to be a columnist and I thought I would make a darn good one. I eagerly handed him a sample of my writing, waiting for him to tell me how good it was. Hey, I thought anything I wrote was just as good anything in the *Chronicle*. Right?

Well, like any good mentor would do, he said some nice things about it. Then, he politely ripped it to shreds. He went on to point out that I had to be a good reporter before they'd let me write any commentaries. I guess that's sort of like paying your dues.

Chuck talked about the difference between being one who reports the news, and one who makes the news. He talked about how as a reporter, you can't be a fan. That is, you cannot root for any team while covering a game. It suddenly dawned on me that Chuck knew me even though I didn't remember him. He had written a story about me the previous year, during the week of the East-West Shrine Game.

My parents quickly took a liking to Chuck when they first met him. Mom asked about his background and was easily impressed when he told her that he was an English major at Colorado. She was soon to be an avid reader of his stories. She also liked how he influenced me.

During the year, Chuck and I went on a couple of outings. First, we went to a Warriors game. We saw them play the Spurs who had George "The Ice Man" Gervin. The Spurs lit up the place and we saw every moment of it, right in the front row. After the game, Chuck took me in the locker room and I got to talk with some of the players.

The next time I went out with Chuck, it was on a bonafide sports story. My paper, the *Millbrae Sun*, had arranged for me to go to see the Giants-Mets game so I could do a feature on local product, Keith Hernandez.

When we got to Candlestick, Chuck reminded me about not showing your allegiance while at the game. He said the press box was a place where people do their work and there was no cheering allowed. I kept my trap shut.

The game was fun to watch and the Giants were keeping the reporters, including myself, happy with plenty of Coke, munchies, and game stats. I didn't even have to take notes.

During the game, Chuck grilled me as to what questions I was going to ask, and who I was going to interview. I told him I wanted to talk to Keith Hernandez himself, and his manager, Frank Howard. I briefly mentioned that I wanted to get my mother a picture of Giants pitcher, Atlee Hammaker. Once again, he reminded me why we were at the game.

After the game, we headed to the Mets locker room where I got to interview Mets skipper, Frank Howard. He looked at me thinking how cute it was to be interviewed by some scrawny lookin' kid in a wheelchair. I opened the interview with a softball—a cupcake. I could tell he thought this was going to be a walk in the park. Sure, throw him another one kid.

"Could you tell me, Mr. Howard, has Keith recovered from his previous battles with drugs?" I asked. It was a tough one, but I had to do it.

As quickly as the words came out of my mouth, Frank Howard's face went sour.

"What are you talking about? Hey, get this kid out of here!"

"Why don't you answer the question?" Chuck replied. He was right behind me when the Mets manager didn't answer my question. That was about the end of that interview.

The interview with Keith Hernandez lasted a while longer. He said that his drug problems were behind him and we spent most of the time talking about growing up in the Peninsula and his parents.

Before leaving, we stopped by the Giants' clubhouse. It was there that Chuck said I could go ahead and get an autographed picture of Atlee Hammaker. I think he thought I had done a good job that day, and this was my reward.

I kept in touch with Chuck while I was going to Chico State. In fact, he came to my graduation ceremony. It meant a lot to me.

Since graduation, I haven't spoken to him quite as often. But whenever I talk to Chuck, he is the one person who wants to know about everything that's going on with me. He has always been supportive of me, and has a knack for knowing what to say, and how to say it.

Nolan Ryan

In an era where it appears that professional sports is headed for the toilet, destined to ruin itself with its obsession for the almighty dollar, there remains a guy whom I consider a role model.

In a day where athletes are willing to pedal merchandise without accepting the responsibility of having others look up to you, there remains a man we can look up to and respect.

That man is Nolan Ryan.

Every person who aspires to do great things in sports, or any other field, need not look very far to see what Nolan Ryan has done, and how he's done it. He has conducted himself with class both on and off the baseball diamond. His graciousness in accepting the accolades of his fans, always giving credit to his teammates, is an example for youngsters to follow. No one can say that Nolan Ryan was a "showboat." Unlike Rickey Henderson, he didn't ask the owners to give him a red Ferrari when he reached another of his many baseball milestones.

You never heard of Nolan Ryan getting in trouble with the law, or beating his wife. Sure, he may have hit a batter or two in his time, but there is no mistaken that Nolan Ryan was a competitor and a winner—a good winner. Though a few players have taken his ninety-mile per hour fastballs out of the yard on occasion, as a model competitor, he never let the opposition get the best of him.

Along with being a class act, Nolan Ryan has given something back to those who see him as a role model. With his vocal and financial support for such causes as Little League Baseball, he understands this inherent responsibility and doesn't shirk from it. You don't see him peddling shoes or memorabilia to children and then whine about how he shouldn't be seen as a role model. Instead, he gives of himself, and quietly endorses products he uses.

Finally, what impresses me the most about Nolan Ryan is the commitment he made to his craft. Okay, the hard throwing hurler was blessed with the natural ability to throw a baseball. But, in order to pitch for as long as he did, Nolan Ryan had to work hard at being the best, even into his forties.

Whether you are a baseball fan or not, Nolan Ryan is someone we can all admire. As a baseball player, he is a master craftsman. As a competitor, he is a winner. And, as a person, he is a class act.

Sure Nolan Ryan is a millionaire, but, he's earned every penny of it.

George Thurlow

When an individual can come into your life at a particular moment in time and leave their mark, George Thurlow would have to be that person for me. He has helped bring to the forefront qualities in me that had been previously untapped. With his guidance and encouragement, he has helped me become a better writer, speaker, and he is largely responsible for introducing me to the world of local politics.

During the late fall of 1988, George and I were having one of our many talks. At the time, I wasn't feeling very good about myself, and I think George knew it. He talked about volunteering to serve on a city commission such as the Affirmative Action Committee. I told him that I wasn't qualified, and I might be moving.

He asked me how old I was. I told him I was 23.

Then he asked me if I was a registered voter.

"Of course, I voted in the last election."

Finally, he told me that since I lived in the city, a block from his house, I was qualified to be on a city commission."

"Yeah, but I'm not a political insider."

"So what? You start with something like the Affirmative Action Committee and you work your way up."

"Well, what if I move away?"

"You write the city a letter telling them that you are resigning because you are moving away."

It wasn't like I didn't want to serve on the commission; I just didn't think I could do it. George told me that I could do it, and that as a committee member, I would represent a group of people like the disabled community.

Soon after George told me about what the Affirmative Action Committee did, I submitted an application and was appointed on my very first try.

George didn't stop there. While serving on the Affirmative Action Committee, he encouraged me to serve on other city committees. He likened it to putting a portfolio together. He told me that by serving on one committee leads to another, and so on. The appointments become more significant, and I would soon become a part of the political scene. George has been the guiding force responsible for doing that.

George Thurlow helped me a lot with my writing while he was editor of the *Chico News & Review*, a left-leaning weekly newspaper. As an occasional free-lancer, I would submit commentaries for his review. Like any good editor, he accepted some, while politely rejecting others. No matter how he felt about one of my submissions, he kept on prodding me to write.

"So when can I expect my next piece?" he would always ask.

There were two things George was looking for when I came to him with an idea for a story or article submission. He either wanted the piece to focus on a local issue, or discuss a topic of general interest, or bring to the article some personal viewpoint. If the article contained both, it was all the better.

For example, one the first commentaries I wrote for him dealt with the closure of a street which was an entrance to Bidwell Park, Chico's crowning jewel. While many in the disabled community opposed the closure because it allowed for easy access for those traveling in cars, I was in favor of closing off the street because I didn't drive. I wanted to keep the area free of cars so that disabled people like me wouldn't have to worry about being hit by oncoming cars.

George was very adamant about what he was looking for in a story or commentary. On occasion, I would discuss a possible piece that dealt with the decay of major league baseball, or the skyrocketing salaries of professional athletes. Hoping that somehow he might give me the green light, he wouldn't hear of it. He felt that readers could find that stuff in other papers.

Instead, George had me write a commentary about a hot-button issue, abortion. He wanted me to discuss my personal views as a person with a disability. Or, he accepted a commentary or two about the goings on inside the Chico State athletic department. Since I was an assistant coach, he thought I could bring the reader some insight.

While C.W. Nevius impressed upon me the importance of reporting the news while not becoming the story, George Thurlow showed me that just by being who you are gives the story a certain perspective.

George usually had me come to his class for a mock news conference while teaching newswriting at Chico State. He had the students ask me questions and write a story based on what I had said during the press conference.

The experience of going into a class and having people ask you questions for over an hour was a learning experience for me. As I did it more often, at least once every semester, I got better with each interview. I was able to decide how much information I wanted to give the students as I articulated my answers.

For instance, if a student asked me a question that I knew would require a long answer, I would often times give a shorter answer and see if they would come back with a follow-up question. This became sort of a game between me and these "budding" journalists. I wonder, would it work with a group of professionals at the *Washington Post*? Probably not.

Like many of my friends, George and his family would appear at my house without warning. They usually came a knocking early in the evening. More often than not, I would have to scurry to get dressed because he would catch me during bath time. I guess he just had a weird sense of timing.

A visit from George and the kids usually included a walk down the street to Shubert's for a juice bar. It was on these visits where we would discuss local politics while keeping the kids happy with their ice cream. His visits always lifted up my spirits and gave me a thing or two to think about.

Even though George and his wonderful family have moved from Chico to Santa Barbara, going from being an editor of a weekly newspaper to a professional in residence, and now a "big time" publisher, I think of him often as I put into practice much of what he has taught me.

Barbara Jordan

To put it simply, when Barbara Jordan spoke, I listened. Whether it was in a one on one interview on the "MacNeil/Lehrer News Hour," or in front of a large audience like the 1992 Democratic National Convention, I enjoyed hearing this woman speak. Few would argue that this woman was a great speaker.

As one who does a lot of public speaking, I have taken a few plays from her playbook and it has made me a better communicator.

Barbara Jordan was probably better known for her accomplishments on the national political scene, however, let me point out a number of qualities which made her one of my favorite orators.

First, she had a strong, powerful voice that commanded my attention every time she spoke. The tone of her voice played with the strength of an orchestra, even on television. During a presentation, her voice could project in much the same way a singer must do with a song. Her voice though deep and strong, it wasn't harsh and loud. In a way, she spoke strongly and softly while wielding a big stick. For myself, I have tried to speak with a strong voice that everyone can hear.

Don't you hate it when you can't hear or understand a person when they speak? That is, they mumble. They stumble. They fumble. You can tell they haven't thought about what they're going to say, and they give a terrible speech? It is so important to pronounce words and names correctly when speaking to anyone.

Well, another thing I liked about Barbara Jordan was that she spoke very well. That is, she was careful to enunciate every word that emanated from her mouth, carefully speaking each syllable, practically to the letter.

Whether she talked about illegal immigration or the Democratic Party,

I could see and feel the passion in her face. She spoke with a believability in her voice that made me want to listen.

Finally, on a technical note, Barbara Jordan used a lot of repetition to emphasize points she was trying to make when she delivered a speech. She repeated key phrases slowly, clearly, and with great deliberation.

In an interview with Margaret Warner on the McNeil/Lehrer News Hour, she constantly reminded Warner that her commission on immigration was concerned about illegal immigration and not legal immigrants that come to our country.

Some may see using repetition as a way to get a big crowd of people, like an audience at a convention to get all fired up. I agree with this to a point. I think she used it to get her point across, and she didn't want the listener to forget it. I use repetition as well in my presentations.

There may be a person who inspires you with the spoken word. It may be a minister, professor, singer, or even a politician. What they say is what they want you to hear. But if they don't know how to say it, you won't listen. Barbara Jordan knew how to say it, and that's why I listened.

James Carville

So, how did James Carville make this list? Maybe it is because of the fact that as I continue to lose my hair, I need someone to look up to? After all, he's bald and married to a political babe!

Or, perhaps he masterminded the election of Bill Clinton as president, thus ending twelve years of laissez-faire, deficit spending, Republican rule!

Sure, that's a possibility.

Or, is it because he's a good ole boy from Louisiana who doesn't mince words when he talks?

That's another good reason.

After listening to Carville tell his story of how he engineered the campaign that propelled Bill Clinton to the presidency, there was one thing he said that I'll always remember.

He said that one thing that made Bill Clinton successful was his ability to talk about one issue in so many ways, to so many people. He could take an issue like healthcare and relate it to blue-collar workers in Ohio, as well as high-tech professionals in California.

I thought about applying this way of thinking to my message, and it has worked for me.

For example, if I give a presentation on the importance of bringing people with disabilities into the workplace, or the ADA, I can't just talk about it as it relates to me, or people with disabilities. Some people wouldn't give a rip. I have to tell everyone in the audience why hiring people with disabilities is important to them. You see, as the make-up of each audience changes, the message must constantly be refined when talking to different groups of people.

When I asked the city to put in strips instead of bricks on downtown sidewalks, I didn't stop by telling them that it would be slower to cross the street for people in wheelchairs. I explained how women with high heels could trip on the bricks as well.

In his book, "All's Fair," James Carville says that Bill Clinton was very good at retail campaigning. Instead of arriving in a town an hour late and giving a speech, only to leave right afterward, Clinton liked to shake the hands of well-wishers and talk to the people in every town he visited.

I believe that a vital element to retail campaigning lies in the message a politician carries to the people. Without that message, people will only shake a candidate's hand for so long if they just think they're a nice person. But, if the message can be tailored accordingly, a connection will be made and it will make that bond even stronger.

I don't try to tailor what I say just to seek others approval. Rather, I hope that there is some commonality we can find when discussing an issue like the ADA.

Like Barbara Jordan, James Carville has influenced the way I talk to others. His influence has more to do with content, than with technique. Whether it be political campaigning, public speaking, or talking to my best friend, it all makes pretty good sense to me.

Keith Cameron

When I was living in the dorms, a friend explained to me that friends are like time. They come and go. You'd think that with moving so often, I would understand what he was saying. But, being somewhat naive back then, I didn't quite see his point.

As time passed and I left the dorms for apartment life, my friends from Lassen Hall slowly disappeared, only to be replaced by other friends.

There is one friend from the dorms who never faded from view. I consider him to be my best friend. He's the kind of guy who I would never want to go to war or coach a football game without having him on my side.

Keith Cameron and I lived on the first floor of Lassen Hall during my second year in the dorms. We also had a few classes together. Everyone called him Cam, and so do I.

Like many people, Cam came to Chico from the Bay Area, Livermore, to be more exact. It was sort of by fate that Cam and I remained friends after we moved out of Lassen Hall. With finals over and everyone having to move out, Cam was one of the last people I saw before leaving the dorms.

Like many, I thought he was going back home to the Bay Area for the summer. I asked him what his plans were and he said he was going to stay in Chico and work on the grounds crew around the dorms. I was elated and told him I was going to be working in the football office. We hooked up a few days later and spent most of the summer doing all kinds of things, including playing "Sports Illustrated, ALL TIME ALL-STAR BASEBALL." We had a blast!

After John Cook left at the end of my junior year, Cam began his first of many stints as an attendant for me. Yes, there is cronyism in the world of attendant care, but he filled in well for John and had his own way of doing things.

In the summer of 1987, the two of us became roommates on what would be the first of three occasions. He was renting a house from a poli-sci professor and helped me out when I needed a place to stay. Later, we became roommates when I moved to Orient Street.

The friendship I have with Keith Cameron has meant a lot to me. He has been someone who I could tell just about everything to without hesitation. He has been a close and personal confidant. I have talked to him about matters I wouldn't discuss with my own family. He has been like an older brother to me.

As close friends, we know when to lift each other up and tear each other down. We do what we can to make sure the highs aren't too high, and the lows never too low. With all of the triumphs and tragedies we have weathered together, we have done what we can to maintain our equilibrium and sanity.

We argue about anything from me casting a vote for a Republican, to Cam's new found interest in the Sacramento Kings. Since we are from opposite sides of the Bay Area, he is a Cal Bears fan, and I like the Stanford Cardinal.

Cam and I know each other so well; we can get into each other's heads at the speed of light. And we do it frequently, mostly just for fun. Sometimes we do it to make a point. And when we're done taking each other's inventory, we'll pick apart the next available person, real or imagined. Whether it is while I am watching him do dishes, or while I'm sitting in the bathtub washing my hair, there is nothing sacred. There are no holds barred.

Keith Cameron has always been there for me. He was never far away. Every time I found myself flat on my back in a hospital bed, I would always find him there sitting in a nearby chair.

While it has grown as we enter our second decade, it is interesting to see that our friendship did not develop as one of two drinking buddies who'd sit up at the bar and tell stories about the good ole days. Sure, we'll go out to dinner and have a make-believe argument about who is going to pay the bill.

"I bought the drinks," he would say.

Or, he'll convince me to go to a movie that he says isn't scary, like "Pet Cemetery. "And, after the first ten minutes, I'll know that he was pulling my leg.

While we have a lot in common, we are different in a number of ways.

For instance, he comes from a family with no sisters while I have a few. Sometimes I wonder how he would feel if I lent him one of mine for a while. Gee, who would it be?

Before moving to Chico, Cam spent much of his childhood in one spot, whereas my family moved around. Before moving to Chico, I always wondered what it would be like to live in the same town for a considerable period of time.

Like so many people, Keith Cameron has helped to fill in the blanks that some of my previous teachers didn't do. I can't forget that.

What one must understand about my friendship with Keith Cameron is not merely to point out that he is a good friend of mine and this is how it happened. It is more.

To list Keith Cameron as one of the people who have had an effect on my life is an understatement. It barely scratches the surface. What is more important here is that our friendship is unique. There is nothing like it. And while I have tried to give you a brief glimpse into it, I cannot fully explain it.

I trust him.

I love him.

It's the uniqueness in our friendship which makes it so special.

Paul Wiggin

Just recently, I had a chance to meet up with Paul Wiggin at the Westin Hotel in Indianapolis. He didn't know I was coming, but I had a slight inclination that I might see him. Perhaps, subconsciously I wanted it to happen.

I was in Naptown to see my cousins, and since I was in the area, I made arrangements to visit Chuck Cook, a friend of mine who works as a scout for the Kansas City Chiefs. NFL scouts and coaches were there for the annual scouting combine, the NFL's version of a big cattle show.

After a number of calls to his room and a peek into the hotel bar, I surmised that my appointment with Chuck was not going to happen. So, my father and I headed back to the hotel bar to see if I could find anyone I knew.

Not long after, I found Sherman Lewis, an assistant coach for the Green Bay Packers sitting at a table. I said hello to him and he invited us to sit with him. It had been a few years since I had seen him at the East-West Shrine Game. We used to spend a few hours talking football at the cocktail lounge at the Hyatt Palo Alto. I felt very comfortable talking around Sherman Lewis. He treated me as I think he wanted people to treat him—with respect.

My father nudged my arm and quietly asked me to look to my left. A few feet from me, at the next table stood a neatly dressed man in slacks and a sweater. As my eyes scanned the tall figure, I couldn't mistake the hair, so even, like your neighbors' hedge.

My eyes started to well-up. I was so happy.

"That's Paul," I whispered to my father. It was hard to contain my excitement.

My father calmly got up and walked over to where Paul was standing. "Hi Paul."

Paul kind of smiled. He knew the face was familiar but he couldn't place it.

"Jonathan is right over there."

At that moment, the lights came on for Coach Wiggin and he quickly came over to my table where I was ready to shake his hand. Suddenly, everything he said to me almost fifteen years ago was playing in my head like a sweet melody.

I could hear him say, "There is no reason why you can't coach football."

It was exhilarating. It was liberating. It felt good. But, more importantly, what he told me made sense.

This man not only told me that I could be a football coach when I grow up. He in effect, told me that I could do almost anything I wanted to do—when I grow up.

He brought it full circle by breaking things down, task by task—like an opponent's game plan. I use what he said back then in my everyday life and in my motivational presentations.

Not many people probably recognize the name Paul Wiggin. I think he prefers it that way. He's not an egomaniac by any stretch of the imagination. But, I know who he is, and that's all that's important.

For myself, Paul Wiggin is the school teacher, minister, mentor, and motivating force all rolled into one. Whether it is football, politics, or public speaking, I have Paul Wiggin to thank for changing the way I look at my hopes and dreams, and the ways in which I should go about pursuing them.

He is my idol.

Mike Long

Some might think that my inner circle is comprised largely of friends who are primarily disabled. I mean, I spent much of my childhood amongst my peers who had disabilities, and as a public speaker, I discuss issues that directly affect me as a person with a disability.

Up until recently, I went out of my way to distance myself from this network of people. It just wasn't my scene.

Mike Long is an exception though.

Mike and I first became friends while I was coaching at Chico State and he helped the guys in the equipment room as a team manager. We used to go out to the bars after games and bathe in our victories or dissect our defeats.

Mike Long is from Dairyville, a small town about forty minutes north of Chico. It is a farming community with its own volunteer fire department. Mike's mother and father, Marilyn and Dudley, raised a huge family while tending to a 400-acre farm comprised of walnuts, prunes, and almond orchards.

When I first met Mike Long, it didn't occur to me that he had a disability. I thought he was just a bit slower than most. Mike later told me has cerebral palsy, a disability which affects some of his motor skills. He walks a little slower than most, and it takes him a little bit longer to process things. Heck, it takes me longer to process things as well.

Because I don't think of him as being disabled, I was amazed to see how he was lassoed into the developmentally disabled community and labeled, well—I'd rather not say.

To me it appeared as a matter of convenience for these "professionals" to do such a thing. And, if I were one of Mike's brothers, I would have made a stink about it.

Contrary to what anyone may think, whether it is real or imagined, I know Mike Long as an intelligent man with a heart of gold. He may be slow, but. stupid he is not.

Mike and I are a lot alike in the way we look at things. We both look at the hows and whys of our challenges and then we go about the business of finding out the answers.

When dealing with a situation in which we want to see a desired outcome, we involve ourselves so much in the process of getting others to see things from our perspective that they are able to do away with any preconceived ideas and misconceptions, and are able to participate with us in trying to solve a particular problem.

Like his late father Dudley, Mike is a very generous man who sees the good in people. He believes in them and feeds off of their energy. In turn, he gives that energy back.

While I was trying to fulfil my dream of moving up the coaching ladder, trying to make it to the BIG TIME, Mike was right there on the roller-coaster with me. At the same time, I was riding on his roller coaster as he was trying to put together a program to get PAC-10 schools to bring developmentally disabled individuals in as team managers.

What became the bond that makes my friendship with Mike Long so special is the support we gave to each other in our quests to make our dreams come true. Yeah, we often talked about our disabilities in the context of reaching our goals, but we never used it as an excuse when something didn't go right.

Mike Long currently works in Sacramento as a governor appointee in the Department of Developmental Services for the State of California. He's in there trying to fight the good fight, helping developmentally disabled individuals achieve their independence and become productive members of society. If you ask me, it's the only smart thing Governor Pete Wilson has done since he's been in office.

Yeah, Mike Long is probably at the top of a very short list of disabled people I am close to. But, the fact that he is disabled is not how or why we became friends. Rather, it is the philosophy we impart as we fight the good fight and spread the good word.

While many callers say "mega dittos" to radio talk show host, Rush Limbaugh, Mike and I usually don't end a conversation without saying, "hip, hip."

"Hip, hip!"

Grandma Elster (Deux)

For a long time, I was known to her as Jonny. As a kid growing up, I didn't mind it at all. My sister Amy still calls me Jonny. I guess your big sister can call you anything she wants. After all, she is your big sister. When I got older though, others called me Jon, Jonathan, or Charles.

Grandma Elster continued calling me Jonny. Finally, when I had enough, my mother told her to call me Jonathan.

Throughout my life, Ruth Elster was the kind of grandmother who always wrote, even when you didn't. Her letters outnumbered mine by about fifteen to one. The letters she wrote were lengthy, so full of detail. She would tell you everything she did in the course of not one, but several days. She documented everything, right down to the number of laps she swam at the pool, the number of roadrunners she saw outside her window, or the number of ladies she had over for her Pen Women meeting. Not only did she write letters, she wrote short stories and poetry.

She and Grandpa (that's what I called him) were married over fifty years before they passed away. And though they teased and bickered with each other, and slept in separate beds, they managed to stick together—until death do us part.

Henry and Cynthia

I have saved the two people responsible for bringing me into this world for last. As a force of habit, I save anything that is important for the end. I save important things to do until the very last minute. In a speech, I reserve the good stuff, or the important stuff for the tail end.

My parents would probably agree that they are not the "perfect parents." Yes, I have had my share of disagreements, periods of rebellion, and downright differences of opinion of what they did, how they did it, and why they did what they did. But, they are the ones responsible for bringing me into this life, and I wouldn't trade them for any set of parents in the world. They have left an indelible mark on me that has made me who I am.

First, without recounting every trip to the hospital, every operation, every fracture, I have to say that these two people had a lot do deal with— and raise three other children.

They had to make some tough decisions about me which had to require a lot of courage. And, after making those decisions, they had to wait on countless occasions to find out results of what was to happen, and then, what lay ahead. They endured a lot as my parents. If I have to do it again with my child, I would want them to be a phone call away so I could ask them for advice.

I think it is important to point out how these people have affected and shaped me, not merely as a disabled person, or a person with osteogenesis imperfecta, but as a human being.

My parents instilled a set of their own "family values" in each of us. They taught us to love one another, and be respectful of other people.

They grew up in the throes of the depression and shared stories of how their family had to work together when times got tough. Such was the case when our family experienced financial hard times, all of us had to come together and sacrifice a little bit.

I have come to understand the importance of the "value of family." Today, we have all been quick to help each other out when a member of the family needs assistance.

Under extraordinary circumstances, Henry and Cynthia Studebaker did whatever it took to get me the best education possible. They didn't buy into all the crap that was fed to them by people who supposedly "knew" what was best for me. They knew better.

They knew that my disability affected my bones and not my brains. My parents demanded that all of their children do their very best in school. They expected me to go to college like all of my brothers and sisters—and I did.

Throughout my life, the two have largely worked together as a unit to mold and nurture me. Individually, I have shared experiences with them that set the two apart.

While he was working sixteen hour days for my Uncle's mother-in-law as a handyman, my father gave me freedom to do a lot of things with my friends. With this freedom came some sacrifice. We didn't have much in the way of material things, but he made sure I was never without the essentials. It was this freedom that gave me the confidence to do things for myself independently.

Since I was a nine year old, my father was largely in charge of making sure that I was ready for the day. Getting me through the bathtub, helping me with my braces, and getting my clothes on were part of the routine. This routine also drew us closer together.

On the day my parents dropped me off at Lassen Hall, the "umbilical cord" was severed. This distance didn't keep us apart. It brought my parents and I closer together—especially my father. It raised our relationship from father-son, to friends and equals.

I talk to Henry on the phone an average of about twice a week. The phone companies must love us. If ten days go by and we haven't spoken to each other, one of us will call.

I consult with my father on a lot of things. I follow his advice on some things, and sometimes I'll do the opposite. Yeah, he still acts like a father should, and tells me things in that father-like way. But, he has the right to do so.

I don't know if I would label my mother a "super mom." I can't picture her wearing a big fat "S" on her front. I don't know if she would want it either. But, I admire her a lot for going through what she did, and I wonder how she did it.

Raising four kids, including one with osteogenesis imperfecta is a big ordeal in itself. But when you throw all of the moves from one end of the country to another together with the financial challenges we had to weather, only a woman with great inner strength could have done what she did.

I credit Cynthia for getting me interested in sports. She is a sports fan herself, a very knowledgeable one at that. Growing up in the Midwest, she was a Cubs fan.

Radios and newspapers were her sources for following sports. As a child, she didn't have the luxury of ESPN and channel surfing from game to game that I had just gotten to know.

Cynthia went to Indiana University and experienced the thrill of big time collegiate athletics and Hoosier basketball. Since most of us kids went to relatively smaller schools where athletics weren't big, I envy her experiencing Hoosier Mania.

My mother got me hooked on listening to the Giants on the radio during our first stint in the Bay Area. Their announcer, Hank Greenwald, had just come to the Giants from Hawaii. Mom liked Hank, and so did I. After the Giants games were over, we would listen to the sports talk shows that followed the broadcasts.

While my parents were responsible for making sure that their son went to the right schools, it was my mother who was the disciplinarian in our house. She made sure that we got our homework done. And if we didn't, we would have to sit through one of her lectures, with my father echoing her sermons with a quip or two in agreement.

She was a giant filter when it came to what we watched on television. She was our family's version of the V-CHIP. It's called being a parent. If I were a student in today's computer age, I guarantee she would be popping into my room to see what I was doing on the Internet. We wouldn't need censorship on the information superhighway if we had more mothers like Cynthia.

Henry would always tell me that Cynthia is the captain of the ship, and he is just another passenger on this vessel. It is so true.

Where would we be without people? Pretty lonely, don't you think? If it weren't for at least two people, you and I wouldn't be here.

If someone asked me to name the one person who is responsible for me being who I am, I couldn't do it. I wouldn't do it. Each person has left their mark on me in their own unique way.

Nolan Ryan showed me through example the importance of hard work, dedication, and what it means to be a class-act. Paul Wiggin told me that I could be a football coach, and he showed me how to do it. C.W. Nevis is the kind of person who asked me about every aspect of my life. Keith Cameron is my best friend. And, my parents? Well, without my parents, I wouldn't be here. Moreover, if it weren't for them, I don't know what kind of person I would be.

I think about all of these people, and a few more, every time I look in the mirror.

When famous people like movie stars, politicians, and Andy Warhol types are asked where they derive their source of inspiration, they tell of how one or two people affected their lives. It may be a parent or celebrity role model. It may be a teacher, relative, or a close friend. For me, simply put, it is people.

I can't pinpoint one or two individuals because I have looked to many people for wisdom and strength at various times in my life. Different people have affected me in different ways. As I get older, there will be many more of them.

People in general motivate me. This is why I get up in the morning and try to make the most of every day. And while I even draw strength from those who say, "You can't do it," it is those who offer positive support and wisdom who have made me who I am. I notice these people every time I look in the mirror.

C-H-I-C-O

For the last several years, my mother will ask me the preverbal question, "So, when are you going to leave Chico?"

Perhaps she thinks I need a change of scenery and explore some new surroundings. Or, maybe she sees I'm in a rut, and moving somewhere else would get me out of it.

She has a point. After all, it's the longest time I have spent in one place. "Sure I'll leave... when I find a better place," I tell her.

I don't know how much longer I plan on staying in Chico. I've thought about leaving a number of times.

I thought about it shortly after I graduated from Chico State in 1987.

I practically had my bags packed in 1992 when I was offered a volunteer internship at Iowa State University. I told everyone I was headed to the land of cows and corn.

From time to time I have entertained thoughts of moving to a bigger city with more excitement. I do this whenever I get bored. Then, I go on a trip and the thought goes away for a while.

There are a lot of things I like about Chico that may not be obvious to your average Chicoan.

For instance, Chico is flat. I can get around fairly easily without having to get in a car every day. In fact, I get around mostly by using my electric wheelchair and public transportation.

Chico is a "disabled friendly" community. With transportation services, non-profit agencies, a university that prides itself on serving the needs of disabled students, and just all around good people. I would recommend the City of Chico to any disabled person, young and old.

Of course, there are the obvious reasons. Chico is beautiful. With its ever-present, Bidwell Park, nature is just a heartbeat away. The town is carefully planned to accommodate growth, while at the same time, preserving its natural beauty.

Chico is a friendly place to live. You can tell just by getting to know a few of the townspeople like Stuart and Sally Thompson. They owned and operated Lee's Pharmacy on the corner of Third and Broadway, a downtown landmark for over a hundred years. I could always count on them to diagnose my coughs and colds, or help me with my Christmas shopping. Sadly, they closed down due to stiff competition from corporate stores.

Bob Pinocchio, owner of Geppetto's, a small Italian restaurant downtown, would always visit me in the hospital with a plate of shells and sauce in his hand. His sense of humor and cooking prowess could cure just about anything.

I like this town so much; I've even tried to get my parents to move to Chico. Imagine that?!

Even though I didn't spend my formative years in the city I currently call home, Chico is a place where many "firsts" happened.

I crossed my first street light alone on the corner of Second and Broadway.

I opened my first checking account at the Bank of America on Fourth and Broadway.

I helped do my first load of laundry in Lassen Hall.

I cooked my first meal in my apartment on West First Avenue.

I lived by myself for the first time when I moved to Orient Street. It is also where I had my first sexual experience.

There is no doubt, I "grew up" in Chico.

Lassen Hall

This is where it all started. With my parents dropping me off at Lassen Hall, I had so many emotions racing through my head.

First, there was the euphoria of new found freedom. Finally, after spending eighteen years at home or in the hospital, I was free at last! The world was my oyster!

There was no one to look over my shoulder, and say, "No."

There was the excitement in doing so many things for the first time. I crossed my first street all by myself my very first day in Chico.

There was fear and apprehension.

What would happen if I got hit by a car when I crossed that street? Would it make me want to rush back home? What about fear in general? What the hell am I going to do if this or that happens?

There was sadness. Unlike all those trips to summer camp, I knew they would not return in two weeks to pick me up. My eyes welled as they drove out of sight. It always happens when my parents leave Chico.

As I watched the car drive out of sight, I bit my lip and held it in, just like all the other times.

It seemed like dorm life had all the trappings of Disneyland while at the same time, felt a lot like purgatory. Every day brought with it excitement and apprehension. Each experience presented some interesting choices to be made, as well as undesired consequences.

There were fantastic days that made me feel as if I were on top of the world. As well, there were gloomy days that made me sick in more ways than one. It was one giant roller coaster, never a dull moment.

Lassen Hall is one of six on-campus dorms at Chico State University. The three-story red brick building sits across from its identical twin, Shasta Hall. A quick trip to the restroom and enough time to put on a baseball cap, and I could get to any classroom on campus within five minutes. In fact, there were times where I literally rolled out of bed to get to class, complete with baseball cap under messy hair and powder-blue pajamas.

My first roommate in Lassen Hall was Eric Peterson, a journalism major from Half Moon Bay. Upon meeting him, I thought he was a nice guy. A die-hard Raiders fan, but I could live with that. With me as a die-hard Chiefs fan, it made for some interesting verbal sparring sessions on Sunday afternoons. Needless to say, I like to go at it with any Raider fan.

Even though we didn't become buddies, Eric and I got along fairly well. He and I ended up liking the same girl in the dorms, Connie Noller. She ended up spending a lot of time in our room with Eric. All I had to cuddle with was my teddy bear I brought from home. It was difficult to deal with and it was a cold dose of reality coming at such an early stage of my "growing up."

Except for my huge crush on Connie, I was basically content with making as many friends as I could. I even went out with girls who had boyfriends. I figured this would be a safe way to check out the landscape. At the same time, I was hoping that my situation with Loretta, my first love back home, would get better. I still had feelings for her—and still do.

Like every other freshman, I was experimenting with my new found freedoms. Sure I wasn't old enough to drink, but I did it anyway. In fact, I spent a lot of Friday and Saturday nights getting blasted at dorm parties. There was one instance where I drank a half a pint of Seagram's Seven and puked all over the top floor of Shasta Hall. Everyone thought I was dead because my eyes were open so they called the paramedics. After checking me over, they just put me in bed and had my attendant at the time, John Cook, watch me for the rest of the night. This would be the first of many huge hangovers.

That year I was also placed on university probation for breaking one of the dorm rules concerning alcohol. Back in those days, you could have alcohol in your dorm room. If you carried it down the hall, it had to be in a paper bag. It was a combination of hear no evil, see no evil and don't ask, don't tell.

One night I was having a nightcap in one of the rooms down the hall. On my way back to my room, one of the girls noticed I had some ice in my cup. She asked me what was in the cup and I told her it was just a little ice. She gave me a weird look and then turned and saw a Resident Advisor walking by.

"Hey Fred, come see what Jonathan has in his cup."

Fred came over and saw the ice and smelled the residual wine. He told me there was some wine and wrote me up a referral.

I went to see the Hall Director and he said they didn't want to be seen as making any special considerations just because I was disabled.

"But I'm not guilty!" I said.

Then, I went to my formal meeting with Lisi Porter, Vice President for Judicial Affairs who asked me how I plead.

"Not guilty!"

"Well, I don't care whether your guilty or not. These are the rules." She explained the rules again and handed me a brown paper bag. I was placed on formal written reprimand for a year.

Now, coming from a rigid, though not a strict family background, it was still difficult for me to explain this to the folks. Oh, my god! I will be disowned or something. Such was not the case. My father told me that I just got caught, and to try not to do it again.

The probation didn't keep me from drinking, partying, and having a good time.

During my first year at Lassen Hall, I also had four fractures. In early October, I was asleep in bed and rolled off onto the floor. I hit the dresser before going down. It made a loud noise and woke Eric up. I would have been alright except that my leg got caught up in my electric wheelchair and I didn't land on it right.

Eric laughed when he heard me fall. I must admit, it was kind of funny.

I was taken to the hospital, put in a long-leg cast and made it in time for my eight o'clock. English class.

My fractures were an inconvenience, but it didn't force me to do anything drastic like drop any classes, or go back home.

I decided to do one more year in Lassen Hall. It was pretty convenient and I hadn't gotten sick of the dorms yet.

My roommate the second year was Dave Bassetti, another journalism major. He was a Cowboys fan. We got along alright. As I found out sometime later, he was not supposed to be my roommate. Dave Garcia, a guy who lived next door, was supposed to occupy Room 168 with me. Apparently, he was uncomfortable about it, so they switched rooms.

The second year was much like the first year. I didn't have as many fractures, but I was prone to doing stupid things when I had too much to drink.

For example, at my whopping thirty-five pounds, I went to one of the last "Pioneer Days." There was a kickoff party at one of the fraternity houses and I drank eight beers. I drove my wheelchair back to the dorms and was alright until I got into the bathroom.

I started doing spins around and around until I made a bee-line for the garbage can. My friends told me to stop. I didn't. I hit the garbage can so hard that I ended up in the garbage can. My friends fished me out of the garbage can and put me in bed. I woke up with a sprained ankle and another bad hangover.

The most difficult part about living in the dorms was battling the perceptions people had of me. For example, if someone told a dirty joke, not much was thought about it. However, if I were to tell that joke, people thought of me as being perverted or something. In fact, I was named as the one most likely to be a "dirty old man."

This bothered me because when you get down to it, I am not that way. I may not be an angel, but I am human.

I think people had a certain picture of me and they wouldn't allow it to change, no matter how hard I tried.

The problem with living in the dorms was that even though we spent almost every waking hour together, eating, sleeping, taking a leak, and using the same showers, we never really got to know each other. Sure, we had social functions and did things like have "secret pals," but these were contrived activities, the kind you'd see on a cruise. Even when we'd be sitting together getting hammered in someone's room, the talk was all too superficial.

After two years in Lassen Hall, it was time for me to take that next step and move out on my own.

Sigma Phi Epsilon

During the spring semester of my second year at Chico State, I pledged a fraternity. You might say it was a mistake, but as I look back on it, I'm glad I did it. I learned a lot about myself and other people.

Before pledging Sigma Phi Epsilon, I had never been to a frat party. I had no interest in going to them. I couldn't get around any of the houses by myself, and while I had many offers of people willing to help me "party," I wasn't going to put myself in anyone's hands but my own. If I was going to a party and get drunk, I wanted to be responsible for myself.

The other thing I didn't like about frat parties were the long lines to get a beer. Blistering hot or freezing cold, who wants to pay three bucks for a plastic cup of beer? I'd rather pay a little more and get a six pack.

Paul Haas, the president of Sigma Phi Epsilon, gave a presentation to a group of us in our study hall lounge. I was curious, so I went. During the presentation, I asked Paul how much money it cost to be in a fraternity. His answer confirmed my suspicions, and re-affirmed my lack of interest in joining.

A couple of days later, Tammy Carter, one of our RA's, asked me what I thought of the presentation. She asked me if I wanted to go to a party with her. I declined the invitation. I gave her my reasons why I chose not to go frat parties. She was persistent though, and invited me again. This time, she offered to go with me and promised she wouldn't drink. Her offer made me even more suspicious, but I took her up on it.

We went to the party, and I got plastered. I mean, she wasn't drinking. I had nothing to worry about. As it turned out, the party we went to was a RUSH PARTY, where they invite those who they see as perspective members to come and learn more about the fraternity. I soon learned that Tammy was going out with Paul Haas, president of Sigma Phi Epsilon.

I was welcomed at the house. All of the guys told me I was a great guy.

"By the way, what's your major?" one would ask.

"Communications."

"Yeah, we need more comm majors in our fraternity."

Even though they didn't know who I was, it still felt great having a group of guys blowing smoke up my ass for three hours while I got hammered. I highly recommend it.

Sigma Phi Epsilon had about twenty members as opposed to the other Greek organizations which were considerably larger. You could say they were hurting for some new blood, and warm bodies too.

The frat was comprised of some interesting characters; some of them fit the typical mold. They had nicknames like "Moose, Meatball, King, and Spud."

Sigma Phi Epsilon had a group of women known as "little sisters" who on occasion, would do things for the guys. As small as the fraternity was, they had about half as many little sisters. I considered almost all of them as nothing more than sisters. By no means would they fit the description as being little. They were more like the cattle on my Cousin Elmer's ranch in Senate, Texas. What few heifers they didn't have, they were already going out with guys in the frat.

Despite the unanimous opposition I had from my parents, I went ahead and became a pledge. I guess it was the "rebel" in me that caused me to do it.

I told the president I would pledge the fraternity under two conditions. First, under no circumstances would I ever be paddled by anyone in the fraternity. My father didn't do it, and therefore, no one else would. Also, I informed them of my income status, and that they shouldn't see me as any kind of money tree. This would later become an issue.

From the moment I decided to pledge Sigma Phi Epsilon, I and all of my pledge brothers went from being great guys, to amounting to nothing more than a piece of scum off the kitchen floor.

In addition to keeping up on my schoolwork, I spent a lot of time doing things with my pledge class. Our big brothers kept us pretty busy. We had to learn the history of the fraternity as well as the Greek alphabet. We had chores to do around the house. My job was washing dishes while reciting my "family tree." It was a lot of fun sitting in a kitchen sink with only a pair of shorts on, scraping spaghetti off a plate that had sat for days.

Pledging did not come without the constant hazing by my brothers. They enjoyed every minute of it.

It didn't come without the massive quantities of alcohol I consumed during the course of that semester. We didn't need an occasion to drink, we just did it.

And, it didn't come without more than a few hits of marijuana. I'll never forget the weekend of Pioneer Week where a group of my pledge brothers smoked our brains out and ate Domino's Pizza while on the night shift, guarding our quad (Or mini house, which depicted a famous person or event in a given time period), on the corner of Sixth and Main Streets. I sat there stoned out of my mind thinking how neat it was to see the pizza guy make a delivery like that.

While all of the other organization on campus had their quads on campus, we joined our neighbors, Tau Gamma Theta, in celebration. They were forced downtown after being suspended by the university. Since we had little money and man power to do things on our own, we joined our neighbors in the festivities.

Make no mistake, I did inhale. And, I probably killed more brain cells that semester, than at any other time in my twelve years in Chico.

With the semester drawing to a close, "Hell Week" was just around the corner. It certainly lived up to its billing.

The week started off with us making paddles for our big brothers. It was more or less a show of thanks for all the things we learned and did over the semester.

One of my pledge brothers, Sam Clifford and I, headed to a local lumber yard to get some wood for our paddles. On our way back, we got rear ended on one of Chico's busiest streets, The Esplanade. Suddenly, I heard two snaps and started writhing in pain. From where we were hit, his car was about a block and a half from Enloe Hospital. There, I was treated for a broken arm and leg. I was sent back to Lassen Hall where I spent the night in my dorm room in a world of hurt. It was not a picnic. It was hell.

My fractures were very painful, but I still had to go to school. Finals were just around the corner and I had five more days of hell week.

Trying to show all of my brothers that I was going to make it through like a good Sig Ep, I kept up with the rest of the week's activities. In order to tolerate the pain, I managed to keep myself higher than a kite. It got to the point where I was popping pills like they were M&M's.

The week's activities culminated in a scavenger hunt where we spent the better part of an afternoon and evening driving the streets of Chico getting all sorts of unmentionable items and bringing them to the house. We even had to stop at one of the houses of our "little sisters" to get one. After a lot of effort, we avoided a circle jerk and got what we came for.

Following the scavenger hunt, we entered the basement of the fraternity house for our official induction into Sigma Phi Epsilon.

What a moment. I mean, despite all of the garbage I went through during the semester, I had fun and I met some cool people. I even bought into all the frat doctrine crap they had fed us. It was like being converted.

Once the fall semester started, things began to go sour. Football season was moving into high gear, and along with school, I was busy with my duties as the Wildcats kicking coach.

My brothers were not happy when I told them I wasn't going on a retreat they were planning for the first weekend of school. I had to go with the football team down to Santa Clara for our season opener against the Broncos. When I returned home from the Bay Area, I found out the retreat never happened.

The next day, I called my big brother, "King," and asked him for a ride to our regular Sunday meeting. I lived quite a distance from the fraternity house and I didn't feel safe driving home in the dark. He said they would send someone by to pick me up.

Seven o'clock came and I was still at home waiting for my ride. The meeting had started and according to the rules, any member who was late was paddled or fined five bucks. I phoned the house once again and my big brother told me that my ride was en route to my house.

My ride never came.

I called the house one more time just after the meeting and my big brother apologized and said that everything was cool.

Soon after, Sam Clifford called. He said I was fined for missing the meeting and I needed to pay my forty dollar monthly membership dues.

"But King told me that everything had been taken care of and I didn't have to worry about missing the meeting"

"Yeah, everything is alright. You just have to pay five bucks or get five swats for missing the meeting. And you owe money for dues."

I went into my room and started to think about whether I really wanted this in my life. At the same time, I still wanted to remain a part of the group.

I spoke to Paul Haas, who was now an alum, about the possibility of going in-active for a semester and returning in the spring. I told him how school and football were taking up my nearly all of my time. School came first and football was a close second because being a football coach was to be my chosen profession after I completed my education. I was firm in letting him know that football was something I wasn't going to give up.

After talking with some of the members, he told me that going in-active was not an option. I was either in or out.

"We don't want you to give up football, we just want you to pay your dues," he said.

"How do I pay my dues for something I'm not going to take part in? I'm busy practically every weekend with football."

"Your dues go toward other things besides parties."

"Like what? You don't even have a ramp to the fraternity house."

"Well, according to the rules of the local chapter, you either stay or get expelled."

I was expelled as a member of Sigma Phi Epsilon and I felt like a huge boulder had been lifted off my back.

This experience showed me that money can't buy you the kinds of friends who will stick with you through thick and thin. If they had been true friends, would they have been there to pick me up for the meeting? If they meant what they said by "don't worry about it," would they have fined me for missing the meeting?

If they had wanted this comm major in the fraternity, would they have made other arrangements to keep me in the group?

What about brotherly love and everything I learned as a pledge? When all of this came down, it didn't mean a thing.

After my unfortunate experience as a quasi-frat-boy, I didn't speak too highly of the men and women who wore Greek letters. I was bitter.

Now, that time has reduced this to just another memory, I believe there is a reason or two for these organizations to exist.

The first is friendship. I don't know why, but there are some people who need this artificial setting in order to make friends and gain acceptance. They need someone to validate their existence. To each his own, I guess.

But, to put a group of people together simply based on looks and money is a bit shallow. After all, I thought I had a lot to offer the group besides the almighty dollar. Maybe it was my looks? Yeah, right!

The second is service. Greek organizations should be in the business of doing community service. Communities need a lot of help that comes in the form of positive energy, unfettered enthusiasm, and a labor of love.

Maybe if I had joined another fraternity, I would have had a more pleasant experience, and I would be writing something totally different. But, that wasn't the case.

Still, I went against my parents' advice and joined. I'm glad I did.

On My Own

Making the initial transition from living in a dorm to an apartment off campus was difficult. Less than a week before I was to get out of Lassen Hall, Tammy informed me that she and a friend of hers had found a place to live until our apartment was ready. Unfortunately, I was not on the guest list.

Our other roommate, Leslie McBride, wouldn't join us until school started. So, as the clock struck two on the last day of school, I was scrambling to find a place to crash for a month. I was desperate.

Pacing outside the Bell Memorial Union, I ran into Bob Wilson. We had a speech class together.

"Hey Bob, are you going to be around this summer?"

"Yeah, why?"

"'Cause, I am looking for a place to stay. Do you know anyone that needs an extra roommate?"

Eureka! Bob was looking for another person to share a house with him and another friend of his, John Thibodeaux, over the summer. It was close to campus, too!

Shortly after moving in with Tammy and Leslie, I discovered many things.

First, living in an apartment with two women is one thing. Sharing a bathroom with them is another. Being responsible for more bills and cooking more meals were things I had to adjust to in this new situation. Believe me, having to think about dinner was a lot more fun than negotiating my share of the bills, especially with Tammy.

Going through my problems with the fraternity put a strain on our living situation. Paul Haas was spending a lot of nights at our place and it got to the point where he became another roommate—who didn't pay rent. So, I had to share the bathroom with three people.

Leslie on the other hand, was a delight to be around. She was beautiful and had a heart of gold to match. She was a PE major and a member of the gymnastics team.

I'll never forget the time I missed my landing as I got into bed one night. I ended up on the floor beside my chair and underneath an end table which I used for a nightstand.

Shortly after hearing the big thud, she rushed into my bedroom, clad in her terry cloth bathrobe, and helped me out of my predicament.

Once I got into bed, I came to the full realization that I had cracked a couple of ribs. Leslie came back with a couple of aspirin and a glass of water.

Living with her and Tammy was like night and day. Tammy was night, and Leslie was a breath of sunshine.

I moved over one street my senior year and had a new roommate, Chuck Graves. Except for the times I lived with Cam, Chuck was my favorite roommate. We got along very well.

Chuck and I had a lot in common. We were both coaching football. While I was in my second year as the Wildcats kicking coach, enjoying our best season in fifteen years, he was coaching at Bidwell Junior High, teaching young kids how to put on a jock strap.

While sharing the same apartment, Chuck and I developed a good friendship. We were kind of like family. We ate together. We sometimes partied together. We shared a lot of what each other were doing. We were there for each other during the highs and lows.

The thing I like about Chuck is that he is a motivator and he loves football the same way I do. If I decided to go back to football, I wouldn't mind coaching with him.

It was kind of interesting though because toward the end of the year, Chuck was pretty secretive about his plans after school got out.

During the summer, I called one of his friends to straighten out some stuff with our apartment. We were getting screwed by the property management. He told me that Chuck had gone to Fort Benning, Georgia, to go into the Army. Chuck had mentioned this to me a couple of times, but I didn't think he was serious.

One day, Chuck's mother called and asked as to his whereabouts. She hadn't heard from him either. I didn't know what to tell her.

I told her that her son went into the army and she cried. She put Chuck's father on the phone and he was a bit more subdued. Still, it was kind of uncomfortable.

Chuck's stint in the army didn't last long. He returned to Chico for a bit and then went back down to the Bay Area where I can imagine he is coaching somewhere.

The 1986-87 school year was probably my favorite year in Chico. I was finishing school. The football team had its best year. I was extremely busy having some fun.

Lion Jonathan

"Lion Jonathan," it has a ring to it. Don't you think?

My friends often chided me when they called me "Lion Jonathan." It was all in good fun.

When Max Lee, a prominent Chico doctor, first approached me about becoming a Lion, I wasn't very excited about it. All that I could think of was that these guys were just like the fellas at the Sig Ep house, only they were my Grandpa's age.

I had given a speech at one of their meetings a few years back, and I remember having a good time. Speaking of Grandpa Elster, he was a Lion too.

With my experiences as a Sig Ep still fresh in my mind, I was determined not to go through another round of this again. On the other hand, not too many people said "No" to Lion Max Lee.

He explained what Lions Clubs International was all about, their main purpose of helping those with sight and hearing preservation. He spoke of the Lions motto, "We Serve," and said that he thought I had a lot to offer to the club. He said that my background in Public Relations was something the club needed.

Max explained how money was not an important consideration and offered to pay my membership dues as long as I would work hard as a member of the club. He insisted that what they were looking for were qualities inside the person that would serve the needs of the club. He would later be my sponsor.

Hard work and dedication to a club service project were critical to making it a success. This club didn't simply cut checks when they saw a need to raise money; they went out and earned it!

It came as no surprise to me when shortly after I was inducted into the club, I was put in charge of getting the club's monthly newsletter out to the members. I spent my first two years as bulletin editor for the club.

Our club was the smallest of three in Chico. Because of the size of our club, it didn't take very long for me to move up the ladder to be the club's president. Before being chosen as club president, I had a challenger to run against in the election. This was a rare occasion as all the previous elections were basically just a formality, a coronation. I ran against a woman who felt I was ill equipped to run the club. I prevailed in the end and she soon left the club to go to law school.

Being the youngest member of the club and president presented some interesting dynamics to work through. I mean, you've got some members who are three times your age and old enough to be your grandfather. Another more significant majority of members are old enough to be your father or mother, and the rest are old enough to be your older sister or brother. They brought a lot of history, personal bias, and life experiences to the table, and this was an education I will never forget.

Lion Glen Williams was one of the elder statesmen of the club who acted as "de-facto" parliamentarian. He was never afraid to give me advice as to what I was doing right and wrong according to the bylaws of Lions International.

Lions Don Nowak and Tony Fasolino were especially helpful when it came to managing the club on a regular basis. I had a pretty good idea of what I wanted the big picture to look like, but they were there to fill in the blanks along the way.

Lion Rick Turner was someone who I could talk to about almost anything. A well-rounded guy, Rick had a sense of humor. He always came to the meetings with a joke or a riddle.

If there was ever a person who I could characterize as being moved by his mere presence, it was Lion "Bald Eagle," or Lloyd La Breacht. I could tell just by looking at him that I had his support.

While I was recuperating in the hospital from my broken neck, Lloyd came to see me just about every day. He didn't speak but maybe fifty words, but I knew he was there.

To merely mention Lion Max Lee as just the guy who got me into Lions wouldn't be complete without saying that through it all, he was always there.

There were many times when he came to my house unannounced at 7:30 in the morning just to talk about the club. Max loved to gossip about anything and everything. But, whenever I needed something, Max always came through in the clutch.

As president, I saw my role as being two-fold. I had to make sure the meetings ran smoothly, and I had to represent my club at other functions throughout the community.

After my tenure as president, I returned to office as club secretary. It would be the last year of the club as membership dropped off and the interest in keeping the club going faded.

Someday, I hope to return to the Lions. I like what Lions International does and I am always proud to tell people, including my friends, what it means to be called "Lion Jonathan."

My Chico Family

From the moment I called Coach Trimmer, "Dad," I could sense our relationship was about to change. I thought that we would grow closer and form a special bond. But, the closeness I have with him extends to their family and it is a relationship that I cherish very much. His wife Barbara is my Chico Mom and their only son, Jeff, is the little brother I never had. He is known as "LB."

To have the Trimmers as my surrogate family made my initial transition to Chico a lot easier and even today, I never hesitate to ask them for their help and guidance.

I remember talking with my Chico Dad about when we first got to know each other. He said it was initially difficult for him to get to know someone in my situation because I was the first person to step into his life and make such an impression.

His wife Barbara is someone who I can talk with about issues that may bring with it a different perspective than my own mother.

They have never been judgmental of me, even when I screw up. Yet they are always willing to state their opinion—when I ask for it.

My "little brother" Jeff started out as being kind of small. When we first met, he was a sophomore in high school. Shortly thereafter, he grew and grew and grew. He was a high school standout running back and ended up going to U.C. Davis where he played defensive back.

There was a time when Jeff worked as an attendant for me. We got very close, like brothers. We talked about his parents and my "Mom and Dad." I asked him if it bothered him that I called them by that name and he said it didn't.

When I am not visiting my parents on a holiday or special occasion, the Trimmers have always made me feel welcome with their love and friendship.

My parents know the relationship I have with the Trimmers. I think they welcome the fact that someone in Chico is looking out for their son. Mom has always said that I am a child of the world and I have many mothers. There have been times when I've looked to my father for help when he passed the baton by saying, "Why don't you ask your Chico Dad to help you with that."

628 Orient Street

"This is the perfect place for you. As long as you stay in Chico, don't ever leave this house," my father said on one of his more recent visits.

I have lived on the corner of Seventh and Orient for almost a decade.

I enjoy the stability of not having to look for a new place, especially since I like living here so much.

It was really by accident that I came upon the single story, red-brick duplex. With the white roof and large parking lot, you'd think you were at a doctor's office. When I first laid eyes on it, I thought it was something out of the T.V. show, "Marcus Welby, M.D."

On a house hunting trip, I was combing the area looking for a place. I was living in the general vicinity with Cam and his friend Jack. I preferred the area compared to living on the avenues because there were more sidewalks and it was closer to downtown.

I peered through the front window and noticed the low counters. I knew at that moment I could be sitting on a land mine. This was it! This was my place. This was my home sweet home.

I looked at the front of the building and didn't see any "FOR RENT" signs. But, when I got closer to the door, I saw the business card of a real estate agent. Bob Browning was his name. I took down the number and went home.

Bob Browning was a nice guy. It wasn't very long into our conversation that he said he knew me from being on the sidelines at Chico State.

I asked about the duplex and he said it was for rent. He said he needed first and last month's rent, plus a security deposit.

I told him I was in love with the place because of the low counters and proximity to downtown. However, I didn't have that much cash to put down on the place and we ended up negotiating an amicable arrangement.

Next, I had to find a roommate—fast. I had a roommate lined up but he bailed out at the last minute. I went down to Chico State and combed the halls of Acker Gym where I found Lisa Nelson.

Lisa was one of five roommates who shared the apartment with me. For the last two and a half years though, I've had the place all to myself. I like it that way.

The neighborhood I live in is vastly different than the one I left behind. Sure, there are college students in the area. However, there are also families, seniors, single parents, blue-collar people, single professionals, disabled people, and just about everyone else that make it a diverse neighborhood.

The best part about living here is the close proximity I have to goods and services. It's not as good as when I first moved here, but I am within wheelchair distance of almost everything I need.

Within a three block radius of my house, I have access to a park, bank, city hall, movie theaters, post office, restaurants, bars, and other stores. It makes life a lot easier when you have everything close to you.

Unless I leave Chico, or my landlord hauls me and my furniture out into the middle of the street, I think I'll be here for quite a while. Nowhere else compares to it. I'd like to own it someday. This is the place I call home.

CHALK TALK

For a year and a half, I did a weekly sports commentary for the local NBC affiliate. It wasn't a real job. It didn't even pay. But, it sure was a lot of fun. I had roughly ninety seconds to make a statement, back it up, and get out as fast as I could.

While I wanted to be serious, the folks in the biz wanted me to be funny. It didn't matter that I thought of myself as a thoughtful, analytical sort when it comes to things, this was television. People don't have time to be analytical while eating dinner, nor do they have the attention span.

"Chalk Talk" was something I could call my own. Despite having to adjust to a different medium, I was determined to get my viewers to stop and think, even if they didn't agree with me. If I was able to accomplish that, I felt like I had done my job.

When it came to putting one of those spots together, I realized it was harder than I thought. The toughest part was getting my topics approved by the sports directors, neither of whom I respected.

I am grateful to Tom Carlson for giving me my start. He is one of the nicest guys you'll ever meet. However, whenever I would get mad at him, he would never fight back at me. I couldn't stand it. He just sat there and smiled while I would go into one of my tirades trying to get his approval on one of my commentaries. Unlike me, he never held a grudge.

Then there was Jeff Peterson a converted weatherman who was nothing more than a pretty face. Like Tom Carlson, he wanted me to be funny. Soon after he came aboard though, his dinner breaks occurred while I was taping. Thus, I practically had total editorial control over everything.

As a professional dedicated to his craft, I was not sucked into the small town confines of the "good old boy network." Chico is not as small as local personalities and sportscasters would like to think. But somehow, the two seem to feed on each other.

When it comes to sports coverage in this community, there seems to be a lack of objective reporting because there exists a tight knit relationship between reporters and coaches that is borderline unethical. Heck, they go out for beers after games.

So, when I said something negative about the Chico State athletic program, I was scorned by everyone, including those in the media, because I told it like I saw it.

If Chico is ever going to grow into a community with a viable athletic program, whether it is amateur or professional, this relationship has to change. Unfortunately, I don't see it happening in the near future.

Doing a sports commentary once a week made me fairly recognizable around town. People either love you or hate you, then they love you and hate you all over again. But, the one thing that made me believe that I was doing something right was when the competition decided to include a weekly sports commentary on their station. It would follow a day after mine.

After being on the air for a year and a half, I was let go without explanation.

"Tonight's your last night, and don't say goodbye," said the station's news director, Paul Unwin.

It was unfortunate that such a thing had to happen. I was crushed when I got the news. I didn't understand it.

As I look back on it, I remember the times when I was right, as well as the other times when I had to eat crow. Either way, I loved doing it.

I can still hear those words echo from time to time, "I'm Jonathan, for Chalk Talk."

Skateboarding

As a child, I went skateboarding. It was nothing really big, just something I did at a friend's house. I would either sit or lie on my stomach and peddle his skateboard with my hands around the front of the house. It was fun to do, but it was nothing special.

Skateboarding seems to be making a comeback these days. And while I have nothing against it personally, I didn't think it belonged on the streets of downtown Chico.

One night, I went before the City Council and asked them to enact a total ban on skateboarding and rollerblading in the downtown core area. It was covered approximately a five by six block area of the business district. A partial ban had been in place limiting the activity to after dark.

For me, this was an issue of safety. It was about the safety of people in wheelchairs, those who use walkers, people with small children, and others who simply aren't quick enough on their feet. When you have to watch out for cars, bicycles, and other pedestrians, those who ride skateboards and rollerblades are an unknown variable that shouldn't be in the mix. I contended that since bicycles weren't allowed on the sidewalks, how are skateboards any different? Sidewalks are for pedestrians. The downtown is a place where people conduct their business. It is not a playground.

After listening to about twenty other people speak against the total ban, the City Council extended the ban on a 4-3 vote.

The main concern that councilmembers who were against the total ban was that there was no other place for people to rollerblade and ride skateboards. It was obvious to me that they didn't consider that the city has the second largest city-owned park in the country. Isn't that good enough? I think we need more basketball courts and football fields too, but that doesn't mean we should play football downtown.

The skateboard issue speaks to something even larger though. It shows how some people don't have concern for their fellow human beings and the lack of control parents have over their children.

Of course, some young people don't care if they run into a person walking down the street. It's a part of being a kid. You just don't think about it. But, when you take this attitude a step further, you begin to ask yourself: Why should young people be out on the streets of downtown at night skateboarding anyway?

It also speaks to the way in which these kids are being brought up in today's society. It shows that whether they were raised by one or two parent families, their parents were most likely products of the sixties—an era where authority was constantly challenged.

Some kids in Chico think that such a ban is somehow a violation of their civil rights. This is something handed down by their parents because they too have lost control of their kids and the only way they can "beat 'me," is to join them in their quest to right this terrible injustice.

Well, let me tell you, in my family, we didn't have civil rights. I lived under a friendly dictatorship. What my parents said and did was the rule. No exceptions.

If I told my mother that I was going downtown with my friends to ride skateboards, she'd tell me to find something else to do. No questions asked.

I know I probably made a few young people very unhappy by doing this, but in this case I did what I felt was right for my safety, and the safety of others.

Chico is very special to me. It is where I did a lot of my "growing up." It is a community where I feel like I can do just about anything while living life to its fullest potential.

There have been times where I thought about leaving. But so far, I haven't found anything better.

Right now, Chico is my home.

The Glue That Holds Me Together

In one of my political science classes, Professor Roy Owen told us that predictability was the glue that held society together. To his credit there have been a few times when this has held true.

When it comes to the relationship I have with those who have helped me take care of my daily needs, getting me in and out of the bath tub, helping me prepare dinner, doing my household chores, running errands, and sometimes performing some difficult procedures that professionals normally do, there exists a bond based on friendship and trust. Ask almost any disabled person who has an attendant, they would agree. There is no other bond like it.

Whether you call them attendants, providers, personal assistants, or caretakers, they provide stability and continuity to my day every day. In essence, they have been the glue that holds me together.

Except for my first attendant, I've had the responsibility of hiring and occasionally firing every one of them. Neither is easy to do.

It's hard to get a quality individual to come to your house every single day at virtually the same time, including weekends and holidays, for a low-wage job that has no benefits. Since I have no other resources, I offer them what I can through the county program. They allocate a certain number of hours per month at the minimum wage salary, and I use every one of them.

I've been fortunate in that I haven't had to fire too many attendants. Usually it's after they've screwed up so many times that it gets old. But, you make the change as quickly and easily as you can and move on.

For me, I like to know a person before I hire them. I have never put an ad in the paper looking for an attendant because I don't know who they are and what they're all about. Doing a personal interview just doesn't cut it for me. I have to know more. If I have a little bit of history with them as a friend or acquaintance, I can trust my instincts as to whether or not they can do the job.

Every person who has worked for me has their own style, a certain way of doing things. Some of them do things better than others. Others just simply do the job, and that's what counts.

John Cook

Upon coming to Chico, John Cook was my first attendant. I was extremely fortunate to have the county pair us up. In one word, I would describe him as a professional. He knew what he was doing and he did it extremely well.

I was one of several disabled people on John's list. He was pretty flexible when it came to what time he was came. But if I was late for our appointment, he let me know it. After all, he had us on a schedule, and he wasn't going to let anyone screw it up.

John was a computer science major, a high strung kind of guy. He would always rush into my room or apartment with his Big Gulp in hand, ready to go. He was never in the mood for wasting time.

I remember one instance where he came to my dorm room during Pioneer Week, Chico State's springtime festival. The RA's were checking people as they came in the front door trying to monitor the flow of traffic. When John came through the door, he was no exception.

I am John Cook and I don't have time for any of that noise!" he stammered. His voice rang with a certain rhythm as he pointed his finger down after every word.

"You tell them that I am here to take care of you and I will not have any more unnecessary delays. Jeez! You'd think they'd know who I am. I come here every day!"

I just sat there and listened.

John was the best at just about everything. He was a great cook. When he cleaned up my room, he had a knack of putting things where I wanted them to be. He could even make a great glass of iced tea.

More importantly, he was interested in my well-being. He equipped me with the right things to know as an impressionable young adult who was adjusting to life outside the nest. He helped me a lot in my early stages of adulthood.

After two and a half years, it was time for John to move on. He left Chico for the real world. At the time, I didn't know how I would survive without him, but following some of the things he taught me has helped over the years. As an attendant, he set the standard.

Keith Cameron

He took over for John and was my attendant for the better part of ten years. After a long stretch, he'd quit for a while and then come back. While he wasn't working for me, he was always available on stand-by in case I got in a jam.

I think our personal friendship played an important part in making it last as long as it did. When he first arrived on the scene, he knew he was following in the footsteps of a guy who knew the tricks of the trade. As our friendship grew, he knew what made me tick. He could read me like a book.

Whenever I ended up in the hospital on an unexpected visit, I always asked him to bring me my Media-Cal stickers.

"Where are they?" he asked.

"I don't know," I replied.

The next day, he showed up with my stickers.

He also knew how neurotic I was before leaving on a trip. He'd have my suitcase packed before I could name everything I wanted to take, and then some. My mother always complimented the way in which he packed my clothes.

Continuity, stability, and quality of care over the long term made him such a great guy to have as an attendant.

Dennis Blaine

After Cam had to leave due to a sudden illness, I looked to Dennis Blaine to captain the ship. He had worked for me both as a fill-in and as a regular over the last five years. We knew each other while I worked in television. Like Keith, he brought three essential ingredients I look for in an attendant. The similarity ends there.

For some reason, Dennis likes to challenge everything I say. He enjoys it.

For example, if I said that the city is doing a good job making things accessible for people with disabilities, he would argue about the cost of doing it and how it only benefits a small group of people.

He's the kind of guy who'd argue that the sky is red, if I said it was blue. The bantering back and forth that goes on between us can get pretty hysterical. There is no real emotion when we argue, it's just something that goes on while he is busy helping me out.

Dennis Blaine is not the most politically correct guy either. In fact, if it weren't for my sense of humor, I'd probably be sending him to get some sensitivity training.

One day, my father bought me twenty-five TV dinners and put them in my freezer. He got just about every kind you could imagine. When Dennis came over to help me out, he put them in two stacks of twelve. Then he told me that after I ate the extra one that evening, we would start from the very top and go back and forth until they were all gone.

"What if we duplicate and I eat the same thing two days in a row?" I asked.

Dennis gave it some thought and devised a numbering system by which I would pick a row and number. What I picked was what I got.

We did all sorts of things that made deciding what I was going to eat a decision arrived by a random outcome, not by choice. He said that I needed structure in my life and that I couldn't make those kinds of decisions for myself. He also devised a system for the clothes in my closet and chest of drawers.

Dennis can get pretty creative when he pokes fun at me, but poking fun is a two-way street and I get my licks in once in a while.

Despite the fact we often trade barbs on a daily basis, I would be remiss if I didn't say that underneath that rough exterior of his lies a person who cares about me. He would deny it, if I asked him, but I think he does.

One day, I asked him to take me to a concert to see the popular eighties rock group, "Foreigner." I probably didn't have a chance in hell of going with him, but I thought I'd give it a shot. I mean, I like the group. Why shouldn't he?

Dennis went into a giant tirade about how their music consisted of four chords. He did this for days and days.

Then, less than a week before the concert, I asked him again.

"Oh, alright," he said.

During the concert, he started counting the chords on his fingers. Soon after, I started to join him.

Then when we got backstage for the last few songs, I could see him rocking out with the other groupies.

On the way home, we did the whole counting thing all over again.

"Dude, tell 'em to learn another chord, okay?" he shouted.

I couldn't stop laughing.

Like many people who have worked for me, on several occasions Dennis has gone above and beyond the call of duty. Moreover, his quick wit and unabashed sense of humor make a daily routine an interesting, unforgettable experience.

Connie Noller

The woman who I fell in love with during my first year at Chico State was the first female to work for me as my attendant. We both lived in Lassen Hall.

So, how do you let a woman who you are sexually attracted to, and extremely in love with, put you in the bath tub every day?

For the first several months or so, the answer was easy. I wore shorts or swim trunks when I took a bath. Then, I let the water completely out and rang them out a bit before getting out of the tub. I didn't want to get the towel soaking wet.

The winter months came and the weather got colder. It seemed to take forever for the water to let out and I was getting the shivers.

"Hey, would you mind if we got rid of the shorts?" I asked meekly.

"What do you mean, would I mind? You're the one who's got the problem. It doesn't bother me any."

Connie was right. It didn't bother her. It never bothered her to see me in any state of undress. I think she had seen it all before.

The next day, it happened. I went into the bathtub in my birthday suit.

It wasn't easy. I turned several shades of red. After a few days though, it got better.

I can relate to people who fall into this kind of situation. It's not an easy one to handle. I don't know what I would do if it happened again. Maybe I'll just have to get another pair of swimming trunks.

I've had a few bad experiences with attendants. But they're not bad enough to write about. I'll let others speak for themselves.

What one must understand is that while these people prepare meals, do laundry, wash dishes, clean house, and run errands, they are not maids, housekeepers, cooks, or caretakers. They are much more than that. For me, it means putting my trust in their hands as they carry me in and out of the bathtub without breaking a bone.

It means doing things that I can't do, like mopping the floors or picking things up from hard to reach places.

Attendants provide companionship whether they are there for one hour or half a day. For some, this person is their link to the outside world. While to others, they become a good friend.

There are so many things a caregiver does, and yet, they often don't get the praise they deserve. Moreover, I think they are underpaid and sometimes undervalued. Sure, those that work for the wealthy are fairly compensated. But for the rest of us, good help is sometimes hard to come by. Not all of us are lucky.

When you can pay someone a decent wage, you are more likely to attract good people. If an individual or agency responsible for paying for the person doesn't offer a fair wage, you face having to scrape the bottom of the barrel. This can have disastrous consequences for both the person giving the care, and those receiving it.

Along with death and taxes, there lies an element of predictability that is an absolute certainty. I will need someone to assist me every single day of the year in order to help me participate fully and subsist in today's society. It is obvious, I can't do it alone.

Attendants are the glue that holds me together.

I Have A Dream

It's been nearly a decade since I was a part of a football program. It has been a while since I last strode along the practice field yelling, "It's a great day to be a Wildcat," during team stretch. A long time has passed since the time my kickers referred to me as "The General."

Being involved with a football program was a routine I had grown accustomed to. There is a big part of me that wishes I were back in coaching and I get a big lump in my throat every time I think about it.

The game of football represents so much of who I am. I have been able to draw so many parallels between football and my life, that the similarities between the two warrant a perfect match.

This does not imply that I view life as one big Super Bowl. It's just that the game of football has taught me so much that no other experience in my life has done thus far. My experience as a coach has given me many fond memories that will remain with me forever.

To be successful on the gridiron, one needs to play the sport with a great deal of energy and quick wit. When it comes to living life to the fullest, I do it with zeal and enthusiasm. I live it knowing that there are times when I have to roll the dice, take a chance or two. Sometimes you have to go for it on fourth down.

If I need to go to the store in a driving rainstorm, I put on a garbage bag and do it. When I wanted to be a part of the football program at Chico State, I went to see Coach Trimmer, and asked how I could help.

When I am tired of looking at the walls of my house at eleven o'clock at night, I go out to be with people.

When Mike Bellotti asked me to be the Wildcats kicking coach, I poured my heart and soul into a facet of the game that is taken for granted and often overlooked.

Sometimes I'll take that chance and ask a beautiful woman out, even when I think the answer is no.

From the late seventies to the early nineties, my interest in the game of football grew to aspirations of making it a chosen career.

"Lakeshore Lancers, we fight for thee..."

I first developed an interest in coaching football when I was a freshman at Lakeshore High School in Stevensville, Michigan. After school, I was supposed to go study somewhere until my ride came to pick me up. One day though, my attention was diverted elsewhere.

I went by one of the classrooms where the football team was watching game film. Peering through the open door, I could hear Lancer Head Coach, Dave Topping, critiquing each play. As I was looking from outside the room, I became an interested spectator. A few players noticed me. So did Coach Topping. He invited me to come in, and I sat in on the rest of the meeting. I asked him if I could watch film with the team the next week, and he said it was alright. For the remainder of the season, stopping by the classroom with the film projector became part of my Monday afternoon routine.

At the same time I was making a connection with Coach Topping, another person who furthered my interest in football was Mr. Clark, the school's vice-principal. He took me to a lot of the games and pushed my wheelchair up and down the sidelines. More than that though, he got me interested in football by talking about the game. On the rides home, we would take each game apart and analyze what went right and what didn't go so well.

Of all of my experiences watching football as a high school or college student, be it at Lakeshore or Mills High School, or at Chico State, nothing compared to watching football on a cold autumn night in small town America, right in the heart of the Midwest.

It was special.

Nothing compared to the smell of dew soaked grass being kicked up on each play, or the aroma of hot chocolate coming from the junior class concession stand. The sights and sounds of the crowd in the stands always got my adrenalin pumping.

Both young and old braved the freezing temperatures, rooting the Lancers on to victory. There was not an empty seat to be found.

Sitting on the sidelines, I could feel the excitement hit me like charges of electricity, coming from all points, both on and off the field. The voices of cheerleaders shouting instructions to the eager crowd were audible, even through the thick sound of screaming fans. Most took the game very seriously and viewed it as more than just another social event. The grunts and groans combined with the grinding sounds of helmets and pads crashing rang between my ears as the action would often come at me with a fury.

While the excitement of the game is contained inside, like a bottle, outside the stadium, the town is still.

As the season continued, I became somewhat of a team mascot. I didn't mind it. I was having a good time.

During the final minutes of the last game of the season, I was surprised when Coach Topping asked me to come over to the sideline where he was standing. The Lancers were behind and the game was well out of reach. Coach Topping asked me to call a play.

I was so shocked, excited, and dazed that I didn't know what to do. I mean, I spent every Monday afternoon studying with the team, and when I got my first shot, the Lancers were hit with a delay of game penalty. After the five yard penalty, Coach Topping gave me another chance.

After looking at the list of plays to choose from, I picked a pass play. The result? The pass was intercepted. First down, bad guys.

I was invited to the awards banquet at the end of the season and Coach Topping talked about how I helped the team. It was good that my first experience as being a part of a football program was a positive one.

California Dreamin'? NOT!!!

Soon after my family returned to California, I discovered that football wasn't as important on the West Coast as it was in the Midwest, at least not at Mills High School.

With the difference in climate and having many things to do on the

San Francisco Peninsula, football was just another thing to do. In fact, our school didn't even have a football stadium. We played a lot of our games on the district field at Burlingame High School.

In my three years at Mills High School, our football teams weren't very good. The win-loss records aren't worth remembering even though we had some good individual athletes like Jon Cox (tight end), Pat Wisecarver (wide receiver), and Inoke Katoa (running back). Mills was better known for its achievements on the hardcourt and diamond. For two years, I watched the games as a spectator in the stands. My wheelchair just barely fit on the bottom level where others would walk back and forth, going to and from their seats. It didn't beat my view from the sidelines. The excitement just wasn't there.

After feeling my oats for a year or so, I asked the head football coach, Mr. Field, if there was anything I could do to help out the football team. Mr. Field, a biology teacher with a cue ball for a head and thick rimmed glasses to match, didn't take my offer seriously thus, I didn't pursue it. As a football coach, he wasn't very impressive, but as my biology teacher, he was great. I guess that's all that counts.

Look Who's Coming to Dinner

The car wound its way through the long and winding road. The excitement in my stomach was building. Finally, I was going to match wits with a guy who was an NFL head coach and a head coach of a major university. I was going to debate a man who I considered my idol as well as a good friend. Moreover, we were doing it at his house—over dinner. The topic was whether offenses or defenses win football games.

Going to Paul Wiggin's house for dinner was going to be special. But, little did I know it would have such a positive influence on my life.

The car made its final stop in front of a huge house located in the Los Altos Hills. I thought we were having dinner at Buckingham Palace. I had never seen a house so big. Coach Wiggin came out to greet us and we meandered our way on to one of the many levels of the house. Dinner was almost ready. There were steaks cooking on the barbecue and baked potatoes in the oven. Coach Wiggin was having some difficulty with the spinach soufflé. I didn't care. I was just happy to be there.

My parents and Coach Wiggin did most of the talking during dinner. You know, your basic family stuff.

Afterwards, Coach Wiggin and I retired to the den. My parents sat and enjoyed the beautiful view from his living room. Our debate didn't last long. He had statistics to prove his point and all I could do was listen and sip my soda.

Paul Wiggin asked me a question that no one ever asked before.

"So, what do you want to be when you grow up?"

"I want to be a football coach," I replied in a cautious, quiet voice. I knew he didn't hear what I was saying.

"What?"

"I want to be a football coach." My voice was louder this time.

"Well, what's wrong with that?"

"Um, everyone told me I couldn't do it. My friends told me I couldn't do it. My teachers told me I couldn't do it. My parents told me I couldn't do it. Everyone told me I couldn't do it." I was still somewhat careful about what I said because I didn't know how he would react.

"And, why is that?"

"Well, because I didn't play the game."

"Jonathan, you know that you will never be able to play football as we know it. I am sure that you would love to play football. In fact, I bet you dream about it."

I nodded my head thinking about all the times I dreamt about playing football.

"But, there is no reason why you can't coach football."

I couldn't believe it! I was being told by someone who I respected that I could be a football coach! Here was a man telling me that I could do something that others said was impossible! But, what was to follow was even more important.

Coach Wiggin asked me a series of questions.

"Can you read?"

"Uh huh."

"Can you write?"

"Yep."

"Can you watch film?"

"Yeah, I did that when I lived in Michigan."

"Can you follow directions?"

"Yes."

"Can you tell others what to do?"

I nodded my head in agreement.

Coach Wiggin then asked questions which caused me to think a little more.

"Are you willing to study the game?"

I sat there in a daze, taking all of this in while sipping my drink. Coach Wiggin was putting a puzzle together for me and I was beginning to see how each piece was falling into place.

"Are you willing to put in the time and commitment into coaching?"

"Yes."

"Okay. Now, when you get to Chico State, I want you to find the football coach and ask him how you can help the football team. Volunteer to do anything. You will have to start out small at first. Then, once you prove yourself, they'll give you more to do."

We talked a while longer about coaching and he gave me a lot of advice. I wish I had brought a tape recorder with me so I could take it all down. I didn't forget the substance of what he said that very night.

There were two very profound things that happened. First, someone finally asked me what I wanted to be when I grow up. When I answered, I didn't get shot down. This was a first for me, and it took someone like Coach Wiggin to do it.

Second, Paul Wiggin not only told me that I could coach football, he told me exactly how to do it. He broke down coaching into the things that I can do. Then, he gave me a blueprint on how to get my start at Chico State University.

When I talk about the way I integrate football as a part of my life, I use what Paul Wiggin taught me. Instead of assuming that I cannot do a particular thing because I, or someone I know tells me I can't do it, I break things down and identify those things I can do. And, I always have a game plan.

First Year As a Mascot

While many students were out buying their books and touring the campus, I was on a mission to find Dick Trimmer, the Wildcats head football coach. I started my search with a trip to the physical education department office located inside Acker Gymnasium.

As I motored through one of the side entrances, I spotted a glass encased sign with a roster full of names and room numbers. Working my way from top to bottom, I found what I was looking for. It read, "TRIMMER—ANNEX."

I thought to myself, "What the hell does that mean?"

I went to the main office and asked where the head football coach's office was and a secretary told me it was outside, behind the gym.

Great!! They've got their own office. That's how it should be.

After making a quick right, I went through a long hallway. On my left were the men's locker rooms while on the right was Acker Gym, the basketball home of the CSU Wildcats. I came to the end of the hallway where I exited the rear entrance, next to the training room.

Outside, I saw two trailers lined up side by side, nestled in the confines of the football stadium. They were painted pink with a faded shade of white trim. Ugly was a better word to describe 'em.

I went up to the first trailer and didn't find a thing. No sign. No people. Nothing. Maybe the gymnastics coaches or track coaches hang out here?

The second trailer confirmed my worst suspicions. The sign on the door read: CSU FOOTBALL: Dick Trimmer Head Coach

I knocked on the door and got no answer. It was around lunch time so I figured they must be out. I decided to come by later in the afternoon.

On my way over to Whitney Hall where lunch awaited my arrival, I couldn't get out of my mind the picture of those ugly, pink trailers. I couldn't believe my eyes! I mean, I know I wasn't at Notre Dame or USC, but didn't these people have any pride?

How could you have a team meeting in an office shaped like a bread box? More importantly, how does the school regard its football program? I mean, if that was my first impression, what did the players think?

I got my food and looked for an open spot at one of the three tables on the main level. I looked to my left and saw a group of men in gray t-shirts and shorts sitting at the table with half-filled plates and cups piled one on top of another. On the front of their shirts was a big blue football helmet with the words: WILDCAT FOOTBALL CAMP emblazoned on the front. I knew I would be able to find something out.

"Can anyone tell me where I might find Dick Trimmer?"

A man next to me set his Coke down and turned to me.

"I am Dick Trimmer."

Eureka, I had found the head football coach! While my ears rang with excitement, I was almost at a loss for words. I told him who I was and that I was interested in helping out the football team. Like Coach Wiggin had told me to do, I offered to help out in any way I could. He invited me to practice.

Dick Trimmer was in his tenth year at the helm with an overall winning percentage hovering around the .500 mark. It was reflective of the team's finish the previous season. The Wildcats went 5-5 in 1982. Briefly put, the 'Cats lost a couple they should've won, and they won a couple they should've lost.

Between adjusting to my first year away from home and catching up on my schoolwork, I found time to go to a few practices during the first two weeks of school. I also went to the annual Red-White scrimmage. This was the final tune-up before the opener at St. Mary's.

Coach Trimmer called me his special assistant. Translation—team mascot. At this point in time, I didn't mind the title. I was doing a lot of watching and listening, feeling my way around. I knew the time would come where there would be something for me to do.

Not two weeks had passed when Coach Trimmer invited me to go on the team bus for the opener against the Gaels. I was particularly excited to make the trip because the 'Cats would be taking on my friend Kevin Shea's alma mater. Kevin was a friend of mine who I met while I was a patient at Shriner's Hospital. He kicked for the Gaels as well as the Oakland Invaders of the USFL. He told me that he would be seeing me at the game.

The drive to Moraga was about three hours as we drove down the morning of the game. I guess if we were Oklahoma or UCLA, we would have gone down the day before—by plane. We stopped at a Howard Johnson's along the way for the team breakfast.

The bus ride was just one of the many indications that led me to believe that Chico State was not your typical "BIG TIME" school. It was far from it. In fact, it played in the only non-scholarship conference in the country.

The Northern California Athletic Conference did not offer any athletic scholarships. The conference was comprised of us, Humboldt State, Sonoma State, Hayward State, San Francisco State, Sacramento State, and perennial power, U.C. Davis.

We got to the stadium about two and a half hours before kickoff. With no wind around us and the temperature making a steady climb up the thermometer, I could tell it was going to be a hot one. Coach Trimmer had his son Jeff push me up and down the sidelines during the game. Jeff was a budding athlete while a sophomore at Pleasant Valley High School.

The stadium at St. Mary's was smaller than ours. What bothered me about the field was the gravel filled sidelines. It made for a most uncomfortable ride that Saturday afternoon.

During the pre-game talk, Coach Trimmer highlighted the fact that even though St. Mary's was a scholarship school, that was no reason for not going out there to kick some butt.

Unfortunately, we lost to the Gaels 39-25. I saw my friend, Kevin Shea, after the game, and he gave me quite a ribbing. He had a right to do it. We got our butts kicked.

Next week was our home opener against Cal-Poly San Luis Obispo. The Mustangs were a perennial power of the Western Football Conference. They had a great team. And yes, they were a scholarship school. They also had neat looking bright gold helmets with a green Mustang on the side. It bothered me that we didn't have stickers on our helmets. I thought we should've had a paw or a cat to show others how mean and tough we were.

The crowd for the home opener numbered around 4,000. The stadium was over half-full. Even though we were only behind 7-3 at half, we couldn't catch up to the Pony's and lost 21-9.

After a home win against Claremont Mudd, we had a week off before our next game against Cal-State Northridge. Coach Trimmer invited me to go on the 6:00 a.m. bus ride to Southern California for the game against the Matadors. I told him I would forgo the day-long bus trip and opt for my choice of transportation, a nice plane ride. I received a letter in the mail from Social Security saying that they owed me some money. Before getting the money, I decided to spend it on a plane ticket to visit my sister Becky in L.A. and go to the Northridge game.

Becky, her hubby to be, James, and I sat in the stands and watched as our offense decided to play dead for three quarters. The Cats fell to the Matadors 24-14.

Even though the Wildcats were 1-3, I was feeling great just being a part of the program. I was starting to learn about what football is like at the Division II non-scholarship level, and was slowly developing a relationship with Coach Trimmer.

I knew it was going to be difficult to prove myself as one who could help the team. It was important for me to show him my passion for the game, even though I had a lot to learn. He would later tell me that since I was the first person with a disability who had expressed such an interest in helping the team, he didn't know how to handle it.

The Wildcats opened conference play with a convincing 50-29 win over Sonoma State. With our modest 1-0 conference record, we were ready for our biggest test of the year against our rivals, the U.C. Davis Aggies. The Aggies came into our place with an undefeated conference streak that almost no school could touch. Their coach, Jim Sochor, was the real deal. It would be my first exposure to this rivalry.

On the night before the game, the players called a team meeting. I listened as many of the players talked about last year's game. They talked about how close it was and how it was time to break the Aggies string of victories over the Wildcats. The Cats hadn't beaten the Aggies since Nixon occupied the White House and Trimmer was an assistant coach.

Despite keeping the score close at half, the Aggies dominated the contest and left University Stadium with a 24-7 win.

With the Davis game in the record books, the Cats kissed their sister and left Sacramento State with a 15-15 tie. We were 1-1-1 going into our next game at home against Humboldt State.

At about this time my relationship with Coach Trimmer had changed significantly. An article about me appeared the weekly athletic department newsletter, "The Sports Tab." In it, the article described Coach Trimmer as taking me on "like a surrogate father."

So, the next time I went into his office, I uttered the words, "Hi, Dad!"

It's been that way ever since.

The game against the Lumberjacks was a critical one for us. First, we were playing for the coveted "AXE," our version of the "Old Oaken Bucket," or "Little Brown Jug," and everything else rolled into one. As we headed into the last half of the conference schedule, there was still a good chance that we could finish with a winning season and win four conference games.

The weather outside was rainy. Almost no one showed up. It was like playing in a cemetery. I couldn't figure it out.

With a 20-19 lead and just 1:25 left in the game, it seemed like we had this one in the bag. We were getting the "AXE" ready to be painted red. That's what the winning team does after the game.

As quickly as we thought we had this one, no sooner was it taken away. We fumbled the ball on the snap and the Lumberjacks recovered. Two plays later, they scored. We lost 26-20, and they had the coveted "AXE."

The week of the Hayward State game didn't get off to a good start. I was on the phone with Coach Wiggin and he hinted to me that things weren't looking so hot down on "The Farm." Stanford was 1-8 in the first year of the post "John Elway" era.

Two days later, I read in the paper that Coach Wiggin had been fired, effective at the end of the season.

"The ramifications of this are far beyond what you realize now," he said.

I felt really bad for Coach Wiggin. Not just because of everything he did for me personally, but because he is a class act and a good man.

I made the trip to Hayward for our battle against the Pioneers. My parents met me at the hotel where the team was staying, and I spent the night at home.

My father drove me across the San Mateo Bridge in a driving rainstorm. As we made our way into the stadium, Dad situated me along our sideline on the red, all-weather, track that surrounded the field. I put on my "raincoat" which was made of a giant-sized, Hefty garbage bag. It fit perfectly and I was able to push my wheelchair along the track with no problem.

We posted a convincing 20-7 win over the Pioneers. Coach Trimmer got nailed on a play during the game and required some medical attention. He made it though. The bus ride home was fun. Finding myself immersed in two hamburgers, large fries, and a Coke, I was beginning to enjoy myself.

We won our final game of the year as we defeated San Francisco State 26-7. We finished the year at 4-5-1 (3-2-1 in conference).

While the Wildcats were dueling it out with the Gators, I was at Stanford Stadium watching Coach Wiggin's final game against Cal. It was a very emotional experience being in the locker room watching the players rally for Coach Wiggin. The Stanford players cried in the locker room as the Cardinal took it on the chin 27-18. Coach Wiggin handled the loss with his players the only way he knew how, with dignity and class.

With my first season of college football under my belt, I barely had enough time to reflect on everything I had learned before another bombshell hit.

In early December, Coach Trimmer was fired.

I cried as he told us the news in a team meeting. He tried to hold back the tears as well.

I couldn't believe it! I must be some kind of jinx! All of a sudden, two men who had inspired me in different ways were having their livelihoods taken away from them—just like that.

I called my parents and told them the news. They couldn't believe it either. They tried to put a positive spin on it, but it wasn't easy to do.

The annual team banquet was held at the Bell Memorial Union. It was a very nice evening. It was also very emotional.

While I was at home on semester break, the Chico State athletic department stumbled and fumbled their way through a national search, hoping to find the next "red hot."

Their first list of finalists included Trimmer's assistants, Gary Houser and Mike Clemons. But, Chico State offered the job to Bob Fortier who was both the Head Football Coach and Athletic Director at Morehead State University.

Fortier declined the first time, but once wasn't good enough. He was asked a second time, and even came out with his family for a second interview. Meanwhile, there was a movement in town to have Houser and Clemons "co-coach" the 'Cats.

Yeah, right.

Fortier turned Chico State down again, and Chico State was still in search of a football coach.

With just a little time left in the recruiting season, Chico State hired Hayward State's Mike Bellotti to replace Dick Trimmer.

When I introduced myself to the new head football coach, Mike Bellotti knew me at first glance.

"You were the one on the sidelines in the garbage bag," he said.

Wow! He actually remembered what I was wearing that November afternoon. After all, while I was sitting in the rain on the sidelines, he was sitting high atop in the press box trying to figure out a way to beat us.

A part of me felt like I had lost a little bit of ground when Coach Bellotti came aboard. After all, it had taken me a whole year to prove to Dick Trimmer that I wanted to be something other than a mascot. And, even though I didn't think I crossed the threshold when the season ended, I felt like I was pretty close. Now, I felt like I had to prove myself all over again.

I pretty much kept a low profile as Coach Bellotti was trying to assemble a football staff and put together a team in a short period of time. During the spring semester, I stopped by the office a few times to see what was going on. For the most part though, I was concentrating on my studies.

A Year of Preparation

Upon returning home from a trip to the Midwest, Coach Bellotti said he needed some help around the football office. He wanted someone to hold down the fort while he and the staff were busy putting things together. There was a lot of work to be done.

Thinking about how Paul Wiggin said to do whatever I could to help the program, I jumped at the chance.

Coach Bellotti offered to let me stay at his house with him and his wife Colleen. I'll never forget the first time I met her.

On our way home, I gave Coach Bellotti the third degree.

"So, is your wife pretty nice, Coach?"

"Yeah, she's nice."

"Is she pretty good lookin'?"

"Yeah, she's not bad."

When the door opened, my nineteen year-old eyes suddenly went a glaze. She gave us a warm hello and thanked us for the cashews.

Coach was right on both counts. I spent the rest of the summer licking envelopes and manning the phones in the football office while enjoying the hospitality of the Bellotti family.

When Coach Bellotti put cat paw stickers on our helmets, I was happy. Every team that has a mascot should wear it on their helmets. What would a USC helmet be without a Trojan head on it? Or, a University of Texas helmet without the Longhorn? A plain helmet shows me that a coach or athletic director doesn't care about his football team. That is, unless you are the Fighting Irish.

We started out the year with two losses to Santa Clara and Idaho State. Then we followed it up with two victories against University of San Diego and conference foe, Sonoma State. Our offensive coordinator, Coach Clemons, had me keep track of who the Cossacks were substituting with on their nickel coverage. I gave him a report at halftime.

Coach Bellotti had me scheduled to ride the team bus for the game against our arch-rival, U.C. Davis. I called my parents and asked them to drive up from the Bay Area and meet me at the game. They made plans to do it.

I awoke that morning with a fever of about 103 degrees. I called Coach Bellotti and told him that I should be better by the time we had to leave, but he wasn't going to take any chances. He made me stay home. I was crushed.

It was no surprise that by game time, my temperature went down to 100.1. This made me even more upset. Coach Bellotti saw my parents before the game and told them I wasn't on the bus. They concurred with his decision.

I stayed in my dorm room perched in my wheelchair next to my radio. Every once in a while, someone would walk in and ask the score of the game. That was the extent to which they cared.

The game was tied 13-13 as we had the ball with a little over a minute to go. We had the Aggies on the ropes and poised to break the streak. I was still brooding over not being at the game. I thought the least we would come away with was a tie which normally isn't great. But in this case, taking a tie was just as good as a win.

With a little more than a minute left in the game, we had the ball in Aggie territory. On third down and twelve we called time-out. There was only one problem. We had no time-outs remaining and were assessed five yards for delay of game. Coach Bellotti sent Jim Mavor in to kick a fifty yarder on third down. He missed it, wide left.

U.C. Davis drove down the field with their remaining time-outs and Ray Sullivan kicked a 48-yard field goal to win it. This was a heartbreaker.

We lost the following week to Sacramento State before a large homecoming crowd of 4,600 fans. I guess when you look at the stands and see only a few hundred folks, this makes you feel like you're at the L.A.

Coliseum. Our defensive coordinator, Coach Houser, had me chart the Sac State offense for the entire first half.

We finished the year by winning two out of our last four games to go 4-5-1. Coach Bellotti probably wasn't excited about it, but I felt pretty good about things.

Summers and Good Times With the Chiefs

I had just finished grazing through a five-pound lobster dinner when the maitre d' handed me the check. I lifted up the bill and saw it was just a little over seven hundred dollars.

"Thanks a lot Jon," one voice said.

"Hey, we'll be seeing you at the hotel," said another.

The crowd started to leave and all I could think of was how many dishes I was going to wash to pay the check. I figured it might take me a week or two. They walked a little further towards the door of one of L.A.'s finest restaurants.

"Hey! Wait a second!" I said. My voice was clearly audible, even to the maitre'd.

"I thought you were going to take care of dinner," said Bob Sprenger. He was the Public Relations Director for the Kansas City Chiefs. They invited me to Los Angeles for the game against the Raiders.

Through my association with the East-West Shrine Game, I was fortunate to live out one of my childhood fantasies. I spent two summers at the training camp of my favorite NFL team, the Kansas City Chiefs.

Shortly after the 1984 East-West Game, I kept in contact with their coaching staff. Later that spring, they invited me to spend a week at their training camp at William Jewell College in Liberty, Missouri.

Once I got out of the car, all I could see were brick buildings with a lot of stairs. Accessibility to them was limited to painting a blue sign on a parking space. It didn't bother me though. I was going to have a good time anyway. I met everyone associated with the Chiefs, both past and present. I was star struck when I shook hands with my all-time favorite quarterback, Len Dawson. Like my father, he went to Purdue.

I also met Chiefs owner Lamar Hunt. He seemed like a nice, quiet, gentleman who talked to me about his son who played soccer. I think he liked talking about his children.

During my stay at training camp, I spent most of the time working in the Public Relations Department and hanging out with the scouting staff after hours. I turned my vacation into a mini-internship.

While working in the PR office, I did little things like answer the phones and put player slides in their proper order. They would be used for the scoreboard. I also wrote a story for the souvenir program about my week at training camp.

I went to practice every day, enjoying that humid Missouri heat. It didn't bother me. I was used to it. Besides, I was too busy watching practice.

I spent most of the evenings talking football with the scouting staff. Most of the time, I just listened intently to what they were discussing. Occasionally though, they would ask me a question and I would put in my two cents. Other times though, I'd hear them share stories and we'd all have a good laugh.

The scouting staff was headed by Les Miller who was the Chiefs Director of Player Personnel. A very nice man, we have grown to be good friends.

Along with Les Miller, you had scouts Chuck Lester, Chuck Cook, Greg Mohns (I used to pronounce it Moans), Bobby Gill, and yes, former wide receiver, Otis Taylor.

Otis pushed me around the grassy fields of William Jewell College. The other scouts called him "Judge" so I followed suit. He would later call me "Judge" as well.

I remember one time while I was down at the East-West Game, Otis drove me to practice. We drove around Stanford University looking for a parking space. The others had been taken because it was just a day or two before the game and people were starting to roll in to town.

"Excuse me, could you please tell me where we can find a parking space?" Otis asked a guy who looked like a parking attendant.

"Hey, I don't speak no English," the man replied.

"Then why are you speaking English?" I asked.

Otis and I were busting up so hard, we couldn't stop laughing. Eventually we found a spot. Thus, our parking story became the talk with the other Chiefs scouts. I'll never forget the expression on his face when I said that.

Otis Taylor is probably thought of as one of the greatest receivers in Chiefs history, but I also know him as a fine human being with a big heart.

The Chiefs played the Saints in an exhibition game at Arrowhead Stadium. It was the second time I had been to Arrowhead, or as I would refer to it, "Mecca." I saw an exhibition game there a few years back when I went to a youth church conference at Unity Village. It was Mecca back then too.

I was down on the field for the coin toss. Ken Stabler, who was in the twilight of his career, came up and handed me his wrist bands.

"Here you go, kid."

I smiled and thanked him. Even though he beat the Chiefs many times as a Raider, it was still nice to meet such a great player.

I watched the game from Head Coach John Mackovic's press box. I got to know his wife Arleen and I spent some time talking with his son, Johnny.

After the game, I went to the locker room where Coach Mackovic presented me with a football with the words, "Chiefs Number One Fan" on it.

The next day, I went home with many fond memories.

I stayed in touch with the organization and managed to see them play the Raiders. That's when I was left with the check and contemplated my future as a dishwasher.

The following year, I was even more surprised when I was invited back to training camp.

I was sitting in my new apartment wondering what I was going to do on a miserably hot Chico day. The phone rang.

"Hello Jonathan, this is General Manager Jim Schaaf. How are you?"

"Fine, sir."

"How's the weather?"

"Well, it's about 118 degrees out here."

"It's hot out here too. Say, how would you like to come to training camp again this year?"

My bags were packed.

There were different things I wanted to get out of my second visit to Liberty, Missouri. Coach Bellotti had just given me the kicking coach position for the Wildcats and I wanted to learn all I could from one of the premier kickers in the game, Nick Lowery, and punter Jim Arnold. Also, I wanted to somehow show them that I wanted to be something other than their "number one fan."

Nick Lowery talked about how he trains, as well as the mental aspects of kicking. I took a lot of notes.

He said that even in practice, every kick has a purpose. He doesn't kick a lot of balls merely for the sake of kicking. He concentrates on the quality of each kick and structures his workout accordingly. Along with kicking, he has a conditioning program.

With regard to the mental aspects of kicking, Nick told me how he goes through a meditation in which he visualizes an entire game day, from the moment he gets up in the morning to when the final gun sounds. He visualizes being called into the game to make an important kick, and then kicking the ball through the uprights.

Jim Arnold also taught me about how much of kicking was in the mind. He used to tell me that I should be careful not to let the "gremlins" get into their heads. He was a comic of sorts.

Throughout the week, I made some subtle overtures about wanting to work for the Chiefs. I started what would be an on-again, off-again dialogue with Les Miller that would last for several years.

On a recent trip I made with my father to the Midwest, we drove by the place I call Mecca. As I reminisced about all the good times, it's amazing how much has changed since then.

A lot of the people I knew have come and gone. And I'm still in Chico, remembering those two summers and all the good times.

"It's a Great Day To Be a Wildcat—Kicker's Coach"

Strolling back and forth through the rows of players stretching their bodies was a common thing for me to do at the start of each practice.

"It's a great day to be a Wildcat!" my voice would bark.

"Hey Coach, it's a great day to be a Wildcat!" a player would answer.

"It's a great day to be a Cat! Every day is a great day to be a Wildcat!" I shouted back.

I began my third year as a real coach with real responsibilities. Coach Bellotti appointed me as the Wildcat's kicking coach because he thought the kickers needed someone and it was something I could do given my situation. I was eager to accept the challenge.

Things changed right from the get-go. First, instead of going to practice when I felt like it, I had to go every single day. Not only that, I had to make my own practice schedule for when I was in the stadium, just me and my kickers.

I attended all the coaches' meetings both in the trailer, and at other coaches' houses. Most of my Sunday afternoons were spent grading films, not watching NFL games.

When you have an All-League kicker like Jim Mavor, the best thing you could do as a coach was leave him alone. Unless he went into a slump, I didn't see us having to make any adjustments.

The greatest thing about Jim Mavor was his leg. Ability wise, he was the best. His leg had the power of a cannon and the accuracy of a dart. We went 5-4-1 that year and Jim was named to the All-Conference squad for the second year in a row.

The thing about Jim Mavor was that when it came to kicking, he was a perfectionist. Sometimes, he let his temper get the best of him and he acted very childish.

Upon missing a kick during practice, he got so upset he took his helmet off and threw it into the ground. I told him that kind of attitude wasn't going to do him any favors if he wanted to kick in the pros.

It wasn't long after that when the tirades subsided.

Along with Jim, I also worked with our punter, Tom Curtin. He too made All-Conference.

I think Jim and Tom liked having someone out there watching and charting them. They liked the attention because it let them know that there was someone on the field, day in and day out, who cared about how they did.

The three of us worked well together and Jim and I became good friends.

The 1986 season was an exciting one for Chico State football. We went 7-3 and had our best record in fifteen years. After being behind our arch-rivals U.C. Davis 26-7 at half, we made a valiant comeback only to fall 33-30.

Coaching wise, this was an important season for me. With Jim Mavor gone, I had to tryout a kicker. Thus, I was a bit more structured with regard to our practice schedule. Tom Curtin returned to handle the punting, so he provided some continuity.

With a group of fresh faces, I started to put my coaching style and philosophy into place. For starters, my players always practiced their kicking with their helmets on. They don't let them kick with their helmets off in a game, why should practice be any different.

One day in practice, one of my kickers, Chris Carter kicked a long field goal in practice with his helmet sitting on the ground next to him. He asked me if I was going to count it. I told him only if he could do it again, with his helmet on.

On the next attempt, he missed. Score one for the coach.

Chris Carter and Brian Denman battled each other to see who would be our starting kicker. Neither one of them were very consistent, so we played musical chairs for the better part of the year.

Coach Bellotti let me have a lot of input in the decision-making process, though he had the final word.

There were times where we couldn't decide who was going to play, so on a few of the road trips, we took two kickers.

Tom Curtin didn't have as good a year as expected. He spent a lot of time in the training room working out his aches and pains.

There was a personal highlight for me during our quest for success that year. Coach Bellotti and I had a deal whereby if we ever got ahead by forty points or more, he would let me call plays.

In our game against San Francisco State, I got my chance. With the ball and a little over two minutes left in the game, I took the controls and began to drive down the field.

"Twenty eight truck sweep," I shouted.

A nice gain would follow.

We were starting to put together a pretty good drive and the players wanted to score one with me calling the plays. Coach Bellotti thought better of it and had our quarterback, Craig Wallis, take a knee.

As it was, the Gator coaches still threw a fit after the game. I wish we had scored.

Then they really would have had something to shout about.

Aside from the loss to U.C. Davis, there wasn't much to complain about. Our kicking game wasn't as successful as the year before, but this is a team game, and that's what counts.

The one thing that really disappointed me about our successful season was our end of the year football banquet. It was the worst planned party ever.

For starters, it was held at one of Chico's sleaziest bars. The Top Flight Ballroom was a dark, smoke-filled place that saw cheesy bands play there five nights a week. A bar it was. A banquet facility it wasn't.

On top of that, the banquet was done buffet style for a gathering of about four-hundred people. There were only two lines and it took forever to feed everyone.

Finally, we had to be out of there at a certain time so they could set the place up for one of their more popular events, Comedy Night.

The football banquet was one of many signs that showed me throughout my coaching stint at Chico State that somehow, the folks that ran the show didn't know how to do the little things right.

I was well-prepared going into the 1987 season. I had more confidence in myself as a coach. I started to put my thoughts down on paper and into a manual. It was my own personal playbook.

In my coaching philosophy, I stressed the importance of hard work and dedication.

Hard work requires punctuality, purpose and perseverance. Good kicking can only come when raw talent is combined with hard work and dedication.

One of the things I had my kickers memorize was the "STUDEBAKER CREDO."

I drilled it into their heads like it was their ABC's. This was my Ten Commandments of kicking:

1. A Kicker is strong.
2. A Kicker is tough.
3. A Kicker is well prepared.
4. A Kicker is confident.
5. A Kicker is humble.
6. A Kicker is an important part of the team.
7. A Kicker is a team player.
8. A Kicker is versatile.
9. A Kicker is only as good as his NEXT kick.
10. Every Kicker needs a coach, as does every coach needs a kicker.

I had an interesting group of guys to mold into shape. Along with a few redshirts, including a straight-on kicker, Bryan Denman returned for his senior year and was to compete against Gerry Fall, a transfer from nearby

Butte College. The coaches said he had a great leg, and likewise, so did the local paper.

It didn't take me very long to figure out that Gerry Fall didn't need a lot coaching. He proved to me what others had previously said. What he really needed was a baby-sitter, shrink, and a garbage man all rolled into one.

When it came to football practice, Gerry was never on time. Like Epstein from TV's "Welcome Back Kotter," he always had an excuse, but never a note from his mother. Moreover, I always got reports from his professors about how he missed class.

I tried to impress to him the importance of being on time for practice and attending classes. Every time he assured me that it wouldn't happen again, it would happen again.

Blessed with a foot that was comparable to other great kickers, most of Gerry's kicking problems were in his head. This was an incredible challenge for me to deal with throughout the season.

Finally, if there was ever a free garbage truck lying around and a driver with nothing to do, I would have immediately sent them to our locker room to clean out Gerry's locker. It looked like a dumpster at your favorite fast food restaurant. He used to let bags of sandwich containers, French fries, and cups sit there for weeks.

Personally, Gerry Fall was a nice guy you'd like to sit in a bar and catch up on the latest goings on in sports. Besides football, his real love was sportscasting. He did it very well.

We started the year with three non-conference losses before our league opener with U.C. Davis. We lost to Sacramento State 14-9 and Gerry had missed a critical extra point. We had taken the lead 9-7 and by not making the kick, it gave the Hornets a chance to win it with either a field goal or a touchdown. As it turned out, they got seven and promptly sent us back home licking our wounds.

In the five years I was on the staff at Chico State, there is one game I would like to do all over again. It was our league opener against U.C. Davis.

The evening started with Gerry coming into the locker room a nervous wreck. I tried to settle him down and he went out to kick a few balls. I thought maybe it would get him focused on what we needed to do—beat the Aggies.

After he kicked a few balls through the uprights, he kicked a few more, and then—a few more. He went to the other end and did the same thing. I finally told the other kickers to pick up the balls. Gerry wouldn't let them.

"What do you think you're doing?" I exclaimed.

"I have to get ready," Gerry responded.

"What do you mean? You are ready. If you kick any more, you're not going to have any leg left."

At this point, I knew I had done something wrong. You just can't kick that many balls before a game.

Gerry settled down once the game got underway.

We went into the halftime down by seven and felt pretty good about our chances of snapping the Aggies reign on the NCAC. Maybe this was going to be the year.

Not long into the second half, we added a touchdown to make the score 17-16 with Gerry set to attempt the extra point.

To my shock and everyone else's, he missed. I was beside myself. I couldn't believe it!

I quickly regained my composure and went over to Gerry who was visibly shaken.

I thought he had seen a ghost.

"Hey! Look at me!" I yelled at him. I was looking at him eyeball to eyeball.

"Gerry, forget about that extra point. You can't do it again. You can't have it back. You are going to have a chance to win this game and you better be ready for it, Okay? We're going to get the ball back and put you in a position to win it! Be ready!"

The Aggies scored a touchdown and we answered with one of our own. Being down by two, we went for the two-point conversion and missed it. With the score 24-22, the Aggies had the ball with just a few minutes left in the ball game.

Our defense did a great job of holding them and we were able to get the ball into Aggie territory. I pulled Gerry over to the sideline next to me and gave him an earful.

"What did I tell you earlier?"

He just looked at me.

"I said you were going to have a chance to win this ball game."

We drove the ball down to the Aggie twenty yard-line. My mouth was watering with anticipation of a chip shot field goal attempt. On third down,

I was looking for us to run the ball up the middle so that we would be in perfect position to kick a field goal of 35 or 40 yards.

It didn't happen.

Coach Bellotti had our quarterback, Kevin Miller roll out and he was nailed for a ten yard loss. I was dumbfounded. I had no clue as to what he was trying to do.

The clock continued to run and we called time-out with seconds remaining. I talked to Gerry once again and reminded him of what I had said earlier.

"I told you that you were going to get a chance to win this game, didn't I? Well, here it is. Just relax and put the ball through and let's win this one."

Gerry nodded.

We got to line up for the field goal and the officials called time-out because there was something wrong with the chains. If that wasn't enough, the Aggies called a time-out to give Gerry a little more time to think about it. Since I had spent all of our time-out with him, I thought it was best to leave him alone.

The crowd was going crazy as Gerry got ready for a 47-yarder. He had a slight breeze but it was negligible. I sat in my chair and prayed one more time.

The snap was good. The ball was placed and I could see the ball in flight. As it hit its zenith, I didn't feel good about it. Still, the crowd cheered as they thought it would make it. It fell short, just as I thought.

The Aggie fans that came went crazy. I was stunned, upset, and visibly shaken. I could hear the disappointment from the stands.

"Yeah look, there's the kicking coach," a voice said.

I went over to Gerry who sat motionless on the field.

"You're probably really disappointed in me, aren't you?" he said.

"No Gerry, I'm not disappointed in you. I am disappointed for you."

It wasn't long after that I went over to Colleen Bellotti and started to cry. We had come so close to beating these guys that we deserved a break or two. It would have been nice to have ten more yards to work with, but it wasn't meant to be.

We won four of our last six games to finish just under the .500 mark. After going 7-3 the previous year though, it was a big disappointment.

Gerry was our place-kicker for the better part of the year. Bryan

Denman fought hard during practice to try to unseat him. But as it turned out, Gerry had the stats to make first team All-Conference.

Throughout the season, you develop a rapport with your players. Seeing them every day for four months during the season makes you a part of their lives, and they are a part of yours. I cared about every one of them like they were my own family.

Reflecting the way in which I ran practice, my kickers called me "THE GENERAL" or "GEN" for short.

Bryan Denman was as close to understanding the philosophy of how I wanted a kicker to be. He was always into the game and very supportive of the other guys on the team. He followed the "CREDO" almost to the letter.

Mike Henle, a red-shirt straight-on kicker was interesting to work with just because of the way he kicked. He also constantly talked about women during practice.

My fondest memory I have of coaching came after our last practice of the season. We had a ritual whereby the seniors would take a dive into a huge puddle of water on one end of the practice field. The trainers had done construction on the puddle from the moment practice began. A couple of the coaches joined in the festivities and we all had a good laugh.

Next, I saw the eyes of all of my kickers look right at me. To my surprise, my kickers carried me out of my chair and put me in the water. There was a big cheer coming from the rest of the players. Then, everyone splashed the cold brown water all over me.

Despite having my wheelchair covered with the sludge and shivering all over, I was happy. I felt like I had been accepted by the players and my peers as a coach. I felt like I was a part of the team.

This was my greatest moment in coaching.

Fall Out of '88

Shortly after the season, I ran into Coach Bellotti at a downtown watering hole. He went out of his way to tell me how I had done a good job with the kickers. We spent some time re-hashing the season, mainly the Davis game. I had a hard time letting go of that one. He pointed out that Gerry Fall still had a pretty good season while receiving All-Conference honors. Coach Bellotti was looking forward to having me come back next year.

I was recovering from a broken leg while spring ball was going on. One day, Mike Henle called me after practice. He was looking forward to competing for the starting job.

"Hey Jon, did you hear we've got a new coach?"

"What?!" I didn't know what he was talking about.

"Yeah, we've got this guy Orlyn Culp out there with the kickers. He's been helping me with my technique."

I asked him if he thought I was being replaced. He didn't think so. Still, when I got off the phone, I became increasingly upset.

I began the process of questioning my own ability as a coach. If Coach Bellotti had thought I was doing such a good job, why was he bringing someone else in to work with the kickers?

I replayed the Davis game in my head and thought it might have had something to do with it. Maybe the folks in the athletic department told Coach Bellotti that there should be someone who could "help me out" with the kicking game. Perhaps my disability was a factor.

What really bothered me was that no one from the coaching staff talked to me about it beforehand. I had to hear it from one of my players.

I called Coach Lou Bronzan and asked him what was going on.

"He'll be in charge of technique and you'll be in charge of practice and player personnel," he said.

What?! This guy who I don't even know is going to just walk in and take over a third of my job? I couldn't believe it! I spent the last five years pouring my heart and soul, and this is what I got in return.

My stubbornness took over and I withdrew from the football program for a while. While I was extremely hurt by what happened, the coaches probably didn't think much of it.

I saw Coach Bellotti a couple of times over the summer. He asked me why I hadn't been around the office. I told him I was busy. I figured he didn't know why I was so unhappy, but I wasn't in the mood to tell him. Sooner or later he would find out somehow.

Football season was fast approaching and I made up my mind not to return as the Wildcats kicking coach.

I called Mike Henle and told him the news. I believe he understood how I felt, but he didn't think I would follow through.

Coach Bellotti did not see hide nor hair of me at the staff meetings. He called and asked me what was up. I told him I wasn't planning on coming back. He asked that we get together to talk about it.

The moments leading up to this meeting were extremely difficult. I talked to my family about it and told them where I was coming from. They were supportive. I talked to my close friends as well, including Coach Trimmer and Keith Cameron.

Both were supportive as well, although sometimes they played the role of Devil's advocate.

We met for lunch downtown. Ironically, it was the same place where we rehashed last season.

The conversation started off by talking about things other than football. It wasn't merely small talk, Coach Bellotti always took an interest in the other things I was doing. He asked me about my health. He wanted to know if I was pursuing any women. He asked me about my family. You name it, he asked about it.

When we got down to brass tacks, I can remember Coach Bellotti telling me that he needed a kicking coach. I think Orlyn Culp had bailed out on them. I told him that in addition to the situation that was going on with the guy who was "in charge of technique," it seemed like as though while I was having more responsibilities, I was getting less reward. Even though I wasn't getting paid, I wanted to go on all the road trips.

"You know, there is intrinsic reward in coaching," he said.

The conversation was very good. I felt as if we were talking to each other as equals. I didn't hold back in telling him how I felt and neither did Coach Bellotti.

He asked me to go home and take a day or two to think about it. While he understood how I felt, there were no promises made, no apologies given.

I sat at home agonizing over the whole thing. My heart ached for football while my head told me to stick to my beliefs.

In the end, the stubborn side of me prevailed. I did not return as the Wildcats kicking coach.

Trying To Make a Comeback

Remember, I didn't leave Chico State football because I was tired of coaching. Are you kidding? Watching the games as a fan got old real fast. It's just not the same.

I wanted to continue pursuing the dreams I had as a kid. I wanted a chance to prove myself. I wanted a shot at the big time.

For the next three years, I sent my resume to everyone I knew in the NFL. I even put a videotape together which covered some of your most frequently asked questions.

Aside from a few "quasi interviews," all I got in return were a lot of letters telling me that I was an inspiration and all that other garbage.

In the fall of 1990, Les Miller invited me to a World League tryout camp in Sacramento. I think he thought of it as a chance for us to get together and catch up on things. I tried to use it as a means to demonstrate my abilities and help wherever I could.

I spent the morning watching the prospects do sprints. It wasn't very exciting but I was just happy to be there, hoping someone would ask me to do something.

Just before the players were about to leave after an afternoon workout, there was a mad scramble to get them checked out before they departed. All the players had to leave their addresses and phone numbers with the staff. While people were scurrying around like a bunch of chickens with their heads cut off, I sensed it was time for me to step in and help.

"Could anyone use a hand?" I asked.

A couple of people looked at me in puzzlement.

"We need to get these players signed, don't we?"

I asked someone for a pen and immediately went to work. I must have signed up a hundred players in a little over an hour. We had everyone out on time.

I received a few kudos for my effort. I didn't think much of it except that I think I surprised a few people by showing them I could write. Amazing, simply amazing.

My performance in Sacramento caused Les Miller to pencil me in to do some computer work at the World League's player draft in Orlando,

Florida. Finally, I thought the door was cracked just ajar and I was going to break it down. I had worked so hard to prove even the simplest of things.

As luck would have it, I broke my neck shortly before I was to go to Orlando.

This was one of the lowest points of my life because I was not only feeling the intense pain from the fall, I felt like my life had been turned upside down.

I spent many a night crying about it. There were times where I was angry and bitter. I felt like I had gotten a raw deal. I couldn't rationalize it at all. It was hard for me to think that there was something better.

I spent the summer of '91 wondering what to do next. Cam came over and we had one of our talks.

"I've got a name you might want to think about," he said.

"Who?" I asked.

"What about Jim Walden? He might talk to you. Why don't you give him a call?"

"Yeah, it's already August and it's probably too late anyway."

"You don't know unless you try."

I made the call and got some encouraging news. Coach Walden asked me for my resume and a copy of a kicking manual I put together. It was a flicker of hope.

Coach Walden told me that it was a little late to move ahead with trying to bring me out. He needed more time and wanted me to start thinking about what I would need to do if I were to make a move to the Midwest. We talked on and off during the season and he invited me to Ames for an interview in January.

Coming off the plane and inhaling that cold Midwest air was exciting. The fact that the temperature was in single digits didn't bother me a bit. Inside, there was a fire burning in my belly. I felt a real sense of accomplishment that a head football coach of a major college program had flown me out for an interview. I finally had my chance to put all my cards on the table.

I had two interviews with Coach Walden. The first one covered the logistics of moving and how I might deal with a myriad of situations. I was pretty honest and left no stone unturned. There were some questions that I couldn't answer because I didn't have the information, but I knew where to get it. We left that part of the interview with a few blank spaces that needed to be filled.

My second interview took place in his office. This was a real football office, not the pink colored trailers at Chico State.

We talked about what I might do for the program. He saw my role as being mostly behind the scenes helping with some film breakdown and academic advising. I thought it was alright although I wanted to spend some time on the field coaching.

The discussions I had with Coach Walden were very substantive. We were frank, open, and honest with each other. Though there were a few instances where he talked to me like a father, I still felt like we were equals.

Toward the end of the interview, Coach Walden was willing to take a chance on me. He offered me a volunteer internship for one-year at Iowa State and depending on my performance, moving me into a paid position the following year. This was the chance I had been waiting for.

I can't describe what I was feeling on the flight home. I was on top of the world. At last, that flicker of hope had turned into a light at the end of the tunnel. I was starting to think seriously about moving to Ames, Iowa and being a member of the Cyclone coaching staff.

I spent the next few months looking for the missing pieces I needed to put my puzzle together and be on my way.

I needed to know what kind of support services I would receive as a resident of Ames. In order to find out whether or not I could make it on a budget, I needed to know how much SSI (Supplemental Security Income) I would receive. I needed to know about Medicaid, and how disabled people get attendants. Do they have a program like the one in California?

I called the State Department of Rehabilitation office in Des Moines and explained my situation to a gentleman on the other end. They seemed like good people who were willing to help me answer my questions. I called the Social Security office in Ames three times and got three different answers regarding the amount of SSI I would receive as a resident of the Hawkeye State.

In doing the numbers, there were scenarios that I knew could work while others made it virtually impossible.

The summer started to creep up quickly and I had almost everything in place. I gave my landlord notice and I as I had the moving expenses figured out, I was one step closer to leaving Chico.

I made one more series of calls to see if I could get the answers I needed to hear in order to make the move.

I called the Social Security office once again and got absolutely nowhere. Even worse, I got chastised by a woman on the phone.

"You're coming here to do an internship? Why don't you have a job?"

I explained my situation and she started asking me more questions.

"How can you do an internship when you're disabled? What do you have? How are you going to get around?"

I guess I should have told them I was born in Indiana instead.

The folks at the rehab office weren't much fun either.

"What do you mean you're doing an internship? I thought you were doing an assistantship?" the voice said.

"What's the difference?" I asked.

"Well, I thought you were getting paid. I'm sorry. We can't help you."

I slammed the phone down in disgust. This was absolutely ridiculous. All I wanted to know was how to play the game, and I wasn't getting a copy of the rulebook.

I talked to my father and he said to go ahead with the move.

"Once you get out there, they'll take care of you," he said.

That wasn't good enough for me.

I gave Coach Walden a progress report. I was extremely frustrated at this point and he didn't do anything to help matters.

"Now I told you in the beginning that we would have to work these things out. You know, life is not a candy store."

At that point, I told him I'd been dealing with these kinds of bureaucrats for almost ten years. I knew what I was doing. It was very difficult for me to convey this to Coach Walden.

We agreed to put the move on hold.

So, where to next?

Well, I went down the road and spoke to Coach Lou Bronzan who was now at U.C. Davis. He was loving life down there in Aggie Land.

I had something put together when he told me how one of their alumni didn't like me because they heard I had said some bad things about the Aggie program while I was coaching.

"Well, what am I supposed to say, Lou? I'm a Wildcat."

Apparently it bothered them so much that Lou made a federal case about it. I took my marbles home and asked my landlord if I could stay.

The Fire Still Burns

Even though I have been out of coaching for almost a decade, there still lies a deep, burning desire to return to football. It's lodged deep inside my gut and rears its head out every time I see a kicker make a boo-boo.

"That guy needs a kicking coach," the inner voice would say.

There is so much about coaching that makes me happy. I like the routine of coaching. In the off-season, you have a certain type of schedule. Then, there's the pre-double days meetings followed by the grind of training camp. When training camp is over, you go into the season with a different kind of preparation. Throughout the course of a season you have hot days, mild days, and cold days. You are almost certain when you will see and feel the hot sun and the cold rain.

You know what you are going to do to get ready for your opponent every single day.

Physically, I never felt better than when I was coaching. Always being on the move and doing things kept the heart pumping and the blood flowing. Heck, even having headaches felt good.

Most importantly though, the thing I enjoyed about coaching were the relationships I had with my kickers, the team, my fellow coaches, and the two head coaches worked under, Dick Trimmer and Mike Bellotti.

I don't know if I will coach again. I don't know if I will ever have a chance to tell another person like Coach Walden how I could help their football program.

All the times I tried to tell so many, so few have listened. Sometimes, I wonder if they would listen if my last name were Walsh, or Shula. If only my brother could have been a better flag football player, I could've ridden his coattails—somewhere. I don't know.

The flame still flickers ever so softly right now. Should the right opportunity ever come my way again, it will burn ever so brightly.

Women

There is a lot to be said about being single. I can go out by myself and if I am having a good time, I can stay as long as I want. If I don't like the music or the crowd, or I am just not having fun, I can leave the joint. I don't have to wait for anyone.

When I am at home, I am in my castle. Instead of decorating my house with beautiful works of art, my walls are plastered with pennants, sports posters, and scantily clad swimsuit calendars of years gone by. Hey, why let a good calendar go to waste?

I eat my Hamburger Helper in the nude. After all, it's usually ready by the time I get out of the bathtub, and I like it while it's still hot.

Another thing I like about being single is not having to worry about my daily sports intake. I can watch as many games, editions of SportsCenters, and old "NFL blooper" shows as I want without having a national crisis on my hands. Believe me, I know it happens.

On the other hand, there is also a lot to be said about having a significant other.

Going out on the town, you don't have to worry about finding a dance partner. Instead of standing in a corner trying to figure out who will dance with you, shaking your booty with your honey is a more pleasurable alternative.

It's always nice to eat dinner with someone other than by yourself. I hate making a great meal and not being able to share my cooking prowess with someone I care about.

Sure it may be cheaper, but it's not always fun to go to a movie by yourself. I would have rather seen "It Could Happen to You" sitting next to someone as nice as Brigit Fonda.

When I get invited to a function, or I am asked to give an important speech, it's nice to have someone else supporting you other than your attendant. I guess the best part about having someone special in your life is sharing the love you have for each other. We all have the need to be loved. We want to be loved and we have the need to give it back.

Telling someone you love them is something we need to do more often. I end almost every conversation with my mother and father by saying "I love you." I love my brother and sisters too, and they know that.

Showing your love by doing something for your sweetheart, or giving them a special gift, is another way we can express our affection.

Finally, sex is another way to express your love and affection for that special someone.

On those rare occasions where I have been told "I love you," from someone other than my immediate family, or when it is not followed by "like a brother," these are moments I hold near and dear to my heart.

I enjoy it when I am on the dance floor in a semi-embrace as my partner who is kneeling looks into my eyes as we slow dance.

Let the word go forth, that I enjoy sex just as much as anyone else. Living with osteogenesis imperfecta has certainly not curtailed my sex drive.

I am not long on experience when it comes to women. Since, I haven't had a serious relationship since high school, most of my experience comes as an observer who often counsels others about their problems. Yes, I have been on a few dates. No, I am not a virgin.

The road to finding that special someone has been largely a frustrating journey, but it's had its funny moments too.

Elementary School Wedding

I'll never forget the first girlfriend I had back in elementary school. Melinda Galloway was her name. We went to the same special ed school in Honolulu. Like me, she was disabled. She had cerebral palsy.

Back then, Melinda was the cream of the crop. She had short blonde hair and beautiful blue eyes. We always played together and I remembered how she laughed a lot. We liked each other so much, we got "married" at recess. I brought a fake diamond ring with me to school. I had purchased it at your basic dime store down the street from my house. All of our friends came to our "wedding." One of them acted as the minister.

A year later, my heart was broken when Melinda's family moved to Utah. It wouldn't have done me any good to wonder what would have happened if she had stayed because our family left the islands shortly thereafter.

Family Affairs

By the time I was a sophomore in high school, I had watched my brother and sisters go through the highs and lows of adolescence. Since I was pretty young at the time, I didn't pay very much attention to Alden's love life. He married Donna when I was fifteen, and I was the ring bearer at his wedding. They met at a church young adults conference at Unity Village.

When they were first going out, the two were insufferable. Some of their antics were difficult for the rest of us to stomach. During the time we lived in Michigan, our family usually went out to eat after church. While we were eating, we would observe the two "love birds" playing footsie under the table and talking German to each other. It was disgusting having to watch this as I sat at the table with my Whopper Junior.

Becky and I used to make fun of them by calling their union the "Alden-Donna Crisis: America Held Nauseous." The Iranian Hostage Crisis was in its infancy along with ABC's nightly reports which eventually turned into "Nightline." Ironically, they got married on the same day Mount St. Helens blew its stack.

Fifteen years and three kids later, they are still together. I am happy for both of them.

While she was in high school, my sister Becky was a model doing commercials for a Japanese soda pop company, Meiji Soda. It was one of her many talents. The guys at school were coming at her right and left. Some of her suitors were armed with marriage proposals. All of this didn't faze her a bit and she didn't have any difficultly taking care of herself.

I was hoping that her opinion of the great baseball player would change.

It didn't. Following in my brother's footsteps, she met Jim Downing through the Unity Church, and is happily married.

Having observed my sister Amy's love life first hand, I would have to devote a whole chapter to explain every juicy detail. But, except for some of my own observations, I'll leave that to her.

Every day after school, Amy and Mom would talk. You know, girl talk. The talk that could go on for hours and hours, day after day. They confided a lot in each other. The two of them were like Bill Walsh and Paul Hackett, plotting strategy like two coaches working on a game plan.

After going to formal after formal, prom after prom, after buying dress after dress after dress, Amy ended up with a pretty decent guy. She met and later married Scott Dennison, a guy she took to her senior prom. We call him Ben and they have three children.

Whenever I get down and start bashing the institution of marriage, I try to think positively about it and reflect on how it has worked for my parents and siblings. I think about all of the things my parents had to overcome to make their marriage work. Having to raise a child whom the doctors called "a bag of bones" may have been a death nail to some marriages, but their inner strength and love for family has kept them together.

I know there's always a possibility that something might go wrong. I know marriages are filled with peaks and valleys. No one is perfect and relationships take a lot of work. But as for right now, they are all together. And unless something happens, it will be "until death do us part." That's the way it should be.

My Turn

Now, it was my turn. After having left my Theodore Cleaver attitude about girls behind, I felt it was my time to follow in the footsteps of my brother and sisters.

To be honest, I really didn't expect all the fanfare my mother gave to Amy. It wouldn't feel right. If I expected any from my father, I don't know how that would have happened either. My Dad is not the cheerleader type. But, if I had to pinpoint exactly what I wanted from my parents, it was a feeling like I had the home field advantage. Like my other siblings, I wanted them to somehow be involved. It never materialized, and thus not having this support made me feel like I was a on a very long road trip.

During my high school years, especially when we moved back to California, my relationship with my parents was a bit rocky. And for me, it was partly to do with how they handled their disabled son's expectations of dating. When it came to the subject of girls and dating, I wanted their advice and support (not patronage), and most of what I got was conflict and acrimony.

The Jonathan Rule

I don't remember if this rule applied to my other siblings, but my parents told me that if I wanted to ask a girl out, I had to ask them first. After playing by the rule for a while, it seemed like all I was hearing was the word "NO!" Unlike a Supreme Court ruling, often times their decision came with no further explanation. I would soon think of this as the "Jonathan Rule."

It was very bothersome. It was frustrating. It got to the point where getting their permission was more difficult than asking the girl out. There was one instance where I was extremely disappointed by their verdict.

I was a senior in high school and I wanted to go to my Christmas formal. I had my sights set on a girl in my youth group, Kelly Wiggin. Yes, her father is Paul Wiggin, a man who I admire very much.

Now, maybe I set my sights too high. After all, Kelly was very beautiful, probably out of my league. She was tall and had brown hair.

Her family is about as conservative as they come. She is the daughter of a famous football coach in the Bay Area and lives in a million-dollar mansion. Why set yourself up for a big fall?

Well, I figured, what did I have to lose? Kelly and I were friends and I thought if she did say "yes," we would go as friends. Even I left my delusions of grandeur at home. Since Coach Wiggin and I were friends, I thought that even though it was a long shot, he might have been an ally for me at the dinner table. Maybe I'm wrong, but I think he would have told her that I was a nice guy and she ought to give it a try. Remember, this was just a date.

For myself, I was prepared to show her a good time. I wanted Kelly to tell her father that she had a great time with me. I wanted her to tell him that it was one of the best dates she went on because I treated her with class. I mean, how else could it be?

First of all, I was nervous enough as it was just thinking of asking her in the first place. I would have difficulty asking her to pass the salt, much less trying to get to first base.

Would I have asked if I could kiss her good night? That of course, would have depended on how the evening went. Kelly Wiggin was not only beautiful, she was nice. She came from a family that would best be described as first class. Whether she said yes or no, whether or not I got a kiss good night, it would have been done with class.

On our way to church I asked my parents for the okay to ask her to the dance. Without much discussion, they did not give me the go ahead.

Not getting the green light from my parents left me to think of what might have happened if I had been able to ask her out. It was a big disappointment.

There were many times when I didn't adhere to the Jonathan Rule. I asked girls out and got shut down. It was frustrating, but hey, at least I was trying.

My First Love

Everybody remembers their first love. I mean, it's the first!!! It has an innocence about it that no other love can match. You think that the first love you have will be the last because of course, it will last forever. More often than not though, the two of you break up. And, that's why it is called your first love.

Do you remember your first love? I know I do. Her name is Loretta DiRicco.

I remember my first love so well, because it was the last time I had what you would call a relationship. Loretta and a group of her friends hung out with a group of us from our special ed class. She was a sophomore and I was a senior. We kind of hit it off and she ended up inviting me to her birthday party.

I had a great time at the party. I danced with a lot of Loretta's friends.

But, the highlight of the evening was a slow dance I had with Loretta. It was magical.

Shortly after her party, I went into the hospital for a short stint. I called her just about every day and she definitely lifted my spirits up.

Easter vacation came and I invited Loretta to go with me to the mall. We had a blast! We talked and laughed a lot as we went from store to store. Loretta had a soft spot for chocolate truffles and I seized the opportunity by getting her one. It made me happy just watching her eat it. Her eyes would light up and she would smile that gorgeous smile. I can still see it.

Shortly after vacation, our school had a spring dance. It wasn't anything formal, just music and refreshments in the gym. Loretta was there without her boyfriend and I asked her to dance with me. With her arms around me, I made up my mind that I wanted to ask Loretta to my senior prom. I happened to remember the Jonathan Rule, but the moment was right, and it was time to do it.

Knowing that she had a boyfriend already, I asked her if she would go to the prom with me. I emphasized that we would go just as friends.

She immediately said yes, except that she had to get her mother's permission before it was final. In the meantime, I explained how there were some hoops I had to go through at home.

The next day at dinner, I brought up going to the prom with the folks.

"How do we know this girl?" Mom asked.

"Remember, I went to her birthday party."

"Does she go out much?"

This was a tough one to answer. If I told her that she had a boyfriend already, I would have been sunk. If I told them she didn't go out that much, they might have thought she was kind of weird.

"Yeah, she goes out."

"Do you think she'll go with you?" Mom did most of the questioning while Dad just sat there.

What was I supposed to say to this one? Like every other son or daughter, you'd think I would be screaming with excitement and jubilation, telling them I have a date for the prom. Whoopee!!! Instead, I am sitting here being interrogated like one of Nixon's aides at the Watergate hearings. Go figure.

"Yes, I think there is a good chance she will go with me."

My parents gave me the okay to ask Loretta to the prom.

At school on Monday, Loretta gave me the good news. We were going to the prom—as friends, of course.

I decided to wait a couple of days to tell my parents that Loretta had indeed accepted my invitation. If I had come home that day and told them we were going, they might have suspected something was up.

In the midst of making all the necessary plans, it seemed like the big night didn't come soon enough. I did have expectations, but I was more concerned about her having a good time.

Ben played the role of chauffeur and after picking her up we returned to my house for pictures. I didn't look too bad in my black tuxedo and Loretta looked great in her long lavender dress with spaghetti straps along her shoulders.

After pictures, we made our first stop at the Magic Pan for dinner. The Magic Pan was one of my favorite restaurants, specializing in crepes. I had my usual order of deep-fried hush puppies drenched in a glaze of honey mustard, a small spinach salad with almonds and mandarin oranges with a spicy vinaigrette, and two seafood crepes that literally melt in your mouth. But, what made this dinner unlike all the other times I went to the Magic Pan was enjoying good food with someone special.

The prom was held at some hot spot up in San Francisco. We had a great time dancing and doing the whole picture thing. Even in that nice dress, she got down on her knees as we slow danced. I felt like I was on top of the world.

We went back to my house after the prom. After helping me into the house, Ben left us alone for a while.

We went into the living room and I took a seat on the couch. Loretta and I were more interested in what we brought home than what my parents left on the dining room table. We sat on the couch and drank a bottle of champagne together. When that bottle was finished, we drank another one. I swear that I matched her drink for drink.

As we sat on the couch listening to love song after love song on the radio, drinking, kissing, and laughing, time seemed to pass by so quickly. It was well into the morning before we got Loretta home.

Loretta called the next day and told me she was going to give the other guy his walking papers. Yeah! With the school year about to draw to a close, Loretta and I went shopping on my Senior Cut Day, and she went with our special ed class on our year-end camping trip.

Nothing happened on the camping trip and I was okay with it. She was a pretty special person and I didn't want anything to spoil what we had.

We continued to do things throughout the summer. Loretta told me that it bothered her mother when she picked me up. God, I only weighed thirty-nine pounds then. Imagine what she would say now. As the summer went on, the strain coming from her mother became increasingly apparent. Loretta would talk about her mother once in a while, but she insisted in not making a big deal of it. Still, it bothered me.

As I headed up to Chico to go to school, I still had feelings for the girl I took to the prom. I carried the picture of the two of us all dressed up in my wallet and looked at it quite often. I called Loretta as often as I could. I rarely got to speak to her though. Her mother screened all of my phone calls and she always had a reason why her daughter couldn't come to the phone. She would have made a great secretary.

Not being able to talk to her made me even more frustrated. When I did speak to her I tried to tell Loretta in a roundabout way that I thought her mother had something against me. I talked about the times during the summer where she mentioned how her mother didn't want her to carry me as well as the time her mother said she didn't like her daughter going out with me because of my disability.

I saw Loretta briefly at Christmas and we wrote each other a few times. But, the longer her mother held up the wall, we grew apart and never came back together. About a year ago, I found out that she had gotten married. I am happy for her, as long as she is happy.

To be honest, I still carry a spot in my heart for Loretta. I regret not hanging in there and confronting her about the whole situation with her mother. Perhaps it would have made it easier to let go of her. It wasn't the typical break-up where you could see some kind of closure. Until someone else comes along and somehow brings some semblance of magic into my heart the way she did before I came to Chico, I can say that I have some very fond memories of my first love.

If I Were In Their Shoes

Time has healed a lot of the frustration I felt as a teenager and I wish my parents had done things differently when it came to girls and dating. Even today, we don't talk about my love life.

I don't know exactly why my parents were so overprotective of me, but if I were to make an educated guess I'd say they were shielding me from the possibility of having to deal with rejection. Plain and simple, they didn't want to see me get hurt.

Is it understandable that they should have these feelings? Of course, it is. They were just doing what they thought was best for me. Would I have done things differently if I was in their shoes?

Most definitely. Knowing what I do, and having a completely different frame of reference from my parents, I would have taken a different approach.

If I were giving advice to a parent of a disabled teenager, I would do some homework beforehand, starting off by making a list of general and specific questions about dating and persons with disabilities. I would make sure this list was complete.

After the list is finished, put together a list of people who can answer these questions. Include friends on this list, but don't limit yourself. They may only give you the advice they heard on a daytime TV talk show.

Consult with your child's doctor and ask if they can put you in touch with anyone. A doctor may not know a thing about dating, but they often know of people who can help.

Should your child have a resource or special ed teacher at school, talk to them about how your child socializes with the other students. Are they quiet and withdrawn? Or, are they popular with their classmates? Maybe it is somewhere in between.

When it comes to answering the more difficult questions about dating and relationships, your best resource may come from the disability community in your hometown. Often times, I will seek the advice of other disabled individuals and listen to their stories. They have been through it already, and might have some helpful suggestions that will put your mind at ease. If you don't know anyone with a disability, contact your nearest independent living center or State Department of Rehabilitation Office.

Finally, if that doesn't work and you have access to the Internet or other on-line computer services, there are plenty of newsgroups and forums that deal with these kinds of issues. Once you have your questions answered and a pool of people to use as resources, you can start piecing together the information you have, and you can formulate some ideas about the best way to deal with this subject. Granted, you may not have all of your fears laid to rest, but at least you know more now than when you first started.

Still, as much as you listen to others, there are core beliefs that are deeply rooted in your soul that you will not compromise. You don't want to see your child get hurt. There is the fear that if your son or daughter has a bad experience with dating, or anything for that matter, they will be scarred for life.

It's a given that you love your child, despite their imperfections. But, you aren't sure whether someone else will do the same. Deep down, you don't think your child is worthy of anyone else's love and affection. Moreover, you aren't sure whether your son or daughter is capable of giving that kind of affection. You shoulder the blame. Your conscience asks, "How could you?" You bear the guilt. You feel not only your pain, but your child's pain as well.

As your child's chief protector, you feel like you let your guard down. You weren't there to shield your kid from the evils and misfortunes of life. Do we as persons with disabilities have to be shielded from this life experience simply because we are short, use a wheelchair, have bones that are fragile, or any other kind of impairment? I have never ended up in the hospital with a bruised ego or a broken heart. Believe me; I've had plenty of those.

Fortunately, my parents were only protective of me when it came to relationships and dating. They were great at just about everything else.

But, what about parents who won't even let their child cross the street alone? What about those who want their kids to live at home well after the age of eighteen? Parents of disabled children don't live forever. What is the "child" going to do when Mom and Dad have passed on?

It's unfortunate that some parents choose to take this route. It does a great disservice to the child as well as the parent. No matter how disabled your child may be, there has to be a point in time where you go from being their parent, to that of a friend and perhaps even a confidant. It's sort of like the relationship my mother has with my sister Amy.

If I were to give a parent advice about their disabled teenager, I would start by saying that no matter who we are, somewhere and at some point in time, we all need someone. Even if the doctor tells you that your child medically, "can't do it," it doesn't matter. There are plenty of couples out there who "can't do it," and you don't even need a doctor to recognize that.

Look, you don't have to be an all-out cheerleader as your child goes through the ups and downs of adolescence. Just be supportive. Make yourself available as a resource to them. Use the information you got from the people you spoke to and share it with your child. Create a climate where they can share their feelings with you. Let them know that you love them unconditionally.

Does this mean you can't be a parent? Hardly. If your teenager is going out with someone who is a loser, say so. If their grades are bad, don't let them go to the homecoming dance.

The point is that we all need to experience as much of life as we can. If there are barriers we need to overcome, then it is important for the parent and the child to do it as a team. It's difficult enough handling the dating scene alone, but if a parent is there for support, it makes it a whole lot easier.

Disabled vs. Non-Disabled Women

I find it very patronizing when someone says I should go out with disabled women.

Would someone tell Senator Phil Gramm that he should marry a white woman? No, most likely he would probably find it very offensive if you told him that. Likewise, I feel the same way.

It is not because I have a preference toward able-bodied women. I have gone out with disabled and non-disabled women.

Though I've had better times with non-disabled dates, it would be too easy to make such a generalization. It also would be unfair because what bad experiences I may have encountered had nothing to do with them being disabled.

During my freshman year at Chico State, a woman named Maria called me on the phone, told me she had osteogenesis imperfecta, and invited me to her house for dinner. All of this took about ninety seconds, give or take a few. She was around twenty-four and I was eighteen. Wow, an older woman!

I showed up at her house, flowers in hand. She brought me a glass of wine and I thought this was pretty cool. She was cute too.

"How many bones have you broken," she asked as she was getting dinner ready.

I don't remember what I said.

"On the average, how much time have you spent in the hospital?"

"About three months," I said.

While reaching for a dish in one of the cabinets, she asked me what I did for a pulled muscle. I told her I put ice on it.

She made a great dinner. We had Cornish game hens stuffed with rice, and a nice salad.

The conversation however, was boring. It seemed like the only thing she was interested in talking about were issues concerning our disability. I was wondering if she was going to ask me what I was studying at Chico State, or what my favorite color was. It didn't happen. Not this time.

During the course of the evening, her mother called at least two times. I thought to myself, "Who does she think we are? Two bulls in a china shop?" Maybe she thought I was going to put the moves on her daughter. She lived in Auburn, about ninety miles south of Chico.

After dinner, we went into the living room and talked some more. I was hoping the topic of conversation would change. It did alright, but it wasn't what I expected.

"So, how do you feel about having children?" she asked.

I know there is a chance of passing on my disability to my offspring, but this one came as a surprise, especially on the first date.

"Well, how do you feel about it?" I asked rhetorically. I took a big gulp of wine.

"My doctor says that it would be very hard for me to carry a child. But if I got pregnant and if I had to choose between me and the child, I would let the child live."

"Before I consider having children, I would want the most recent information there was about the risks of having a child with osteogenesis imperfecta," I said.

The next question was even better.

"Would you rather marry someone with a disability, or one who is not disabled?"

Not knowing what to say, I threw it right back at her.

"What do you think? Would you rather marry someone who is disabled or non-disabled?"

"I'd rather marry someone who is disabled," she said.

For some reason, I thought I was undergoing an interrogation. She wanted certain answers to her questions.

I was honest when I told her that I didn't take the disability issue into account. If I like the person and there is a mutual attraction, it doesn't matter to me whether or not they are disabled. There are disabled women I find very attractive.

I went out with Maria again, and this time she asked me about school. Three days later, I broke my leg. I didn't want to go into any rehash of all of my fractures, so I never called her again.

If I did have a preference between disabled and non-disabled women, it shouldn't be regarded as anything more than preferring blondes over brunettes, tall women versus short women, brains or no brains.

Dating Experiences

During my freshman year in Lassen Hall, I went on a few dates. Call me crazy if you will, but almost all of the women I went out with had boyfriends.

Why subject myself to this kind of torture?

At the time, just going out was good enough for me and I thought it was more important to make a lot of friends. It worked for a while, but I wanted more.

In the fall of my sophomore year, I was pretty determined to get a date for the dorms annual semester formal, the Knad's Ball. I didn't go the previous year because I couldn't get a date and I didn't take rejection very well. On the night of the formal, I went to a dorm party and almost drank myself to death. My thirty-nine pound body couldn't handle a half pint of Seagrams Seven, and I puked my guts out all over the place. After being assured that I didn't require additional medical attention, the paramedics had me put to bed and I woke up with a giant hang-over that lasted about three days.

This time, I had a date for the formal. Her name was Nancy. It was kind of interesting how it all happened.

Early in the semester, she and Cam kind of had something going on. It hadn't reached its peak yet and he went out of town for the weekend. I came by her friend's room where she was watching T.V. and we started to talk. When it was all over, I asked her to the dance and she accepted.

As everyone found out that we were going, things started to get shaky. Cam didn't mind that we were going. He wasn't big on formals anyway.

One day, a group of us guys were in my room talking about Knad's Ball and what we thought was going to happen. You know, guy talk.

"So J, are you gonna get some action?" one of my hall mates asked me.

"I just want to show her a good time," I said.

"Yeah, but don't you wanna get laid?"

What was I supposed to say? No? Of course, I wanted to get laid. Every guy on our floor wanted to get laid.

"If anything happens, that would be great. Otherwise, I just want to have a good time."

As it turned out, what I said in my room came back to her in a different way.

She was told that I was expecting something from her other than a kiss good night.

This wigged her out so much that she asked Cam to talk to me about it. Cam knew what I was all about and he said nothing about it to me. About the only thing he told me was to have a good time.

Going to the dance with Nancy was like going out with a talking porcupine. She was so worried about what I was going to do that we ended up having a miserable time.

The evening did have its moments though. One of the guys on our floor left the dance early because his date told him that he wasn't going to get what he was expecting.

He raced through the front door of Lassen Hall in an alcohol induced fit whining about how much money he had spent on the evening and there was nothing for him in return.

When going out on a date, it is important that they know how to operate a wheelchair and handle me at the same time. Such was the case when I went out with a Delta Zeta named Lisa.

What I liked best about Lisa was among other things, her smile. Of course, the first time I saw that smile, I was three sheets to the wind.

In the second semester of my freshman year, I went out to the bars. Alright, so I was eighteen and the legal age was twenty-one. It didn't matter to me.

My friends and I were bar hopping with members of the Oakland A's. I knew a few of their players from the visits they made to Shriner's Hospital and I had gone to some A's games the year before.

We were about to leave one of the bars that had a huge flight of stairs. My friends were trying to figure out what to do with me while they got my electric wheelchair down the stairs, so they practically tossed me like a rag doll to this woman.

I looked up at her and saw a gorgeous smile. I thought I was in heaven. I said hello and asked her name. Then I asked her if I could stay in her arms for a while. Remember, this is heaven we're talking about.

My friends pried me away from her arms and we headed home. After that night, I didn't see Lisa for a while, or so I thought. You see, I would always go by her on my way to class and she would smile at me. The problem was I couldn't put two and two together.

At the end of the semester, we passed each other again. I went by her about twenty feet before turning around.

"Hey, I remember you!" I said.

"It's about time. Do you remember my name?"

"Yeah, it's Lisa."

"Do you remember what I was wearing?"

"Sure, you were wearing a black dress."

"Do you remember what you said?" smiling broadly.

I smiled meekly.

"Do you remember what you did?"

"Sort of." I smiled again.

So, we went out a couple of times and had some fun.

The funny thing about Lisa was that she was a klutz, a lot like Lucille Ball in "I Love Lucy." While watching her put my wheelchair in her car may have been funny, having her put me in her car was risky. Oh well, who cares. She never dropped me.

If there is ever a feeling worse than rejection, it's the anguish that goes with being stood up. I have been stood up more times than I'd like to think about. Every time it happens, I get a lump in my stomach.

Once I invited a woman over for dinner. She called an hour before and told me she was going to be a little late. She never showed and I ended up eating my dinner with my friend Phil who told me to ask her out.

If at all possible, don't ever stand anyone up. If you don't want to go out with someone, "just say, no." Believe me, it feels a whole lot better.

Once I went to a dance with a gorgeous, drop dead, babe! I felt like gold sitting next to her. We were sitting having dinner and she turned to me and said.

"Jonathan, do you know what I like best about you?"

I sat across from her in great anticipation. What could it be? Was it my hair? I still had most of it back then.

Maybe it was my body. Nah, she hadn't seen it—yet. Okay, it's my personality. That's it!!! Right?

"What I like best about you is that you're a safe date."

She couldn't be serious. Did I really hear what I thought she said? Did she call me a safe date?

No, it couldn't be that!

She went on to tell me how comfortable she felt with me because I wasn't like everyone else.

Well, just because I'm a gentleman, doesn't mean you have to call me a safe date.

S-E-X

There has only been one instance where a woman asked if I am able to have sex.

"Sure I can," I said, hoping she would come back with some sort of offer, nothing happened.

It's not that women haven't inquired as to my ability to have sex; it's just been something they would rather ask my friends about, instead of me.

After being a virgin for twenty three years, I began to wonder if it would ever happen. One person told me it was good being a virgin because once you had it, you will always want it.

One January night, it happened. It came without any fanfare. It came without warning. There was no build-up, no pre-game show.

It was shortly after nine and I was heading to the computer lab at Chico State. I had just finished taping one of my weekly sports commentaries. As I was going down Fifth Street, I heard a voice call my name.

I waved hello and proceeded along.

"Can you wait up a minute?" the voice said again.

I looked around and saw a woman walking toward me. She looked as if she had a couple of drinks under her belt.

"I was wondering if you would do me a favor and walk me home," she said.

"That depends where you live."

"I live on Eighth Street."

"I can probably walk you to Eighth Street, but I don't know how much farther I can go."

We walked two blocks to the corner of Fifth and Main and she asked me if we could sit in the city park for a minute so she could rest her legs.

"You used to stay at Shriner's, didn't you?" she asked.

"Yeah, how did you know?"

"Oh, my kids were at Shriners too. I think they were there while you were in the hospital."

She told me her name was Debra and her kids were at Shriners because they had polio. She started getting very emotional while talking about them.

At this time, I was wondering when I was going to get to the computer lab. It was getting a bit nippy out, and I still didn't know exactly where she lived.

We talked for a while. Debra started to go on a religious tangent and asked me if I had faith. Of course, I told her I had faith.

As much as I enjoyed it, you wouldn't believe all of the stress I was under. No, I'm serious. I was three days away from going down to the Bay Area for the East-West Shrine Game, and the last thing I wanted to have happen was to break a bone while having sex. How would I explain that to anyone? It didn't happen though. I survived while having an alright experience.

When it was over, she left a mailing address where I could write since she didn't have a phone. She called a friend to pick her up.

I wrote her once and never got a response. She left about as quickly as she came in. There was no fanfare. There was no post-game show.

I turned on the eleven o'clock news and my mind replayed everything that happened that evening.

My sex life has been nil ever since. It figures.

Where Do I Go From Here???

So, where does this all lead? Will I ever meet that special someone? Or, will I be disappointed in love like my Great-aunt Mildred Studebaker?

Sure, I want to fall in love with someone special. I want to show that person how much I care about them. I want to have the kind of relationship that is unique to any couple.

Does this mean I want to get married?

Well, when I look at my family, including my brother and sisters, I can see how they have been able to make their marriages work so far. It makes me think it can happen with the right person.

On the other hand, I'm not so sure.

Maybe it's just me, but I have noticed a lot of couples my age who are getting "unhitched." What does that tell you about the institution?

Unless something strange happens, I envision having a long courtship before I get married. For a guy who hasn't been on many second dates with the same person, it's important for me to really get to know the person I plan to spend the rest of my life with before I take the plunge.

There are times when I wonder if meeting the right person is in the cards for me. I get down on myself sometimes. I think to myself, maybe the naysayers are right? I mean, today's society is very appearance oriented. It seems that what you look like, what you own, and what material things you can give, are tantamount to who you are on the inside and what you have to offer another as a person. As much as I work myself into a deep funk about it, I still believe that there is someone out there for me. I also believe what Coach Bellotti said to me one day after a coaches meeting.

He said, "Jonny, it is better to have loved and lost, than to have never loved at all."

I think there is someone out there for me. I mean, who could pass up such a wonderful guy?

Oh God!!!

There is an inner faith inside where I have gone to in times of great need. It is a faith unlike any others, as it should be.

Your faith in God is unlike any others, as it should be. If you are expecting to read an inspiring story of how I found Jesus Christ and now I accept him as my Lord and savior, you will be disappointed. You see, that would be too easy. This belief in some ways defies human logic, and it provides us with an easy way out. So, what's wrong with giving people an easy way out? Nothing. I just don't ascribe to this philosophy and its methodology. It doesn't make sense to me.

Does this mean that I should do what I can to be a good person? Does it mean that I should forgive others for their mistakes as I would want them to forgive me for mine?

Does it mean that I have faith in myself and others?

Of course, it does.

So, do I believe in God?

Do I believe in Jesus Christ?

The answer is yes. However, it's still not what you think it is.

I have spent a lot of time to evaluating the role of religion in my life, and my relationship with God. It has become an on-going process that brings with it a constant flow of new ideas. Though you may not agree with my viewpoint, I hope it causes you to reflect on religion in your own life. Maybe it reinforces some of your own beliefs. Or, it raises a question or two in your mind, and causes you to think for a moment—about your own relationship with God.

It was a typical Sunday night in my dorm room at Lassen Hall. I was sitting at my desk scurrying to get my act together for the upcoming week. There was always a paper to write, a book to read, or a project to finish. Of course, I always waited until Sunday night to do it.

I heard a knock on the door.

"Come in."

"Hi Jon, how's it going?"

It was Mark DeSio, a floor mate who, like me, was a PR major. We were pretty good friends as we took several classes together. He was a big Raiders and A's fan.

"Hey, I'm getting ready to go to church. Do you want to go with me?"

"No, I've got some studying to do."

Always bemoaning the fact that he had to go to church, Mark asked me to go with him a number of times while we lived in the dorms. He would recount all of the "screw-ups" of the previous week which would serve to justify his going to church. I could tell he felt really bad about what he had done.

Frankly, I was amused to hear Mark tell me of his "sins." This was because I characterized his "confessions" as someone just having a good time in college. You know what I'm talking about—the party scene—the countless trips to the bathroom standing over the porcelain god. If you are lucky, you'll meet a babe and get laid. I did practically the same things Mark did. Well, almost.

While some may deplore such behavior, I find nothing sinful about it. Mark never committed any felonious acts. As long as it didn't hurt anyone else, there was nothing wrong with it. It's all a part of living life, and learning along the way.

When I moved away from home, I stopped going to church regularly. I was suffering from church "burn out." I just did not want to go.

Growing up, I rarely missed a day of Sunday School.

I was baptized in a Unitarian Church in Beverly Shores, Indiana which lies between Gary and Michigan City. They called it "the Old North Church" because the building was a replica of the one located in Boston.

Shortly after we moved to Hawaii, our entire family went to the local Unitarian Church that was a short distance from our house.

One summer day, about a year later, my mother received a phone call from the head Sunday School teacher. He was also a minister who was a little gray around the edges. My mother told him that she was planning on having all of us go to Sunday School, including me. The teacher told her that there were two schools of thought as to my going to Sunday School. One idea was that having people like me would broaden the horizons of the kids around me. The other was that it would frighten them. They would be scared of me because they would be afraid that something like that would happen to them. This made my mother feel like I wasn't welcome in the church. She would later hang up the phone. We stopped going to the Unitarian Church.

Shortly thereafter, my mother went to a lecture given by Dr. Maxwell Maltz, author of the bestselling book, *Psycho Cybernetics*. The lecture was held at the Unity Church of Hawaii. After attending the lecture, she was impressed by the minister of the church, Reverend Stan Hampson.

It wasn't long before Mom was attending services at the Unity Church And, one by one, we started going to Sunday School. Alden was the last one to join the pack. He was at home in front of the tube watching NFL football games. Smart guy, eh? He later became a Unity minister.

The Unity Church is a positive, practical, Christian based denomination. The movement was founded in the late 1800's by Charles and Myrtle Fillmore. Over the years, it has grown to an international ministry and has over 600 churches worldwide. The world headquarters is located in Unity Village, Missouri, just outside Kansas City.

The church views Jesus Christ as a master teacher, not just the Son of God.

Why, you ask? Well, because we are all the "son" of God. In fact, we are all children of God.

Instead of dwelling on the historical footnote of his death, the church celebrates the life and the resurrection of Jesus Christ. It teaches us that there is a Christ light within each of us. And, that we too, can aspire and do the great things that Jesus did. The Bible tells us this.

"Jesus said, 'I tell you the truth. Anyone who has faith in me will do what I've been doing. He will do even greater things than these because I am going to the Father.'" (John 14:12, NIV)

"During the fourth watch of the night, Jesus went out to them walking on the lake. When the disciples saw him walking on the water, they were terrified. 'It is a ghost,' they said, and cried out in fear. But Jesus immediately said to them, 'Take courage, it is I. Don't be afraid.'

And Peter replied, 'Lord, if it is you, tell me to come to you on the water.' And Jesus said, 'Come.'

Then Peter got down out of the boat and walked on the water to Jesus. But when he saw the wind, he was afraid. And beginning to sink, cried out 'Lord, save me!'

Immediately, Jesus reached out his hand and caught him. Jesus said, 'You of little faith. Why did you doubt?'" (Matthew 14:25-31, NIV]

In looking at these two passages, I believe that Jesus himself was a motivator. He was more concerned about people realizing their own greatness, rather than his own. He commanded it by telling Peter to have faith while walking on the water. Aside from the stories of Jesus' birth and resurrection, these are my two favorite passages in the Bible. I apply them to my life and every challenge that awaits me. In fact, when I go to a church to give a talk, I use them whenever possible.

Going to Sunday School in Hawaii was fun, whenever I wasn't in the hospital. We sang a lot of uplifting songs like "Joy, Joy, Joy," and "I'm Ready For a Miracle." We also learned a number of prayers, like the Prayer of Faith by Hannah More Kohaus:

> God is my help in every need.
> God does my every hunger feed.
> God walks beside me, guides my way.
> Through every moment of the day.
>
> I now am wise. I now am true.
> Patient, kind, and loving too.
> All things I am, can do, and be.
> Through Christ the truth, that is in me.

The environment was one of unconditional love, a stark contrast from the Unitarian Church just down the road.

When I was in the hospital, Sunday School came to me. Reverend Stan's wife, Helen, would come to the hospital with "get-well" cards from the other kids. She even brought in a tape of the Sunday School kids singing joy songs to me.

When I was in high school, I continued along the route that my brother and sisters had taken by becoming president of my youth group (Youth of Unity), and going to Y.O.U. Conference at Unity Village, Missouri.

When I moved to Chico, I put going to church on the back burner as football on Sunday mornings was now part of my routine. But, I didn't think that not going to Unity Church, or any other church on Sunday, made me a bad person. It gave me a chance to think about myself and my relationship with God. This new found freedom gave me an opportunity to try new things. It gave me a chance to go to different churches, talk with people of different faiths, and formulate my own recipe for living a good life, and becoming a good person.

Here are some ideas that have worked well for me.

Religion should make you feel good

I remember my mother telling me to do something not necessarily because it felt good, but because it was good for me.

She told me to eat my prunes. She told me to do my homework. She told me to go to church. That's what mothers are supposed to do, I guess.

Oftentimes, we are told to go to worship because doing so will make us a better person. We need to do it. It's good for us. We become saddled with a heavy guilt trip.

Well, I'm never one to argue with my mother telling me to eat my prunes or do my homework. Even if I happen to be at their house on a Sunday and she says we're going to church, I go. But, with all of the physical and psychological pain we endure throughout our lives, the last thing we need to deal with is having someone coax or coerce us into going to church.

I never go to church because I have to go. I go because I want to go.

I go to church because I want to sing. I love to sing. I love singing joy songs that are uplifting and carry me through the day. During the Christmas season, I love singing Christmas carols. They get me in the mood for the holidays. Singing makes me feel good.

I go to church because I want to hear the minister speak. As a public speaker, I draw ideas from others. I listen intently to their presentation. They may discuss a topic that interests me. Or, I like the way they deliver a talk. They have a voice that is easy to listen to. They know how to deliver an inspiring message.

How many times have you gone to church and found yourself dozing off five minutes into the minister's talk? My father used to do this and Mom had to keep shoving Life-Savers in his mouth to keep him awake. I did it too. I couldn't understand why we had to repeat the same experience the following week. I know it made the Life-Savers people happy.

Think about it. If you believe in making every minute count, what are you doing sleeping in church? If you're going to sleep, you might as well do it in bed.

If you are looking to hear an inspiring message on Sunday morning, or whenever you go, shop around. Preachers of every denomination are vying for your attention. Like performers, they open their doors for the public to see and hear their performance. They seek your approval. They want you to come back.

What you have to remember is that you are the consumer in the church-going business. It's like choosing between NBC and CBS, or Willie Nelson and Randy Travis. Go to as many different churches until you find the right one, or two. That's what I do.

Another reason why I go to church is for the fellowship. I like being around people.

We all know that going to a place of worship is good for us as people. But, does it have to make us feel bad—and even cry? Hardly.

Such was the case when I attended an Easter Service at the Neighborhood Church in Chico. The church put on a program dramatizing the last days of Jesus' life. As the man playing Jesus was on the cross having his hands "nailed," young children in the audience were bawling unmercifully in their seats as they saw the fake blood dripping down from the sides. This disturbed me greatly.

For me, getting spruced up to go to church is an event. I go because I want to do it, not just because it's good for me. Choosing your place of worship should be a happy, eye-opening experience, not a Sunday morning chore. It should make you as happy as eating your favorite candy, or watching your favorite T.V. show. If you don't like the minister or the church, go somewhere else. It's not just in God's hands, it's in yours too!

Religion has got to make sense

You are a reasonably intelligent person, aren't you? So, don't you believe that whatever faith you worship, you do so because it makes sense to you—intellectually?

You're not still worshipping in the same church because your significant other said you better do it, or you're not getting any nooky tonight. Or, are you not going to the same church because you've been doing it since you were two, and even though your mom is off in another world, real or imagined, she's going to come down and crucify you if you go to another church.

You choose a church because what is being said makes sense to you. There are some concepts around organized religion which I don't agree with strictly because it doesn't make sense to me.

Upon my first visit to the Neighborhood Church in Chico, a fundamentalist Christian denomination, I heard one of the pastors exclaim to the congregation that we were all going to heaven.

Great! We are all going somewhere, why not "heaven?" That makes sense.

About a minute after he said that we were ALL going to heaven, he started changing his story.

"If you don't believe that Jesus Christ is your Lord and Savior, and believed that he died for your sins, you are going to end up in the burning hell of Judgement Fire!" he exclaimed.

"Wait! I thought we were all going to heaven," I said to myself. He asked us to close our eyes and raise our hands if we hadn't already accepted Jesus Christ as our Lord and Savior, and if we were now ready to do so.

Like a ten year-old, I snuck a peek through my right eye and looked to see if anyone was buying into this stuff. They did, as a number of people raised their hands. I was still trying to process it.

Think about it. This guy opens the service by telling us that we're all going to heaven. He did say ALL of us. And not a minute later, he puts conditions on it.

Jesus Christ was a lot of things. He was a master-teacher of his time and he taught us many things. He wanted us to be good people, live and do great things, and most of all, learn and grow.

The next part of what the pastor said was when he eluded to the burning hell of Judgement Fire. What in the world is that, a suburb of Los Angeles?

I think what the pastor was referring to, was heaven and hell. For which I ask, "Is there a heaven and a hell?"

That, I believe is true. Where we believe it exists is another question. For me, heaven and hell are one in the same place. It's not a magical place with angels and cotton candy. It's not a burning fire with devils and demons either.

Heaven is right here. Hell is right here, too. It's all where you are in your head.

Think about it. How many times have you heard someone say that, "Life is great?"

Or, "Life's a bitch. Life is hell!"

I believe that this is where it's at for all of us.

What happens when we die? Well, since I believe that the soul is indestructible, we merely start the whole process all over again and live our lives as another human being. It's called reincarnation.

The Catholic Church does a number of things that just doesn't make sense to me.

The first has to do with communion.

When I was at a Catholic service, my friend asked me if I was Catholic. I whispered that I wasn't. He said that I was not allowed to take communion. He went up and got a blessing from the priest, and I tried to make sense of it all.

Perhaps I missed something here, but I didn't remember Jesus saying that some of us could take communion, while others had to sit in their seats and watch. That's not the Jesus I know. He loves us and accepts us unconditionally, no matter who we are. Would he approve of this sort of thing? I hardly think so.

If worshipping a given faith should be something I do because it feels good, and it makes sense to me intellectually, then am I just playing by my own set of rules with no personal accountability? Am I taking the easy way out?

I don't think so.

Unlike my friend Mark, I have never gone to church because I "had" to go. Well, maybe when I was a kid, I did. But, this business of going just because you screwed up, or, in the eyes of someone else you did something bad, just doesn't wash. Mark would go to Mass, get forgiven, and then go to Mass again to get forgiven, for the same things he did a week later. Again, these were things I did not find "sinful" or bad.

When it comes to the role religion plays in my life, I try to apply the concepts I learned through the Bible, Unity, and other sources that will make me a good person and will challenge me to do great things. For right now, this has been good for me.

Be open to change

I know people who don't get together because of the "religion" issue. There is a tug of war to see who is going to which church, and with whom. I think it's kind of funny, yet also very sad.

I don't necessarily believe it is something to be worked out, or compromised.

No matter what faith you belong to, whether you are Catholic, Jewish, Protestant, Christian, Muslim, Hindu, or belong to a church like Unity, your relationship with God is one of a kind. It belongs to you.

Because it belongs to you, you can choose to go to any church. If your mother wants you to continue to go to the Catholic Church you had gone to since you were a pup, and your new spouse is a Fundamentalist Christian, you can do either of those or decide on a faith that is right for you. Be receptive to change. Change is good, but don't change churches just for the sake of changing.

Respect other people's beliefs

I'll never forget all of the crap my sister Amy and I used to get when we told people that we belonged to Unity. They used to say that our church was a cult. Maybe they thought we were an off-shoot of the People's Temple, led by the infamous, Jim Jones. I don't know.

Anyway, I was really disappointed whenever I heard this kind of talk. After all, I never told them that they belonged to a cult.

One person who didn't react this way was Coach Trimmer, who is a fundamentalist Christian. I think there is a mutual understanding that we have differences when it comes to each other's faiths, and we discuss it once in a while. But, I have never told him that his religion is wrong or unworthy, and he is likewise respectful of my beliefs.

While I was a student at Chico State, I ran into Father Lynch of the

Newman Center. He was a true Irishman with white hair, and a big fan of Chico State football.

He led a number of our team prayers and roamed the sidelines during most of our home games.

When he invited me to his church, I told him I wasn't Catholic. It didn't bother him. He told me that he didn't care what religion I practiced, he welcomed everyone who came to the Newman Center. He even found occasion to mention this as I enjoyed myself the few times I attended his services.

As much as we preach to folks in other countries about how free we are to worship our own God, it's amazing that we are so quick to criticize other people's faiths, and label them unfairly.

Though I may not agree with someone's faith, I respect their right to believe, and leave it at that.

The reason why religion is one of those taboo subjects that you don't discuss is because it's very personal. It should be that way. Your faith may not be exactly the same as mine, but it's one thing you have that you can call your own. It's not your mother's or father's. It's not your significant other's. It's not your best friend's. It belongs to you.

I have a special relationship with God that no one else can have. Why, because we all have a special relationship with God. My relationship with God is centered on being the best human being I can be, giving of myself to others and society, and doing the great things that Jesus Christ and all the great master teachers challenged us to do.

A Law For Everyone

In 1990, President George H.W. Bush signed into law the Americans with Disabilities Act. For the disabled, including myself, this was a great day. It is by far the most sweeping piece of legislation since the Civil Rights Act of 1964. On the other hand, the ADA has given many in both the public and private sector a lot of headaches. It has caused some friction between the able-bodied and disabled communities. Furthermore, in an era where there is a movement to roll back government regulation and civil rights laws, there are those out there who are trying to weaken the ADA to the point where it's not worth the paper it's printed on.

Some believe that this law is strictly for the benefit of a few. I take exception to this by saying that the Americans with Disabilities Act can and will affect every one of us in some way, shape, or form during our lifetime.

Before we take a look at the law, there are some things I need to tell you right up front. These are probably going to be things you don't want to hear, but they must be said—sometimes more than once. You could call it a reality check.

First, in your lifetime, you will have some kind of disability. There is no question about it. While some choose not to admit it, as we get older, it becomes increasingly difficult for people to get around. Most of us won't walk at the same speed when we are eighty, than we did at twenty. We may lose a step or two. Therefore, it takes us longer to do things. For some, growing old may render some sort of disability that requires one to use something other than a cane or a walker. It may require the use of a wheelchair.

The aging process presents different circumstances for each of us. And as our senior population continues to grow, we need to be more understanding of these needs.

The second thing you need to understand is that being disabled can happen to you at any moment in time. It knows no race, gender, political, or religious orientation.

Let me say this again because it is really important. Due to sudden illness or accident, you can become disabled at any moment in your life. It could happen twenty minutes from now. Or, it could happen twenty months, or twenty years from now.

When you think about all of the people who are injured on the road because of bad weather, a sudden mishap, or some drunk slammed into the side of their car, accidents occur every day. If they are lucky, or not dead, some are faced with having to face life with a whole new set of circumstances. It can happen to anyone.

It can happen to you.

My best friend, a very active schoolteacher in his early thirties, went to the doctor one day because he had a pain in his hip that he thought was the result of a playing a little too much softball. It was later diagnosed that the pain he was having was caused by a cancerous tumor. The doctor immediately put him on crutches and ordered him not to drive his car anywhere.

Soon after, he called me to see what kinds of services are available in the area. I was ready, willing, and able to help him out.

For me, even though I have a severe form of osteogenesis imperfecta, there are many things I can do for myself. But, even I don't think I am immune from having a serious accident or sudden illness. After all, in the last ten years, I have broken my neck, twice. This has left me with some reduction of movement and considerable pain.

I know that it is not a pleasant thing to discuss our own fragility and mortality. It is not something that we need to dwell on and mope about. It is, however, something we need to think about once in a while. I do.

Those who have some sensitivity when it comes to issues concerning people with disabilities acquire this as a result of knowing someone with a disability. The Kennedy family acquired their sensitivity toward these issues because one of Joseph and Rose Kennedy's daughters, Rose Marie, was mentally-retarded, or developmentally disabled.

Senator Tom Harkin, D-Iowa, has a brother who is hearing impaired.

You may also have a relative, or know a friend with a disability. Or, you are disabled.

So, what I am pointing out here is that the ADA is not just about a group of people in wheelchairs. It is not just about the blind or hearing-impaired. It is not just about "Jerry's Kids" or Vietnam Veterans. It's about me. It's about you. It's about all of us.

So, what is the Americans with Disabilities Act all about? Like anything, it means different things to different people. Surprise! Yes, even the disabled have different viewpoints when it comes to how they interpret the ADA. For me, it means a number of things.

First, it's about participation. Many in the disabled community call it a "bill of rights." I see it as something even greater. This law, written and signed into law under the leadership of two Republican presidents, was the clarion call from the political establishment for people with disabilities to participate in society.

The ADA is about access. Without access, it is difficult, if not impossible, for people with disabilities to participate in the mainstream of society. It can make it easier for the hearing impaired to communicate by phone, or provide accessible public transit for a wheelchair user to get to work.

This law is about opportunity. As the ADA is integrated into our nation's infrastructure, there is an inherent responsibility that must go hand in hand, in lock step with the intentions of the law. That is, the disabled community, including myself, should use the components of this law to better ourselves as not purely participants in our society, but as contributors to the common good.

So, what was life like for me before the ADA? Well, even though I may not have a long history of injustices to draw upon, I do have my fair share of horror stories that give me more than a few reasons to support the substance and intentions of the ADA.

My first real encounter with an access issue came when I took a weekend trip from San Francisco to Los Angeles to visit my sister, Becky. I was to fly down on TWA and return on Pan Am.

The flight down went without a hitch. The flight crew was nice and very helpful.

When we returned to the airport early Sunday evening, it was a different story.

Upon entering the terminal, we found the walkways crowded with Washington Redskins and Miami Dolphins fans. Decked out in all sorts of garb, these folks were returning home after the Super Bowl. After finding our way through the lines of people, we checked in my bags.

The man at the ticket counter asked my sister to sign a release form. He said that just in case something happened, the airline wouldn't be liable. He gave her a song and dance, but Becky didn't seem to mind. After signing her name on the dotted line, he put my bags on the conveyor belt, and off they went.

We meandered to the gate and waited for my boarding call. While waiting, I chatted with a couple of people who had seen the Super Bowl in person. The boarding call came over the PA and we expected that I would board the plane first, since I required some additional assistance. As it turned out, all of the passengers got on before me.

"Are you going with him?" the attendant said.

"No, he's going alone," Becky replied.

"Excuse me," she answered. The attendant walked into the airplane and returned a couple of minutes later.

"I'm sorry, but he can't go on the airplane unless he is with someone."

"Why not?" Becky fired back."

"Well, if the plane were to crash, there would be no one to assist him in case of an emergency."

Becky explained to her that I had flown down by myself and my father would meet me on the other end in San Francisco.

"I'm sorry but the pilot will not let him board the aircraft."

Becky was upset to say the least. We headed to the nearest phone booth to call another airline that would take me to SFO. By this time, my bags were on their way to the Bay Area without me.

We called airline after airline. Almost everyone refused to take me, even United.

This made Becky particularly upset since she knew their Vice-President had muscular dystrophy. She used to see him talk to Jerry Lewis on the MDA Telethon.

After talking to the folks at PSA (now defunct, Pacific Southwest

Airlines), we received the green light to take one of their "midnight flyers." We made the long track from the Pan Am terminal to the PSA ticket counter. It was especially difficult for my sister to do this because there was no easy access, the airport was undergoing some construction work, and it was raining hard outside.

About an hour after the Pan Am flight had departed, my father was awaiting my arrival. The plane landed, along with my bags.

When the folks explained to my father why I was not on the airplane, all they got was an earful. Dad let 'em have it.

"What do you mean, what if the plane crashes? My son understands the risks that go with flying. He's prepared to die just like everyone else!"

I wish I had been there to see it.

Meanwhile, Becky and I waited in line to board yet another plane. We never made it to the front.

The airline personnel ushered us to the side and explained to my sister that I could not go on the flight alone. They used the same line as the folks from Pan Am. It was shortly before midnight and Becky was too tired to be upset.

We called TWA and explained our situation to them. They were more than willing to help us out.

After a long wait in line, getting out of the parking lot, our adventure at LAX came to an end. We headed to Bob's Big Boy for a late dinner before going home.

First thing Monday morning, Becky had to call her boss at work and tell him what was going on. This was no picnic either. She had to miss a day of work because if what happened. On the other hand, I didn't mind missing a day of school.

That evening, I took a flight home and met my father and my bags a day later.

Shortly after moving to Chico, I ran into another access problem when I went with a bunch of friends from the dorms to a movie playing at the Senator Theatre.

The theatre, located in the center of downtown, is an old building, complete with lots of stairs. There were four movie screens, two upstairs and two downstairs. The movie we wanted to see was upstairs on the second floor.

Before going to the show, I explained to my friends that I would need some help getting up the stairs. They understood and told me they would carry me up without my chair, and set me in a regular seat.

As we all paid for our tickets to the show, it suddenly dawned on theatre personnel that I was intending on seeing the double-feature upstairs. The manager came over and told all of us that I couldn't see the movie because there was no way I could get up the stairs. My friends told the manager that they were going to carry me up the stairs to see the show.

Then, the manager said that I wasn't allowed in the theatre because their might be a fire in the building. They ignored him and picked me up for the "lift-off" to my seat. Seeing that he was out-numbered, the manager gave up, and we watched the double-feature. The seats were great and there was no fire.

My biggest fight when it came to access in the "pre ADA" days centered around a dining hall on the Chico State campus, my alma mater.

While living in Lassen Hall, I ate the majority of my meals at the dining commons in Whitney Hall.

The dining room, located on the first floor, was split into three levels. As you enter the dining hall, you are on the middle level where you get your food. There is an upstairs and a downstairs by which many of the residents could find a table.

On the middle level, there were three tables available for people to choose to sit if they wanted to eat there. Often times, these tables were taken by the kitchen staff that saw them as very accessible, especially at break time.

For the first few months, I didn't mind eating with those who worked in the kitchen. They were very nice people. After a while though, I wanted to eat with my fellow dormies—especially the babes who inhabited Lassen Hall. I asked the Food Service Director, Roger Becker, about putting in a lift that would go up the stairs. After telling me that he would look into it, he came back later saying there was no money to get one installed. With that answer, I dropped the subject for a while.

As one year rolled into the next, I became increasingly frustrated with not having access to the upstairs level. Why was I feeling this way? Well, I couldn't get anyone to sit with me at the table. It was in plain sight of everyone and I think it made them feel a bit squeamish.

The situation made me feel uneasy, and I proceeded to take the next step. I went to the housing office with Paul Karlstrom, Director of Disabled Student Services, and met with the Director of Housing, Jim Moon.

I tried to explain the situation to Mr. Moon. He basically told me that since they had set aside a certain number of tables on the main level, where everyone gets their food, it met any requirements in terms of access. I looked at him in utter amazement.

I couldn't believe what this guy was saying. I mean, I paid the exact same money as every other resident who lived on campus, and I had to sit in a designated area! To me, this was a simple case of separate but equal.

After a very unproductive meeting, I met with Paul and we commiserated over the issue. And for a while, I slept on it. I also moved out of Lassen Hall.

Even though I had moved out of the dorms, I still paid for a meal card. I didn't want to have to go home all the time between classes, and this proved to be convenient. Still, the situation was left unchanged.

At this point, I thought I was running out of options. I had tried just about everything and I became increasingly frustrated with the university. I couldn't believe that after all the bragging these folks did about how accessible Chico State was, they weren't planning on fixing the access to the dining hall. Moreover, the fact that they didn't see this as a problem was even more disappointing.

In October, I sat down and wrote a letter to Jim Moon and told him exactly how I felt. Knowing that his direct subordinate was an African-American, I explained to him that sitting in a designated area in the dining commons in the eighties was likened to sitting in the back of the bus in the fifties and sixties. Then, I backed those words with a common threat used by many, as a first option. I stated in the letter that if the problem wasn't fixed, I was going to sue the university. I gave them a month to respond to my letter.

Two weeks later, I got their response. In a letter to me they informed me that they had found the money. They would have the lift installed by the spring semester and it would be operational shortly thereafter, sometime in February.

Everything went according to plan and we even had a ceremony commemorating the installation of the new lift. I let the university take credit for it even though it was a dog-fight. I did explain to those who attended that having the lift would make it easier for future Chico State students who are disabled, to have a barrier-free experience when eating at the Whitney Hall dining room.

Using litigation as an option to right certain injustices is not the only way to get things done, nor should it be considered from the get go. It doesn't do a lot to help implement or enforce the components of the Americans with Disabilities Act. However, in this situation, I felt it was the only thing I could do. I tried for over two years to get them to listen, and they put me off by saying there was no money. They followed it up by not recognizing there is a problem and telling me to "sit in the back of the bus."

While litigation is an option, it should be used sparingly, and as a last resort. Though you may achieve a desired outcome, don't expect those on the other end to kiss and make up with you afterwards, because they won't. In fact the more people hear about lawsuits arising because a certain entity didn't comply with the ADA, they target their anger and frustration at those who the law is trying to help, the disabled.

Sometimes though, it becomes necessary to hit those who fail to comply right where it hurts, in the pocketbook. Yes, it does work.

When you encourage a person who uses a wheelchair to go with you to the local pub or movie theatre, their first thought is most likely centered on how they are going to do it rather than if they want to do it.

Access to goods and services is a vital component of the law. However, when it comes to ADA compliance, the most likely responses you are going to get from those who may not be so willing to comply may go something along these lines.

"Why do I have to do it?"

"How much is it going to cost?"

Even though I was able to argue that everyone had the right to eat on the upper level of the dining commons, one may find this argument a bit less palatable if you are trying to get access to a private business such as a deli, or movie theatre. You may be one hundred percent right when it comes to this, but the business owner may not be so understanding, and will start asserting their civil rights as being more important than yours.

For example, if there are three delis in a city block and only one of them is accessible, where is the disabled consumer going to go? Why, they are going to go to the deli that is accessible. And, the other two? Well, they will simply be out the money they would have received from those consumers.

Remember, people with disabilities carry the same money as those who are able-bodied. It is just as good as anyone else's.

Let's say that you are a theatre owner, and your business features four screens, like the Senator Theatre in downtown Chico. There are two upstairs, and two downstairs. You are getting lobbied by a group of disabled activists who want you to put an elevator or lift in the building that will go upstairs so they can take advantage of watching movies on all four screens. Meanwhile, you are sitting there having a total cow wondering how you could pay for such an accommodation. What are you going to do?

Well, if you live in a community like Chico, which has a significant disabled population, making four screens available instead of two increases the chance of you getting my money by fifty-percent. Hence, if there are three hundred disabled people in a given community and half of them go to the movies frequently, you could have such an accommodation pay off in no time.

We need to do what we can to modify existing buildings so that as many people can participate in as many activities as possible. What is even more important is the fact that when we plan our communities for the future, we need to keep access first and foremost in our mind. While buildings are made accessible to many by car, we need to make pedestrian access a priority as well. In Chico, my main source of transportation is my wheelchair. For others, getting around may involve walking with the use of a seeing eye-dog, a cane, crutches, or a walker.

Another component of the Americans with Disabilities Act centers on employment and the workplace. While some public and private entities have embraced this part of the law, there are others who shirk from it.

In order to think about it in this context, I can't help but stress to you again that you can suddenly become disabled at any time in your life. Let's say that you are a well-known scientist who is on the verge of discovering something really big, like a cure for breast cancer. You are driving home from a hard day's work, on a snow covered road. All of a sudden, the person driving along side of you loses control of their car and slams into you. Your car spins out and they end up using the "jaws of life" to get you out.

While you are in the hospital, the doctors tell you that your spinal cord is damaged and they are not sure if you will regain movement in your arms and legs. You may have to spend the rest of your life in a wheelchair.

What are you going to do? Is your life over? Should you just go ahead and call Dr. Kevorkian and end it all? What about all of your work? No one else knows what you have already learned. Are you going to throw it all away?

What about pro football players like Dennis Byrd, Mike Utley, and Darryl Stingley?

Are their lives over with just because they can't play football anymore?

What about those who are born with disabilities? Not just those token few, I mean everyone. I'm talking about those who are born with the slightest case of Down syndrome to those with the most severe form of osteogenesis imperfecta. While some can do more for themselves than others, each individual has a contribution to make.

What about all of those people on welfare? You know, not all of them are single mothers who spend their days in front of the tube eating bon-bons as some would want you to believe. There are many people with disabilities who can, and should work.

In dealing with issues concerning job discrimination and reasonable accommodation, the ADA provides the initial step toward getting people with disabilities into the labor force. The next step involves dispelling myths and changing attitudes. And that is accomplished by those like myself, who seek employment opportunities, and those who provide them.

To those who may oppose the substance or the intentions of the Americans with Disabilities Act, I will throw this bone out to them by saying that this piece of legislation is by no means perfect. That can be said for just about any law. Among the people you have who oppose the law are those with disabilities who don't want any of "your" help, thank you. Don't bother holding a door open for them either.

Another group of people who deem the ADA to be unnecessary are those who think making such things as reasonable accommodations voluntary. They believe that people who make their businesses accessible do it out of the goodness of their heart.

They want to do it, but they'll be damned if Uncle Sam is going to tell 'em to do it!

Well my friend, if they were so kind and generous, we wouldn't need the ADA in the first place. We wouldn't need the Civil Rights Act of 1964 either.

There are those able-bodied people whose livelihoods are threatened if "those poor helpless people" get anything that will enable them to live their lives like the rest of us. What would become of them? If we could somehow make it so that a vast majority of disabled people could lead totally independent lives, they might have to look for other work. Then you have people who feel the same way about people with disabilities as they did about blacks in the pre-Civil Rights era.

Some who oppose the law use the price tag argument as a means for holding it back. There is no doubt in my mind that the ADA will cost our nation some money in order to make it worth the paper it's printed on. If we don't spend the money now, we will find ourselves in deep trouble as our population grows and ages. It's kind of like the old FRAM oil filter commercial, "You can pay me now, or you can pay me later."

It has been over five years since the ADA was signed into law by President Bush. In that time, I have learned a lot about what the law means for disabled individuals, like me. I know that the ADA is not the only answer. By no means is it the be all to end all that will make life easier for people with disabilities.

As I think about the ADA and do what I can to make it work for me, there are five things I keep in the back of my mind. Whether you are on the front lines in Washington fighting the good fight, or back at home in your community, perhaps you will find these helpful for you.

ADA, What?

Remember, not everyone knows what the ADA is all about. Sadly enough, there are many disabled people who don't have a clue as to the ADA, or how it is supposed to help them.

Education

As a person with a disability, I feel it is my responsibility to educate others in the most positive way about the spirit as well as the substance of the law. Education is the only way we can break down the barriers, dispel the myths, and provide opportunities for people with disabilities.

Dealing with the Opposition

In discussing this issue with an unsympathetic ear, present your views with a controlled passion that comes from your gut. Don't be a phony.

When talking to this individual, view it as a discussion and not an argument or confrontation. Don't show your anger at this stage of the game. It will only make you look immature.

Instead of making the focal point of your argument about your wants, needs, or desires, discuss your views in ways that makes it important to them. For example, if you can't get into a hardware store to buy a hammer, you might tell the owner that they are missing out on having you purchase your hammer from their store.

Make yourself available as a resource. If the person you are talking to needs information on how to make a reasonable accommodation, take it upon yourself to get them pointed in the right direction.

Quietly ask them if they know a person with a disability. You may get someone who says, "No." And then they talk about their mother who has diabetes, or their friend with the "bum" leg. Bring these people to life and get them to talk about their friends and family. Again, you are making the discussion about them, and not you.

Humor never hurts. When you are talking about a subject that is important to you, perhaps using a little humor will take the edge off what could be a contentious discussion.

If you can't get them to see where you are coming from the first time around, try again later. There may be circumstances in their life which causes them to see things differently.

Stick by your principles

If you think you are getting the run-around on a particular issue, or your efforts are falling short to a group of "rubber stamp do-gooders," continue the fight and stick to your principles. Don't allow yourself to be railroaded by people who compromise your principles for their own personal and political gain. I had this happen to me just recently, and I didn't put up with it.

While reading an article from my local paper, *The Chico Enterprise-Record*, I found out that my State Senator, Tim Leslie (R), opened an office on the Chico State University campus. Though I found it interesting to read he was going to be on campus, I was glad to see the senator was going to have an office in my hometown.

In reading further, I discovered he was going to occupy an office on the second floor of Sutter Hall, a twenty-five year old, temporary building. There was no wheelchair access.

After scratching my head wondering what was going on, I called Chico State's Disabled Student Services. Their initial response was that they did not know about what was going on, and I was the first to let them know about it.

Soon after, I received a call from Senator Leslie's office. They told me they knew of the access problem and that if I wanted to meet with the senator's staff, I would have to call them ahead of time and they would arrange a time and place for us to meet. They also invited me to a reception that afternoon, announcing the opening of the office.

"Well, that's fine for me, but what about everybody else?" I said.

Now that they had an office, they needed to arrange another "rent-free" space for us to meet?

They told me that they were able to get the office rent free, and they were saving the taxpayers money. Since the university is a state supported school, I use the term "rent-free" loosely. This argument didn't wash with me and the access issue became even more important. After all, his Republican counterparts in the State Assembly and U.S. House of Representatives have offices that are accessible. Everyone should have equal access to their elected officials. Again, I am not just talking about people in wheelchairs. My mother would have a hell of a time walking up those stairs.

I took them up on their offer to attend the reception. On my way over, I visited my friend, Bob Pentzer, Public Information officer for Chico State University. I explained to Bob that I would have a problem here if they went ahead and let the Senator have an office on the second floor of Sutter Hall. He agreed and pointed me in the direction of the university's ADA compliance officer, Zaida Giraldo, Zee for short.

I found Zee to be a sympathetic ear and she assured me that she would look into the matter. At the reception, I went looking for the university's top dog, President Manuel Esteban. He's a big diversity kind of guy and I thought for sure there was a place for me under his tent. I was wrong.

"That's the only building we have. They take what they can get," he said.

I was shocked. After saying a brief "Hello" to the senator, I left in disgust.

I spent the weekend stewing over the matter and planning out various strategies.

I knew it was pretty early in the game to do anything and there were some things I needed to find out. Still, I made some contingency plans.

I called Independent Living Services of Northern California (ILSNC), our local advocacy group that is supposed to help us in these kinds of situations. They had never been of any help to me in the past, but I wanted to hear their take on this one. Perhaps they could provide some additional support in getting this situation resolved—in the right way.

Their response to my phone call was pretty weak. They figured since it was the only office the senator good get that was "rent free," then he had to take it.

Zee called a few days later and said they were looking at alternatives to the Sutter Hall office. I thought for sure they could find the Senator another office. After all, they had just completed several new buildings on campus in the last few years, all the while they were handing out pink slips to profs and staff like cotton candy. Enrollment had been increasingly declining as well. Heck, give me fifteen minutes and I'll find him an office. No problem!

The university decided that there was no other place on campus for the senator, except the Sutter Hall office. They brought the problem to the university's ADA Transition Team, a committee that looks into ADA compliance issues on campus.

While all this was going on, I did some more research. After numerous unsuccessful attempts, I was able to reach the State Capitol and found out that the Senator's office budget was around $24,000 a year. This excludes salaries for office staff. I was beginning to wonder if he really needed a "rent-free" office, or was this just a cozy deal between him and Chico State University.

I talked to another friend of mine who works at Independent Living (ILSNC) and is on the university's ADA Transition Team. We discussed the Leslie situation for quite some time. She pointed out that there were several people in the disabled community who were questioning my motives, and there were rumblings that I was going to pursue litigation. She advised me that I should be more concerned with the process in which this was being handled, all the while accusing me of being myopic.

I told her my efforts were sincere and the bottom line here was that the university had made another boo-boo and I wanted to see them fix it in the right way. Litigation was not an option I was considering, not yet.

The Transition Team received a recommendation from Rocky Burks, Executive Director, ILSNC, who basically said that if the senator posted signs outside directing everyone as to how they could meet with the senator's staff, it would take care of the problem. The Transition Team agreed with the recommendation and forwarded it to the president's office for his approval.

I disagreed with this wholeheartedly.

The question at hand was whether posting signs informing everyone that they had to call in advance to set up an appointment constituted meeting the "equal facilitation" clause of the ADA.

I felt that this policy didn't meet the spirit, nor the letter of the law. What would stop an able-bodied individual from walking up those stairs and meeting with the senator's staff? Nothing. Therefore, I don't believe it constitutes equal facilitation. I also thought the solution was archaic, as if it were something brought out of the 1950's. You know what I'm talking about. Remember, the days where there were signs telling blacks such things as which restroom they could use?

Posting signs telling folks how to make an appointment with their elected officials was not a viable solution. While the university categorically denied it, I still thought there was another office on campus for him. I was very angry with the Transition Team's recommendation. I believed that this whole thing was just being "rubber stamped."

Several weeks later, I was interviewed by the campus newspaper, *The Orion*. Not long after, I received another phone call from Robert Dougan of the senator's office. He was not happy with my remarks.

He took exception with my comment that the parties involved did not consider the access issue. He said they did. He also pointed out that they had tried in vain to secure another office but that there weren't any others that were accessible, and "rent-free." He asked me if I wanted them to shut the office down.

I found what he said to be quite interesting. If they hadn't thought about the access issue, that was pretty bad. But, if they had thought about it and then ignored it, that was even worse. They couldn't win either way.

I said that the university has a habit of not doing things right and they needed to get hit between the eyes once in a while. I mentioned the Whitney Hall incident and a few others. I told him that I didn't want the office to close. I just wanted things done right.

He then explained that they were looking for another office and asked me if I knew of one. I took his remark as a challenge and went to work on it. I knew there was a place to put the senator, and the building was brand spanking new. Yes, it is completely accessible. The City of Chico had just completed construction of a new Municipal Center. There were offices available. The only thing in question was whether Senator Leslie could get the office "rent-free." His office had spoken to the city in the past, but there was no offer made to the Senator about it being "rent-free."

I spoke to a number of council members about the situation at the university, and asked them if they would consider such an arrangement. They did consider the matter and offered Senator Leslie an office, "rent free."

I was elated!

See what happens when you stick to your principles? In this case, there was no room for compromise because I was on the right side of this one. If you hang in there and explain to others how and why you are right, they will come around. It will have been worth the effort.

Litigation won't solve everything

It comes as no surprise to say that various aspects of the ADA will be decided by the courts. We live in a very litigious society and lawyers love it because it makes more work for them. Some see it as the first and only way to resolve disputes. As I said earlier, it doesn't need to be this way.

If you're dealing with an ADA issue, I sound a word of caution as you consider your strategies. Even if you think you won't get anywhere using all the options available, exhaust all of your plans before calling a lawyer. Make litigation a last resort, not a first option. You might be surprised if your issue is resolved, and you'll save a lot of money.

The Americans with Disabilities Act is by far the most sweeping piece of legislation which seeks to open the doors to opportunities for people with disabilities. It is also a very complex law. It means different things to different people. This law also comes with a price tag. Some would say that it's a hefty price tag.

As with other civil rights laws, the ADA serves as a benchmark toward changing the ways in which we view people with disabilities, and bringing us into the mainstream of society. That my friends, is what the law means to me.

Politically Speaking

There is no doubt, politics is important to me.

It wasn't always that way.

Until I graduated from college, my interest in local and national politics was limited to following the issues for a class assignment. You know, the dreaded current events quiz or term paper. It didn't bother me though. My parents told me on more than one occasion that there was life beyond the sports page.

Politics were discussed a lot in our family. My parents educated me about the issues and had me follow the election returns.

I remember sitting in front of the television with a plain white map of the United States and my colored pencils. Our teacher had given it to us to take home and fill in as we watched the presidential election unfold. I used the red and blue pencils to match the colors the networks were using to keep track of who won each state, Jimmy Carter or Gerald Ford. I recall how elated I was to have colored more states for President Carter.

As much as I was energized by the election of President Clinton, Jimmy Carter remains my favorite President of my lifetime.

In 1980, I sat in front of the tube once again. Only this time, I was bemoaning the fact that we had elected an actor as our President. During my sophomore year in college, I watched in disgust as Reagan won a second term by a record landslide. At the time, I was taking a debate class which took up the question of whether or not Reagan should be re-elected. Ironically, I got a better grade arguing for his re-election than against it. Who knows, maybe I'd make a good actor—or president!

Since I left coaching, my interest in politics took center stage. It meant something more than getting a good grade on a current events quiz. I started to see how issues were affecting my everyday life. In some ways, politics helped to fill a void left by football, but by no means did it replace it.

Whether it is family or friends, there has been a contest of influence over my political soul. I like that. I always want to hear what others have to say. Those who know their words have meaning, never hesitate.

Right now, I have two friends who have made sure to it that I neither veer too far to the right or left. How do they do it?

Well, you could call it vigorously pulling on both ends with their thoughts and ideas while we discuss and debate the issues. There haven't been many times where the three of us go at it. When that happens, it turns into a love fest and everyone comes to an agreement almost immediately. Then, we turn to sports.

But, when I have discussions with them individually, the gloves come off and each of them espouses their differing viewpoints with such sharpness, it cuts with clarity.

Since I have known Keith Cameron, he has always been there to make sure that I don't lean too far to the right.

In the last few years, Phil Midling, another friend who I knew from college, has tried to see it that I don't veer too far to the left.

Phil is a Republican, who upon one of my interrogations, confessed to me he voted for Walter Mondale in '84. It's hard for me to imagine a "Mondale Republican." That is, except for Phil. He hates it when I bring it up.

As a person with a disability, there is a different set of dynamics that come into play when considering the issues from this perspective.

For the most part, it is life's experiences which have helped me to understand the issues and articulate my views to others. To agree or disagree with me is not as important as knowing that they are there, and they're a part of who I am.

Affirmative Action

I wasn't as passionate about the issue of Affirmative Action per say as I was at the opportunity of serving on a committee. I would have served on any committee, but George Thurlow thought this one would be good enough to get my foot in the door.

One of the charges of the Affirmative Action Committee was to see that the city was moving forward in bringing protected group members into the city's workforce. As a member of the committee, I always held to the belief that an Affirmative Action goal was just that, a goal. It is not a quota.

I am not in favor of quotas primarily because it places a numerical value on the "what" aspect of a person rather than the "who." It causes us to think of people as being one dimensional.

What I tried to do as a member of the committee was to make sure that the avenues to opportunity were open to all protected group members.

Did we have enough advertisements placed in minority based newspapers so that we could reach protected group members? Are the testing procedures such that everyone gets a fair shot? Is the process for moving up the ladder amicable for all? Did we create a climate that made everyone who applied feel welcome? Is the City of Chico living up to the spirit as well as the letter of being called an Affirmative Action/Equal Opportunity Employer?

In the four years of serving on the committee, two years as chair, I learned there was a lot more to this committee than just goals and objectives. We're talking about the city's workforce. We're talking about human resources. We're talking about people's jobs. I realized how important this committee was and took my work very seriously.

The Affirmative Action Committee was noted for its high turnover rate. People were getting on and off the committee like it was a passenger train. I couldn't seem to understand why? We only met four times a year unless we had a hot issue come up. In spite of this constant change, there was an interesting cast of characters on this committee.

Mike Skram was a libertarian who by some wild stretch, got on the committee. A proverbial council candidate, he was always taking on the establishment every chance he got. If he belonged to a protected group, I don't know which one. I didn't think libertarians fall into any category.

In accordance with his political ideology, Mike came to the committee with one purpose only, and that was to get rid of it. As chair, I recognized this and dealt with it. It made things interesting at times. Although he and

I disagreed on the big picture, we found common ground on a number of other things and we got along alright.

Penny Thomas was an African-American woman who saw things a bit differently.

Despite knowing the city had met its goal with respect to the hiring of blacks and Hispanics, that wasn't good enough for her. From my perspective, she wouldn't have been satisfied until every new employee was African American.

My closest peer on the Affirmative Action Committee was Linda Balbutin. We became close friends while serving together.

After meetings, we used to go to Gina Marie's for iced teas. We had a lot of laughs and enjoyed each other's company.

While I was in the hospital recovering from my broken neck, Linda came to visit me and we talked about what was going on with the committee. At about that time, the chair position was opening up and she knew I wanted it.

"So what do you say if I nominate you for Chair, and you nominate me for Vice-Chair?"

"That sounds alright to me." A smile grew on my face.

At the next meeting, we were able to pull it off without a hitch. I wasn't surprised. No one else was interested in doing it.

At one of our post-meeting get-togethers, Linda told me she had cancer. She spoke frankly about it, but remained upbeat. She vowed to stay on the committee as long as she felt alright.

Unfortunately, she didn't make it. Linda went to a better place and I lost a trusted friend. She was a kindred spirit and a shining light. The city lost an individual who was committed to service, and cared about her community.

So, if you aren't for quotas, why are you for Affirmative Action?

Contrary to what those on the other side of this delicate issue believe, the present landscape is not equal. We need to continue our efforts to even the playing field.

Through my own experience, I have found that a culture exists which assumes that some people are presumed inferior, or thought of as being less than when it comes to their abilities. blacks, Hispanics, Asians, are often judged by the color of their skin. Women face sexual discrimination in the workplace.

The same can be said about people with disabilities. Often times, a person will be presumed as not having the ability to work just because they have a disability. These perceptions are much more pervasive than you think and carry a long history with it. They have helped to create a high unemployment rate amongst working age people with disabilities. Instead of tapping into this valuable human resource, we have a society where the disabled are thought of as tax takers and not taxpayers.

If they are deemed as having the ability to work, what falls into question is the value of that work. With the advance of programs such as sheltered workshops, those who work there are paid on different scale which suggests wages that are comparable to those in countries that have unfair labor practices. Those involved and profit from the system find a thousand reasons for this system. They cite performance standards that they use to judge workers' performance and keep their wages low in order to preserve their SSI benefits. This practice depresses wages. I accept none of these and go even further to call this practice, "cotton candy" slavery.

So, how does this affect me? Well, if my work is valued as being less than of another group of disabled people, or even a group of able-bodied people, then how do you think that makes me feel? The comparison is not warranted. I had a person tell me that I should give a presentation for free simply because that's the way he judged my work.

I don't give that much credence to those who believe Affirmative Action is wrong because the system assumes that protected groups are inferior. I hardly think that a program intended to even the playing field assumed that those who benefit would be thought of as inferior. It doesn't make sense. I think the system was set up to help those who are disadvantaged. There is a difference.

Let's say that I was given a job to work for the Kansas City Chiefs simply because they could check a box and fill a quota. Would that bother me? In the short term it might gnaw at me a little bit. But if I knew in my heart that I could to the job, then I would take it upon myself to prove them otherwise. I've done it several times.

If people assume that others are inferior, we need to ask how and why they feel that way.

Is it because they were brought up that way?

Did they have an experience that affected this perception?

Or, are there underlying causes which contribute to their point of view? Maybe they think minorities aren't educated as well as others.

Even though I don't give much energy or thought to it, I don't totally dismiss the notion that an inferiority complex exists with those who support Affirmative Action. Nothing is squeaky clean. But, the forces outside the mainstream that say that groups of people are inferior to others and oppose Affirmative Action are far greater than the few inside the system.

By the same token, I don't believe we can use two-hundred years of past discrimination as a reason for Affirmative Action. We can't rewrite history or say that we have to make up for the past.

The reason why it's ludicrous is because the protected groups that have used this have not offered a meaningful solution to its end and are convinced with the status quo. They will continue to use this as long as we have Affirmative Action.

I don't know exactly how to fix Affirmative Action. There are those who think we need to end it. Unless those who seek to end it provide a reasonable alternative, then I would be in favor of reforming these programs rather than ending them.

Our country needs to have a serious discussion about race, gender, class, and how we treat different groups of people. That's what it's all about. There are a lot of nice things that are said in public about how everyone should be given an equal opportunity to be the best person they can be. But, we all know that what we say in public isn't necessarily what we do in private. We must be honest with ourselves on this very point, or we will never get to the bottom of this issue and bring people together to realize the American Dream.

What a Riot!

In the fall of 1990, I was appointed by Councilmember Dave Guzzetti to be his representative on a task force that looked into a series of melees that occurred between students who were having a little too much of a good time, and police from around the area who, in some instances didn't use the most tactful means to control a bunch of rowdy partiers.

The task force did a six-month study of the causes which led to this event and prepared a report for the City Council with a list of recommendations. It was an interesting exercise.

I remember listening to a lot of testimony from folks who really cared about their community. They came from all walks of life and presented us with some interesting observations and ideas.

One of those interesting observations came from liquor store owner Bernie Richter who attributed the rowdiness to almost every other cause known to man—except alcohol.

"Alcohol didn't cause the riots," he said.

"Then what were they throwing at police, coke bottles?" I said to a fellow taskforce member.

Bernie Richter is now in the California Assembly.

Go figure.

My presence on the task force was the scene of one of my most embarrassing moments.

In a joint meeting with the City Council, then Councilmember Mary Anne Houx asked how she was going to abide by one of our recommendations. I think she thought adults were being targeted for something a bunch of young people had done.

I told her that she was just going to have to adhere to the rules like everyone else. The only problem was that I referred to her as "babe."

The conference room hushed for a moment of silence and then everyone broke out laughing.

As soon as the word left my mouth, I wanted to take it back. I was embarrassed.

I told her I was sorry.

Fortunately, Mary Anne had a sense of humor and was pretty good natured about it.

Still, I took some ribbing about it from fellow task force members as well as some in the media. I hope no one has it on tape.

Transportation

Many people wonder why we need public transportation. They claim that the buses are always empty.

Our transit system, CATS, has transported over half a million people just in the last year. In addition, the city runs a paratransit service, the Chico Clipper, that serves people with disabilities and senior citizens. These numbers continue to grow, and I am proud to say that I am one of those people.

After two failed attempts, I was appointed to the City of Chico's Community Transit Advisory Committee, or CTAC. As I watched the Council discuss the candidates and tally the votes, I was getting my first taste of local politics.

The third time was the charm and I was extremely happy to make it on the other side of a 4-3 vote. My appointment to the committee also made me a member of the county's Social Services Transportation Advisory Council (SSTAC).

At our first CTAC meeting, we had to pick someone to chair the meetings. Seeing how no one else was interested in doing it, I volunteered. I also volunteered to chair the SSTAC at my first meeting as a member of that committee. Like a running back going through an open hole, I seized the opportunity to do more.

Don't mistake this as some guy wanting power merely to satisfy his own ego. I thought being the chair would bring me closer to the people who are dealing with these issues on a day to day basis. You get to know what makes them tick. There is a lot to learn about issues such as transportation and I thought being the chair would give me the best perspective.

I had somewhat of a rocky start as chair of both committees. At the county level, I had to deal with some underhanded criticism of the previous chair, Bill Brashears.

In my first few months as a CTAC member, I was getting increasingly frustrated at the lack of attendance by my fellow committee members. There would be times where we would have as few as two members at a committee meeting. As far as I was concerned, I was sitting in on a glorified staff meeting.

Since I had tried on two other occasions to get on this committee, I wished I had known about the lack of attendance. That way, I could have written a letter to bring this to the City Council's attention in hopes it would lead to an earlier appointment. Why appoint someone to a board or commission if they aren't going to show up for meetings?

I wrote a letter to my fellow committee members expressing my disappointment and said that if they didn't plan on attending the meetings, they should resign from the committee so that someone else might have a chance to serve.

My letter drew praise from some members. It infuriated others. One member went so far as to write a letter to the City Council and the Board of Supervisors saying that I was a disgrace to the community and I should resign from the committee.

The City Council responded by instituting a policy where staff was to notify them if a committee member misses two consecutive meetings and the reasons for it. In spite of the crap I took, I think I did something right. They obviously agreed.

I get along very well with the city's Transportation Coordinator, Lynn McEnespy.

She has made herself readily available to me whenever I had a question, and she has been pretty open when it comes to new ideas about how to increase ridership and make the system run better.

I told her that we should shift some of our advertising dollars from print to television. I thought we would reach a lot more people who would consider riding the bus by purchasing air time on the local cable system.

Her initial response was less than favorable. She explained that the city had paid a huge sum of money to have a commercial produced and it didn't get them the return on their investment the first time around.

I told her I could get her a better deal than the outrageous price she had paid to a firm in Sacramento. She said she was willing to listen to any offers.

I arranged a meeting and two months later, we had bus commercials running up and down the cable system.

Who was in the commercial, you ask?

I'll let you figure that one out.

My interest in transportation comes primarily because I am a consumer of public transit. Despite what others may think, there are people who ride the bus. I ride the bus.

Since public transit is important to my quality of life, I want to take an active role as a citizen in doing what I can to make sure that it works for those who use it.

Triple-A Ball

"You don't know the difference between a sub-division and a cul-de-sac," Keith Cameron jokingly said as I told him I was applying for a spot on the Planning Commission for the City of Chico.

I certainly do now. In fact, I have learned a lot about city planning and local government since my recent appointment to the seven member panel. Shopping centers, sub-divisions, and parks don't appear by magic. As I contemplated running for a spot on the City Council, I looked at what I did and did not know about local government. There were some things I knew and there were important things I needed to learn, some gaps I needed to fill. Getting a spot on the commission would help to fill those gaps and expose me to another area of local government.

In my interview with the City Council, I recounted my years of city service and explained that while I was a green banana when it came to city planning, I felt I would bring a unique perspective to the commission. Remember, this is different than telling them they should pick me because I am disabled. I explained that this was another way I could serve my community and I would work hard to learn and understand the issues.

There were about twenty five people who applied for the four open slots. As the first two were being filled, I came up one vote short each time. I thought I was going to have to wait another day to crack this field.

Then, Dave Guzzetti joined Jim Owens, Michael McGinnis and Kimberly King to put me over the top. I cracked a smile and clenched my fist in elation when I saw what happened. I was also shocked and stunned as I went home to call Mom and Dad.

"Well Jon, you're at Triple-A ball now. People are gonna be looking at you," said Mike Hawkins. He's one of those who I talk politics with from time to time. He also works for the local Democratic Party.

Of course people are going to be looking at me. The meetings are on television.

When Melrose Place or Monday Night Football isn't on, they channel surf and watch the Planning Commission at work. Yeah, sure they do.

I will be the first one to tell people that I came to the Planning Commission as a green banana. I have spent a lot of time reading materials and asking questions of those who know the ins and outs of city planning.

I spent a lot of time in the outset with Planning Director, Clif Sellers, to get down some of the terminology. On the afternoon before Planning Commission meetings, he and I will go over questions I have regarding the agenda.

As part of being on the commission, the city pays for us to go to a conference once a year. I attended a Local Government Commission Conference in Los Angeles with Senior Planner, Tom Hayes. He helped me out a lot while I was at the conference. I learned a lot about the city's General Plan by being around him and I think he got a new perspective about me in the course of the time we were together.

When it comes to planning, you're not just coming into contact with the Planning Staff. You are exposed to other departments as well.

There may be an instance where I need to talk to Bob Boehm, the City Attorney about a conflict of interest issue.

The Director of Public Works, E.C. Ross, is generally in attendance at most of our meetings answering our questions.

As a planning commissioner, I have discovered that as the issues grow, so does my interaction with city staff.

Sometimes I wonder if my very presence on the commission hasn't caused a few heads to turn and wonder how this guy made it. Think about it. How many disabled people do you know are on their city planning commissions? I would venture to say not many.

At the Local Government Conference in Los Angeles, I was the only disabled person in the gathering that numbered over 600 people. I was kind of surprised at this judging by all that's being done to implement the Americans with Disabilities Act. You'd think the two would go together.

Whether they like it or not, those that depend on the recommendation of the Planning Commission, as well as the general public, have to deal with a guy whose situation might make them uncomfortable. If they want my support, they have to talk to me as someone other than a poster boy. Though it may make some people feel uneasy, I enjoy it.

Disabled Politics

If you are a farmer, you are probably going to keep your eyes on legislation that has to do with agricultural issues.

If you are woman, you are most likely to follow women's issues like funding for pre-natal care or breast cancer, education, and abortion.

Likewise, as a person with a disability, issues like healthcare, government assistance, and the ADA are more than just a passing interest to me.

In large part, the disabled community has relied on groups of individuals to get their message out. Personally, I am not aware of any large organizations or PAC's who represent people with disabilities in the same way as the AARP (American Association of Retired Persons) does for senior citizens, or the National Organization for Women advocates on behalf of women.

Don't get me wrong. The disability movement does have its advocates and lobbyists. A political machine exists.

Independent Living Centers that grew out of the fifties and sixties have taken up the mantle as being one of the primary advocacy groups for people with disabilities, especially in California where the idea was first born. These groups were started by people with disabilities who were the pioneers in fighting for our civil rights.

In my independent living class, I was taught that whenever I had a problem, I was to go to them and they would fix it for me. Everything would be all better.

Well, after a number of experiences with them, both in Chico and the San Francisco Bay Area, I think Independent Living Centers do some things very well, others not so well.

The director of the Independent Living Center in Chico is Rocky Burks. Like me, he's been around for a while. He has both supporters and detractors.

Rocky and I were both presidents of our respective Lions Clubs at the same time. I'm sure we both feel a commitment to giving something back, and likewise, he knows how to use his connections to benefit his agency. I don't have any problem with that.

Rocky and I agree on many things that have to do with the way in which we want to see the disability movement go. We also differ on a number of issues as well.

What has made our relationship the "love-hate" kind that you see on soap operas has been the path we take to get to our own destinations. Oftentimes, we just don't agree with each other's methods and it has made things a bit acrimonious.

Now, you may find this a bit trivial. I mean, who cares how you get there, as long as you get what you want? Right?

That's not necessarily so, especially if you think you're not getting your desired results.

Rocky has been at odds with me since the mid-eighties when we went head to head at a City Council meeting. We disagreed over the closure of a road to Bidwell Park. He wanted the road open. I wanted it closed.

I told the Council that as one who goes to the park without the use of a car, having too much car traffic would make me a vulnerable target. This would free up other wheelchair users to go about the park as they pleased.

He said that having car access to certain picnic tables was the main reason why he wanted the street to stay open.

The Council decided to make another set of tables accessible by car, and close the street.

While I have since moved on to other things, I have heard that he still carries a grudge over this one.

This was the first time I could see that I could be my own advocate and not rely so much on the "system."

A number of times, I considered going back to the old ways of doing things.

I remembered what my teachers had told me, but I have since learned that while they remain a resource, they are not always a good army to go with into battle.

Why is this so?

First, as an advocacy group, their interests may be totally different than mine. They have different agendas and people they want to look after and protect. If what I am doing doesn't fit their agenda or interferes with the relationships they have with certain politicians, they'll either ignore you—or fight you.

Second, an agency like that has so many things on their plate. In all fairness, they are too busy.

They are faced with placing people in housing while finding attendants for others. They deal with people coming in and spilling their guts out to them. Lord knows, I've done that a few times.

For many, they are a primary support system for those who need it.

Are they going to have time to assist me because I want some bollards taken out because there isn't enough room to cross the street? Are they going to drop what they're doing when I see that the downtown crosswalks are being decorated with a brick pattern which will make it more difficult for people to cross the street? Are they going to intervene on what I deemed a safety issue when it came to a skateboard/bicycle ban on downtown sidewalks?

I chose not to go to them because of several reasons. On one hand, I don't think any of these things would have been high on their priority list. This is neither good nor bad. It's just the way it is. They are an agency with a bureaucracy. Time was of the essence on some of these things and their support might have been too little too late, especially in the case where they were laying down the crosswalk.

Again, their interests might be different than mine. They might have certain people they want to kiss up to and there might not be enough time to tell each other who your friends are and who you are kissing.

Finally, I had built up a rapport with city staff that made me confident that I could do it alone.

Just before I culminated a two-year effort to get bollards (a 1920's style cement blocks shaped like cones that were used to keep cars from cutting street corners) removed from several downtown street corners, staff informed me that they were having some problems with the Chico Heritage Association. They wanted them to stay for historical purposes.

"Hey, if they are a part of history, we ought to take 'em out and put them in a museum with a little caption underneath. They no longer serve their intended purpose and have since become a hazard," I told one staff person. I don't think they expressed my entire sentiments to those folks. It probably would have taken a lot longer.

Yes, I did get a call from the Heritage Association and I very politely explained my position.

Shortly after that, the bollards were taken out.

As the crosswalks were being laid, I got a hold of someone just in the nick of time.

"Do you plan to put those bricks going across the walkways?" I asked.

"Yes," they said.

"Please don't."

"Why?"

I explained that the brick pattern was quite bumpy and it would take longer for people who are mobility impaired to cross the street on such a short light. I also told them it might cause those wearing high heels to trip on a wet surface.

"So, what do you suggest we do?" they said.

"Why don't you put a solid strip that goes down the middle of the street?"

When the project was finished, they had what some affectionately call, "Studebaker Strips."

The skateboard ban was a lot more difficult, but I was confident that it would go through if done the right way.

The issue was first brought up to the City Council a couple of years ago. The main proponents of the ban were downtown business owners who didn't want skateboarders around their businesses.

After hearing arguments which basically attacked those who rode skateboards, the City Council opted for a partial ban during business hours and would re-visit the issue in a year.

I was the only one who talked about skateboarding downtown as purely an issue of safety. I left the meeting a little bit frustrated at what happened.

A year later, I wrote a letter to the City Council asking them to implement a total skateboard ban on downtown sidewalks. They kept their word and put it on the agenda.

I pleaded my case in front of the City Council in the late hours of the evening. That's exactly how I wanted it.

The council directed City Attorney, Bob Boehm, to start the process of amending the current ordinance.

The next hearing was not like the first. Oh, I was alone alright. But, there were many on the other side that were waiting to take their shots. Most of them were young people who weren't old enough to vote.

I kept my remarks fairly brief the second time around. I had already done it once, and even though some of the councilmembers were new, I had talked to them previously about it.

I took some shots that night, but in the end, I was on the right side of a 4-3 vote.

I was very pleased about what happened because in my heart I knew what I was doing was right. This was about safety. It was about my safety and the safety of others.

Those over at Independent Living weren't especially pleased with me on this one.

They said that what I did hurt the movement and that everyone was going to target their wrath on people in wheelchairs.

I wasn't surprised by their reaction. Since it didn't come from them, of course they are going to oppose it.

These three instances are just a part of my overall philosophy when it comes to trying to make a difference. City service is just as important.

If people see that a person is someone other than a complainer, an individual that reacts only in times of crisis, you're not going to have as much credibility as when you have something else to offer.

In many instances, this is how the "system" reacts. They don't follow issues. They are not prepared. And sometimes, they get caught with their pants down.

So, what does this all mean?

It means that the disability movement needs to go back to its roots while at the same time redistributing the workload.

Independent Living Centers should stick to helping people on the most personal levels and remain as a resource to which we can look to for information. They should go from being in the front seat on political issues to taking a behind the scenes approach.

Remember, some of those disabled people who started Independent Living Centers are being replaced by "social engineers" who just don't have a clue when it comes to politics.

Next, people with disabilities need to get involved just like everyone else, in a pro-active manner. It is important to participate in the activities of local government.

That's where it all starts.

To those who have said, "I can't do it,"—try again. I said the same thing almost a decade ago.

Protests and arrests have their place, but developing relationships with decision makers and not waiting for a crisis to occur in order to get something accomplished is even more important. Issues should be discussed year round until solutions are reached.

Do I think the disability movement needs to go the route of the AARP? Well, maybe not exactly. However, we should learn lessons from those groups that have the ears of those in government. A big-tent lobbying group is worth consideration.

As far as my relationship with Rocky and others who preach the virtues of the "system," we each sail our own ships. He is the captain of his vessel and I am the proud skipper of my ship. If we clash while sailing the high seas, so be it. I'm just going to keep on sailing.

The Players

If the Planning Commission is the Triple-A level of local politics, then the City Council must be the big leagues. It is unless you want to be a supervisor, state legislator, member of Congress, Senator, or President. I don't know if anyone has actually started at the bottom and worked their way to the Presidency without missing a level. Maybe I should give it a shot and see how far I go.

Over the last few years, I get closer and closer to making a run for a spot on the Chico City Council. Each time I have thought about it though, two reasons cause me to put it off for another election cycle.

First of all, I have been pretty content with what I have done as just an ordinary citizen. I can pick and choose my battles and not have to worry about every little thing that goes on in city government. It's a comfortable position to be in.

The other thing that bothers me about making such a run centers on money. A person must be crazy to raise thousands of dollars for a seat on the City Council that pays around fifteen dollars a week plus health benefits. Is it worth being heckled by folks who call in their comments anonymously to the local newspaper, or being misquoted by reporters who are more concerned with getting an interesting story than an accurate one? Rarely do you ever get a chance to go after your critics. That would suggest that you are weak. You can't take the heat. Is it worth having to put in many hours of preparation, long meetings, and constant scrutiny for such a measly wage? I say there is a price for hard work, accountability, and responsible leadership. You have to give something if you want to attract good people.

There are people from both sides of the political spectrum on the Chico City Council. I like that. I mean, I wouldn't want a council of only liberals, conservatives, or even moderates for that matter. You'd have group think and wouldn't be able to get anything done. I have learned two things in my dealings with "the players." In trying to get something through, I or anyone for that matter, needs just four votes. That's it. So, don't exclude anyone because you never know where those votes are going to come from.

The other is to view victory and defeat as something that can change at a moment's notice. If I leave a council meeting on the short end of a decision, I look at what went wrong, and change my game plan accordingly.

Each victory reminds me never to be complacent. Always be on your guard because if you are not prepared, someone will come out of nowhere and snatch it away from you.

Who Am I, Politically? What Do I Stand For?

Along with my involvement in local politics, I spend a lot of time reading about the issues and staying on top of current events. As a Planning Commissioner, I have to keep tabs on what's being talked about. This gives me a chance to learn about the issues and the people who want me to vote for or against certain projects, support or oppose the commission's recommendations.

Once again, I can't help but say that putting one more notch in my holster with this latest commission assignment has opened my eyes to the complex nature of government. You cannot appreciate what I have said unless you are involved as a direct participant in the process.

While there is no doubt as to the political nature of government, I have come to realize that the role of government is about resolving problems with a look to the future. You can apply this to both local and national issues.

For example, I may choose to support or deny a use permit because our General Plan, a document that covers a period of time, says it may not be an appropriate use for the area.

Likewise, whether the President supports or opposes the sending of troops into a hot spot half-way around the world has a direct impact on what we do today, tomorrow, and the next day.

When it comes to the role of local government I see those elected officials as the custodians of the vital services that affect our quality of life. Police, fire, public transit are just a few of those things that are essential to our day to day activities.

Good planning, which includes a mixture of goods and services that are accessible to everyone, is an essential to the function of local government. When it comes to the big picture, I also have a vision of how I see the role of state and national government

For example, I see government as a tool for helping people who are in need of assistance. Even though it is not directly expressed in our Constitution, I believe that everyone has the right to quality healthcare, no matter who they are. As far as I'm concerned, it is just as much a part of life, liberty, and the pursuit of happiness as anything else. If we are going to be a society that says life is an inalienable right, then we better be willing to place a value on the quality of that life as well. As I see it right now, society has chosen to ignore this very point.

It sickens me that there are so many people that either don't have healthcare, or can't get it because the private sector won't let them have it. I know. I am one of those people.

"I want the members of the Congress to work with me, and I will work with them, so that at long last we can make good on Harry Truman's commitment to basic health insurance for every family in America," said Michael Dukakis in his acceptance speech at the Democratic National Convention. Dukakis was on the right track and I was moved by this statement.

As we all know, Dukakis lost. Bush won. I was depressed for a few days. We got a kinder, gentler, laissez-faire president, and healthcare was shoved back into the freezer of American politics.

In the 1992 presidential race, healthcare was taken out of its cryogenic state as Bill Clinton sounded the clarion call for healthcare reform almost everywhere he went. I was excited. Finally, I thought we were going to get something done.

While Clinton was able to use this issue to help get him into the White House, the only thing it guaranteed was healthcare for him and his family.

I believe that this was the biggest domestic policy failure of his presidency thus far.

To blame the First Lady for the healthcare fiasco is too easy. Republicans have done a great job of painting her as the evil witch who is going to take away everyone's health insurance. This couldn't be farther from the truth, but everyone bought it.

Of course I didn't think she should have been the one leading the troops on this one, but, I was willing to wait and see how it was going to play out. After a very good State of the Union speech by President Clinton, the foundation that was built in hopes of getting something done was whittled away to sawdust. The subject of healthcare lost another life and will not be seen or heard from in the foreseeable future.

Even though many blame the First Lady and all those "rocket scientists" for coming up with a healthcare plan too long to read, and too difficult to comprehend, I point to Clinton's inexperience with the Washington establishment as the real reason why healthcare reform failed. He thought he could do it all by himself and didn't realize he would need to reach a broad national consensus.

If I were in President Clinton's shoes, I would have put together a bi-partisan blue ribbon commission to craft a bill with the features he wanted to see in such a package. Such a bill with bipartisan support would be more likely to pass the Congress and hopefully make a difference in the lives of the American people, like me.

If a healthcare bill didn't pass, Clinton could have shared the blame with Congress instead of shouldering it all himself. Then, he could have made it a campaign issue in the next election. Instead, it could come back to haunt him.

When it comes to welfare reform, I think it should be a system that requires work for those who are able. If childcare is needed, it should be provided. People need to have a sense of understanding that they were put on this earth to make a contribution to the common good. Thus, we better be willing to pay for it instead of expecting something for nothing.

While I may be a Democrat, issues are more important to me than party. My interest and involvement in politics is a part of who I am, not necessarily that I am a Republican, Democrat or Independent.

Who Am I? And Why Am I Here?

So who is Jonathan Studebaker, you ask? And, why am I here?

The who is easy for me to answer. The why is a bit more difficult.

Let's deal with the who first.

It just so happens that I apply the same philosophy about living life to defining who I am.

When it comes to my own self-actualization, I know who's in control—me. Even though I may be influenced by people, I am the only person who can best define me, no one else. Other people can judge me, but they don't know who I am.

If at some point I don't like who I am. I can change that. Much of what I have written describes who I am and what I believe. Though it goes very far in painting my self-portrait, it remains incomplete. There is more to me than what the eye can see.

For starters, I am a happy person. I like myself and I enjoy what life has given me up to this point. I believe that life has more to offer in the years to come, just as I have more to offer it.

Am I happy all of the time? No, of course not. I have my down moments just like everyone else.

There have been a few times where I have asked, "Why me?" There have been instances where feel I got a bad break—no pun intended.

But, those who say that I am a bitter person are totally wrong. They don't know me.

Moreover, I don't think they've considered getting to know me.

I am not a bitter person. Nor has the thought of being bitter even entered my mind—ever.

Now, I don't consider myself to be intelligent in an academic sense. Neither do I think I'm stupid. Let's just say that I am a quick learner and I have acquired a thirst for learning from those who know what's going on.

With the various committee assignments I've had, this has become especially important in knowing the issues in order to make responsible decisions. When it comes to being in the public eye, I have not confused being presentable with putting on a happy face. That is, what you see is what you get.

I may choose my words carefully, but I am not one who plays games with anyone. Furthermore, I don't mince words either.

I have a sense of humor and often allow my close friends to make fun of me when they get the chance. I know for a fact that others would be offended by some of the things they say, but I say them as well and it doesn't bother me. If you can't laugh at yourself, who can you laugh at?

Do I make fun of them? How about others?

Of course, I make fun of other people. We're all guilty of that at one time or another.

While I can't describe what it is exactly, there is a force that drives me to go on living life. There is an inner determination that causes me to continue to shoot for the stars, and continue reaching for the top. For someday, I believe I will get there.

What people may not know is that there exists a side of me that has a lot to offer in the way of love and affection. Sure, I love my family and close friends, but until I find that special someone, this part of me will remain a hidden treasure.

On the other side of the coin, I am impatient. I am a slob. I have an ego. I have a penchant for holding grudges. And when it comes to male-female roles, I liken myself to Fred Flintstone.

Like any Taurus, I am stubborn and I love the smell of money.

What I mean by being impatient, I think of it in terms of not being able to wait to get something I want. I have what my family calls, an "I-G complex." I-G stands for instant gratification. At one time or another, everyone in our family has had an "I-G attack."

When someone is having an I-G attack, those not involved would say, "I-G! I-G!!"

I had more than my fair share of I-G attacks as a child. Today, I can say they happen on occasion.

One of my more visible faults is that I am a slob. Neatness is not one of my virtues.

Part of what makes me a slob is that I am a pack rat. I like to save everything. It is extremely difficult for me to throw something away. Once I keep something, I am more likely to find the closest spot available for its home. I am not very organized. Sometimes, finding an important paper is likened to finding a needle in a haystack, literally.

When others step in and try to clean up my messes in hopes of assembling some kind of order, it bothers me because I don't know exactly where they put things.

You see, I have convinced myself that my messiness is part of my being organized.

My parents' house is very similar. They have piles of papers and stuff scattered about the house.

Thus, I attribute my lack of organization skills to the idea that I inherited it from my folks. Hey, I've got to blame it on someone, right?

Big or small, each of us has an ego. No doubt about it. While growing up, my parents were always cognizant of not letting my head swell. They insisted that with notoriety came responsibility. By their example, I understood that the best way to accept a compliment was to be gracious and humble.

When I am out in public, I keep my ego at home. That's where it belongs.

But when I am at home, it's a different story. My home is my castle, and it is where I tend to let my ego run rampant, like a teenage runaway.

For starters, I have pictures of myself all over the house. Cam always jokes with me how I don't have enough of them around.

"I think you need to put up another picture of yourself," he said.

Along with the pictures, I have awards and plaques in various rooms scattered about my humble abode. To me, they're nicer to look at then those gaudy animal pictures my roommate Lisa used to hang up.

When I did sports commentaries for Channel 24, I always recorded and watched them, sometimes over and over again. Even today, I have a good laugh when I take out an old tape.

I never miss the opportunity to let my friends and family know when I make the newspaper or land on the tube.

"What did you do now?" is my mother's response.

Only amongst my closest friends do I let my ego run amok. Every time I do, they are always there to rein it in. It's all done in good fun.

While I have on occasion let my ego grow to the size of a boulder in the privacy of my own home, it provides a release for the times when a darker side of me has emerged and grown to similar proportions. There have been moments where a lack of self-esteem rules my world. I see how the two extremes counter each other to strike a balance. However, one should not mistake it as being two different personas. I keep both of them tucked away somewhere in my house.

One of my biggest faults is that I like to hold grudges. I don't forget the times where someone has done me wrong. I have a hard time letting things go and forgiving others. It is one of those things I need to work on.

If there is ever a question I think about most, it centers on the future. What lies ahead for me? How am I going to fill that niche? Or better yet, why am I here?

Will I find that rightful place in society doing something that makes me happy and puts a few bucks in my pocket? Or, am I going to remain a pauper, doomed to a life on welfare and government assistance?

Is there a chance that with a lot of hard work and a little luck, I will be successful? Or will another golden opportunity go awry because of a freak accident?

Does there exist a life of champagne wishes and caviar dreams? Corn dogs and iced tea will do just fine for me. Or, is there an alternative on the horizon, worse than anyone could imagine?

I vacillate back and forth when I think about the future. Sometimes it can be described as a delirium filled with hope and anticipation. Other times it is a deep, dark, picture etched with fear and paranoia.

If you think about the future too much, you forget about today. So, I think about what I can do today in order to make things better for tomorrow, and the next day. Former Denver Broncos running back Floyd Little once said, "Play each play as if it were your last, because someday, it will."

Though Little was better known for his exploits on the football field, I thought what he said to be inspiring, and quite profound.

Most football coaches see this statement as inspirational. I also view it as a reality check.

If you change this just a bit, it could read this way:

"Live each day as if it were your last, because someday it will."

This definitely puts things in a different light.

To think what the future may hold doesn't come without a brief look at the past, and a careful examination of the present.

For the most part, the past meant football. It meant pursuing my hopes and dreams.

It meant paying my dues as an assistant while going to school. It meant spending five years to get someone to offer me a job interview. It meant having the opportunity to get my foot in the door being shattered by a freak accident. It meant finally landing an interview I had worked so hard to get.

It meant having to deal with state bureaucrats who thought I was trying to take advantage of the system because I told them I was doing an internship that didn't pay. It meant turning down a chance to pursue my childhood dreams. It meant having to turn down the chance to prove myself at a major college program. It meant not knowing what would have happened if I had left Chico and gone to the Hawkeye State.

Who knows, I could be some big time assistant right now. They'd be doing all kinds of stories about how I overcame the obstacles of my disability. Or, they could have found me frozen solid in a snow drift. Either way, I'm a hero. One as a dead hero, but still a hero.

It didn't happen though.

My old boss, Mike Bellotti is now the Head Coach at University of Oregon. I haven't heard from him.

Have I bothered to pick up the phone to see if he needs a kicking coach?

No. I guess that's my fault. My mother has said many times over the years, I would be happy doing just about anything for a professional football team or Division I college program.

She's right.

I would love to find a place in the corner of the front office of the Kansas City Chiefs and make whatever kind of contribution that will help them win the Super Bowl. I would do it in a second.

So, let's consider going back to football a long shot and explore other possibilities.

The moment I got off the phone with Jim Walden, I had to consider my options.

Yes, there was disappointment. I was angry and frustrated. I felt like the system had given me a raw deal.

Once the anger and frustration wore off, I realized something very important had taken place. That is, I accomplished a very important goal.

I was able to sit across from the Head Coach of a Division I football program and explain how I could make a viable contribution.

This was important because in the five years previous, all I got were letters. Up to this point, I had done a lot of talking, but Coach Walden was the first to listen.

Accomplishing this goal left me content for the time being to put my childhood dreams on the back burner. I sat in my wheelchair and thought to myself, "What else do I like to do?"

The first idea that came to mind was public speaking. After all, I love to talk.

I went to my back bedroom and shuffled some papers trying to find something I had doodled on a while back. I don't remember exactly what it was, only that it had to do with public speaking. Bound and determined to find it, I knew it was somewhere.

Eureka! A natural-born pack rat struck gold!

In a stack of papers, I found a sketch of a megaphone with the words: PROJECT SPEAK OUT scratched on it.

At first glance, I wondered when and where it came from. I couldn't remember if it was something I had spent some time thinking about, or was it one of those ideas I so frequently come up with at some ungodly hour of the night.

While gazing at the sketch, the wheels started churning. I got out another piece of paper and jotted ideas down as fast as I could write them down.

The Iowa experience gave me reason to believe that there should be someone who can educate others about the abilities of people with disabilities. I scribbled on my paper some target audiences that would be receptive. Most of them were civic groups and local organizations.

Next, I thought about the children. I thought about all of the times I was stopped at the store by kids with questions. I thought about starting a school program.

Finally, I knew that I had to do something other than disability awareness. I would get bored very easily if I didn't have anything else to offer.

I thought about the few times I spoke in church for my brother. This gave me the idea to be a motivational speaker, not a minister.

I spent the next few weeks working tirelessly, like one of Santa's elves. I put together a series of presentations I could use.

George Thurlow gave me some ideas about my brochure. He said I needed a catchy phrase or slogan to catch someone's attention. He offered up "education through motivation."

It sounded great to me.

When I told Cam about the slogan, he asked what it meant.

I said, "I don't know, but it sure as hell sounds good."

We had a good laugh.

With my speeches on paper and my type-set copy ready to go to the printer, I used the money my Grandma Elster lent me to go to Iowa, and launched PROJECT SPEAK OUT.

Grandma didn't mind. She said I didn't even have to pay her back. I got my first gig as a keynote speaker for Disability Awareness Week at my almamater, Chico State. I called a few of my friends to see if they would come.

I thought there would be at least fifty people for my debut.

Nancy Hermanson, Director of Disabled Student Services, was expecting a good turn-out. She said there was a lot of publicity surrounding the event. As my eyes scanned the smattering of faces in the room, I was disappointed at what I saw. Yes, a few of my friends were there, and a reporter from the school newspaper showed up. Unfortunately, that was about it. I counted twelve people in the audience. Despite the small gathering, I was determined to give those twelve people the best I had to offer. Afterwards, everyone came up and talked to me. I thanked them for listening.

Not long after my speech at Chico State, things started to pick up. I got some positive feedback from a mailer I had sent to area schools. I was able to go to eight schools during the first year and nine schools in the second year. I enjoyed every moment of it. Seeing the kids' faces looking straight at you, their eyes with curiosity written all over them was thrilling. I knew I was doing something right.

Anticipating their questions and responding to them, I was able to see a myriad of expressions from each child.

"How do you sleep?" a student asked cautiously.

"In my bed," I replied.

The face said it all.

Heck, I was having so much fun talking to kids, even school lunch began to taste good again. I always liked school lunch. Weird, eh?

After watching me do my thing, a few teachers thought I should give their profession a try. I thanked them for their praise but politely declined the invitation.

With one year under my belt, I spent the summer writing grant proposals in hopes of expanding my school program and take it around the country. I was fairly successful in my own school district, but I knew that it wouldn't be long before the well would run dry. Also, there is some truth to the fact that some schools are strapped and by taking the funding question out, I would reach a lot more children.

All of my efforts came up empty. I sent a grant proposal to the Dole Foundation. You know, the one set up by the infamous Senator from Kansas who as many of us are aware, was injured in World War II. Their organization funds grants to help disabled people get jobs. I knew I was going about it in a roundabout way, but even for a first time grant writer, I felt good about my submission.

In turning down my proposal, they said I was unable to prove that my program was actually going to guarantee that disabled people were going to get jobs because these kids heard my presentation. They wanted quantitative, tangible results. I was befuddled by their request and thought what they were asking was unreasonable. How was I to determine, much less prove, that when a six year old child grew up to be a business owner, that they gave a job to a disabled person as a result of hearing my program? If I had been doing it for twenty years, I might be able to do it, but this was a pilot program. I didn't have time to go through the mental exertion of trying to figure that one out.

Furthermore, I couldn't believe my program was being held up to such scrutiny. Do they hold others like the D.A.R.E program up to the same microscope? I highly doubt it. In fact, I don't know what they can prove. I think it just happens to be one of those programs we support because it makes us feel good.

On the other hand, I had letters from children who shared stories of how they were no longer afraid to play with kids with disabilities. Some of them explained how they could adapt their games so that other kids could play.

I may be very naive when it comes to grant writing. But I think like many other entities, the non-profit industry has its own good ole boy network that is prone to stifle good ideas because they came from those outside the system.

As I continued doing my school program, I spend the better part of my second year trying to expand my audience base. I did this by traveling to government agencies around the Pacific Northwest and giving presentations on the importance of putting people with disabilities in the workplace.

I got the idea from a friend of mine, Jennifer Jones, who was working for the Bureau of Land Management in Washington D.C. We were both in television as she worked as a news producer for KHSL-TV while I was at KCPM. We all used to hook up on Friday nights and shoot the breeze at one of Chico's watering holes.

I told her I was trying to make it on the circuit and she suggested I send out a direct-mail piece to all of their regional and district offices I had some degree of success with her idea. The audiences I spoke to were generally friendly and eager to learn. I enjoyed doing this and really felt like the message I was delivering was getting through.

During my excursions to these offices, I got to see a lot of the country. I traveled throughout the northern region of Nevada by car, giving speeches in Winnemucca, Elko, and Battle Mountain. The trip didn't come without some R&R in Reno where I won a hundred bucks playing keno and a stop at a local Hooters for their famous chicken wings and friendly waitresses.

I took another road trip with my father to Boise, Idaho where I gave a keynote speech to the employees of the Boise National Forest. The speech went really well except for my voice. For some reason, the gremlins had gotten to it that day.

This trip was a memorable one for me because he and I got to spend some quality time together. We talked a lot while passing the time on the road. We ate at diners we wouldn't have considered going to if mother had been with us. For instance, we went to a diner called the T and A Cafe.

This was a good old-fashioned father and son trip with a heavy splash of male bonding. I hope we can do it a few more times.

Now that I have explained both the past and present, it still seems difficult for me to tell you why I am here. Why am I here? Is it something I need to be preoccupied with, or should I let others decide that long after I am gone?

I would be happy if I could return to football in a way in which I felt I could make a contribution to the success of an organization or program. Once you've been a football coach, or involved with a program, you can't escape it. There is no feeling like it. This door will always remain open, even if it's just a crack. I still have dreams about being a head football coach and winning the Super Bowl.

Public speaking is something I hope to continue doing because there is still a lot of work that needs to be done in terms of educating people about individuals with disabilities.

I enjoy sharing the good word with others. I never miss a chance to talk and listen to people as we exchange ideas and information. This is the information age and we need to spend less time listening to ourselves in front of the mirror and talk to each other a lot more.

If I were to line up my ducks in threes, I would have to include the possibility of making a contribution in the area of public service. I have come a long way since I was appointed to the Affirmative Action Committee, and I think I have done some good things. But, if you follow the rules of negative entropy, the work is not done.

I will consider my options in terms of moving up the political ladder. Heck, I wouldn't mind living at 1600 Pennsylvania Avenue. If FDR could do it, why can't I?

I believe public service is noble and is something we should all do in some way, shape, or form. We should all make a contribution to the common good. It's never too late and anyone can do it.

I want to be happy. I want to be healthy. I want to live life to the fullest and make the world a better place than when I arrived here on May 20, 1965.

There are some things I wish I could change, but I can't. There are some things I want to do, but haven't. Perhaps I can share those things with you thirty years from now.

But, if I were to tell you what the future holds, I would probably say that I have nowhere else to go but up.

Who Are You? And Why Are You Here?

The alarm clock goes off at 6:00 a.m. telling you it's time to get up. What do you do?

If you're like me, you probably wish the darn thing didn't go off. After all, you could use a bit more sleep. Right?

Your first instinct is to hit the "SNOOZE" button so you can sleep just a little bit longer. Depending on how quickly you get showered, shampooed, and shined, you may hit that button two or three more times.

I keep my alarm clock far away from my outstretched hand so that in order for me to turn it off, I have to get into my wheelchair and go over to do it.

Whether you are an early riser, or a night owl who likes to sleep in, each day presents us with many decisions to be made, many questions to be answered. Some of them are easy.

What am I going to wear to work?

Do I want a Big Mac or a Quarter Pounder for lunch?

What's on the tube tonight?

Where will I go on my vacation? Disneyland or Hawaii?

Others are a bit more difficult.

Where do I want to live?

Can I really afford a new car?

Or, how about the ever popular: What do I want to do with my life? What do I want to be? Where do I want to go?

In one of her classic songs, Diana Ross asks, "Do you know, where you're going to? Do you like the things that life is showing you? Do you know?"

Waiting until the last minute is usually our first response in answering the hard questions, in dealing with tough decisions. We all like to procrastinate, right?

Perhaps dealing with difficult decisions causes us to question our own ability to make important decisions. Then, we second guess ourselves once the decision or choice has been made.

Maybe we worry too much about what others will think.

Or, we put undue pressure on ourselves when we see these choices as a burden rather than an opportunity.

As you read this chapter, I want you to seize this opportunity and ask yourself two very important questions.

Who am I? And, why am I here?

That's right. Who am I? And, why am I here?

When I think about these two statements, I can't help but remember when I first heard these words so profoundly spoken. It was during the 1992 presidential campaign when during one of the Vice-Presidential debates, Ross Perot's running mate, Admiral James Stockdale, uttered these words in response to a question. You could tell the guy was very uncomfortable on the stage in front of a large TV audience, but it was obviously something he really wanted to say.

Before you ponder these two questions, I want you to keep in mind a few things.

First, know and trust that what you are about to embark on is NOT a burden.

Rather, it is an OPPORTUNITY! It is not a chore. It's an adventure!

When you ask yourself these two questions, think of it as painting your own self-portrait. You are painting a picture for you, and everyone to see. Like any good artist, we need to allow ourselves plenty of time to paint our picture. We need plenty of time to find these answers. It's not something you can do in an hour, a day, or even a month. Right? After all, Rome wasn't built in a day. It took twenty years to build the Sistine Chapel, and over two hundred years for the pyramids.

When painting our self-portrait, we must be aware that there are no right or wrong brushstrokes. This is not a paint-by-numbers experience. Whatever is right is what makes us happy.

And if we aren't happy with our picture, what can we do with it?

We can change it by simply touching it up a little bit. You know, add a color here or there.

Or, if we really don't like it, we can get a new canvas and start all over again. And it is okay to do that too.

Once we are satisfied with our picture, we should look at our work of art. See it! Feel it! Touch it! Admire it! Then, it is time that we let others know who we are, and why we are here by showing them our "work of art."

Keeping these things in mind, it is time to begin to answer these two questions.

Who am I? And, why am I here?

A good place to start with this would be with your name. That is, your full name. Do you know how you got your name? Where did it come from?

For myself, my mother liked the name Jonathan. Peter came from my great-great-grandfather. Later, I would incorporate Charles as a part of my name. It came in a roundabout way.

When I was a wee tike, about four or five, my mother used to take me out of the bathtub and wrap me up in a bunch of towels. She carried me from room to room, calling me her "chickie, peep-peep."

From age six to about ten, I was referred to as "the chicken." Mind you, they never called me chicken, it's just that in everyday conversation they would refer to me as an object. For instance, if Mom and Dad needed to go out, one of them might ask, "What are we going to do with the chicken?" I was too young to get all PC about it, and since they never called me "chicken," I didn't care.

In junior high, I went from "chicken" to "Chicken Charles." And when I reached high school, my parents called me Charles. It has been that way ever since.

Perhaps as a child, you were given a special nickname by your parents. Or, maybe you have a unique name that means something in another language or has a special significance in a given culture. As kids, we may not have liked some of the nicknames our friends or relatives gave us, but hey, we were kids then.

Next, let's think about the personality traits that make you special. What are the qualities about you, which make you who you are? For example, is it love? Are you a loving person? Do you like others? Do like yourself? Are you willing to accept the love that others have to give you?

Are you a responsible person? Do you take responsibility for your actions, or are you always looking for someone else to take the blame for something that may have been your fault?

Do you trust others? Can others put their faith in you? You know, aside from love, trust is a very important word in my vocabulary.

During the course of a day, there are many things I can do for myself. However, there are times when I need some assistance. For example, even though I can give myself a bath, I still need someone to lift me into the bathtub. With my bones being fragile, I have to put my trust in whoever is helping me. I have to feel comfortable knowing that they will do their best not to drop me. While I feel it is important to trust others, I have to let people know that they can put their trust in me as well. It may sound like something a politician would say, but it's true. Trust is a two-way street.

So, are you a determined individual, or do you let obstacles stand in your way? Do you give up easily, or do you fight the good fight, knowing that there's a pot of gold at the end of the rainbow?

Now, let's focus on the things that are of interest to you, the people you care about. That tells us a lot about who you are.

First, how about your family or close friends? Are there a few people in your inner circle that have helped to make you who you are? I have talked about a few of mine in this book.

What about your religious or spiritual beliefs? Are they important to you? So often, people are criticized for not belonging to a "certain" religion, or the "right" religion. I think that's a pile of crap. If you are a Catholic, great. A Protestant? No problem. A Muslim? Sure, what's wrong with that? Hey, I don't care if you're an atheist, or you belong to the Church of Monday Night Football. It is important for you to know that whatever you believe, whatever makes you happy, is what is right for you. Your religious or spiritual beliefs are a part of who you are.

As you identify your religious beliefs, why not throw in your political ones as well. There is nothing sacred here. Are you a conservative or liberal? Or, is it somewhere in between? Are you a "Reagan Democrat" or a "Clinton Republican?" Maybe you are an Independent and voted for Ross Perot? Perhaps you are conservative when it comes to some issues and liberal when it comes to others. No matter how simple or complex your political orientation might be, it is a part of your picture. It's part of who you are.

The next part of our self-portrait involves the things we like to do for fun. Let me ask you, when was the last time you had fun? I mean, really had fun? What do you like to do for fun? Are you a sports fan or a movie buff? Do you like to cook? Fish? Hunt? Read or sing? Do you have any hobbies like stamp collecting or bird watching? My mother loves birds.

Part of living life means having fun. If you like your work so much that it is fun for you, so much the better. On the other hand, we get so wrapped up in our work that we neglect the things that interest us, the people we care about. Getting stuck in the same routine without having some sort of recreation or leisure activity makes life less fulfilling and somewhat meaningless.

Speaking of our work, whether you currently have a job or volunteer your time, deciding on what you want to do with your life is an important part of your self-portrait. It is the most recognizable aspect that communicates to others who you are.

Let's say you want to try something different and possibly make a career move. You don't want to spend your entire life at the same old job doing the same old thing. I bet you know more people who don't like their jobs than people who do. I mean, can't you see a bunch of people complaining about their work in the smoking lounge at break time. It's become tradition.

So, is it alright to make the "dreaded" career move?

You bet it's alright!! And there is nothing dreaded about it. Remember, whatever career you choose, you can always change it. Experts say that today's worker will have many different jobs doing many different things.

For myself, I started by coaching football. When that didn't quite go according to plan, I chose public speaking. Now, as I try to make it on the speaking circuit, I am looking to further my opportunities in other areas, like public service. The key here is to open as many doors without closing any. Even though I am not involved in football right now, I may find an opportunity to go back into coaching someday.

Sure it may be difficult to just go ahead and make that move from one career to another. I know it's hard enough just to find one job, let alone look for another. It's not that easy. What's important here is that you allow yourself to explore other possibilities. If you don't like what you are doing, change it. Think about doing something else. No matter how you may feel about your current situation, remember to view this as an opportunity to make a positive change in your life. I guarantee your mind will be more readily available to new opportunities.

If there is something out there you really want to do, and you feel in your heart that you have the capabilities to do a particular job, are you going to put those dreams aside just because a couple of people tell you that you can't do it? HELL NO!!! If you believe you can do it, there is no one out there who will bring you down, except yourself. Don't believe the people who tell you that "you can't." Use them as your source of inspiration.

As you think about these things, your name, your interests, your hobbies, your beliefs, and your work, let us suppose that each of these aspects is one color. When you put these colors together, you have a picture. You have a self-portrait that tells others who you are, and why you are here.

Too often that we let others define who we are, and why we are here. We allow them to label us as being something we aren't. When we allow this to happen, a number of things occur.

It allows others to paint our picture according to how they see us. They pick which brush. They choose which color. They decide what your picture is going to look like. When they get done with yours, they start telling others how to paint their picture.

Handing your paintbrush over to others so they can paint your picture, keeps you away from the drawing board. It takes you out of the decision making process. The more you let others decide things for you, the greater the chance you are going to question your ability to make important decisions. You will fall into a trap of seeing these choices as a burden rather than an opportunity. Or maybe, you will decide to fold up the tent, and just give up.

More importantly though, when you allow others to seize control you relinquish the power to make your own decisions. You give up the right to self-determination. You give up the opportunity to answer the question, "Who am I," and "Why am I here?" Too many of us are handing our paintbrushes to others. Don't let others tell you who you are. Only you know that.

Just as we want others to look at us for whom we are, we must do the same. We should be more careful when judging other people. It is not as important to define others as it is to define ourselves. Instead of rushing to judge others as simply this or that, we must go deeper in our understanding of each other by asking more questions. Also, we need to be more accepting of the differences that make each of us unique. It is the diversity within us that should be used as a source of strength within our country. Instead, it is being used as a wedge to divide us as people.

Once you have finished your self-portrait, it is time to look at your picture. Again, see it! Feel it! Touch it! Admire it! This is your picture, painted by you!

Show the world your work of art! Let others know who you are, and why you are here. How do you do it?

You do it like any good artist would. You do it by showing and telling.

By telling others, you communicate your thoughts, feelings, wants and desires. In doing this, you let them know that you are a person first. It keeps others from defining who you are.

By showing others your picture, it enables you to take this process one step further by letting your actions augment, or enhance your words. You can do this by taking a more active role in the causes that are important to you, the things that are in your self-portrait. Perhaps you are active in your church, or you are involved in various political causes. You may participate in cultural or ethnic customs associated with your particular heritage. Or, you may belong to a service organization that represents ideas and values that are important to you.

Being involved in a number of activities makes you a participant in the "everybody movement." It is the first step toward self-determination. It is the first step toward self-empowerment. It also shows others who you are, and why you are here.

Most of us hate it when others take our inventory. Much more, we detest the thought of taking our own inventory. But, if you take the time to paint your self-portrait, using your brush, starting with each color, then, combining each color to make a picture, you will find this experience likened to recharging your batteries. You will discover something about yourself that you never thought about.

Now is the time for you to seize the opportunity and begin to answer the question: Who am I? And, why am I here? See this as not a burden, rather an opportunity. See it not as a chore, but as an adventure.

Start with your name, your full name.

Don't let others define who you are. Only you know that.

Once your picture is complete, show it to others. Display your work of art for everyone to see.

Most of all, be proud of your picture! Be proud of who you are!

Photo Gallery

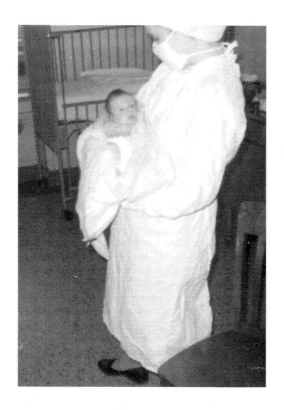

Newly born Jonathan being held by his mother, Cynthia.
Porter Memorial Hospital, Valparaiso, Indiana, 1965.

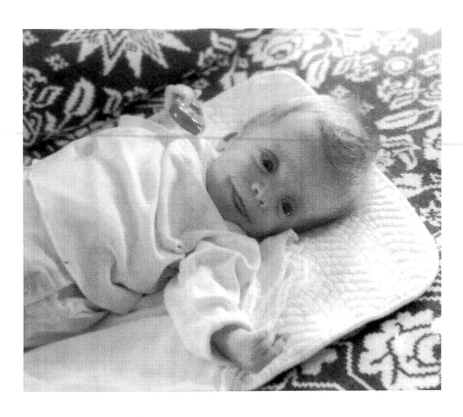

Jonathan, home from the hospital, laying on his Grandma
Elster's bed. Dune Acres, Indiana, 1965.

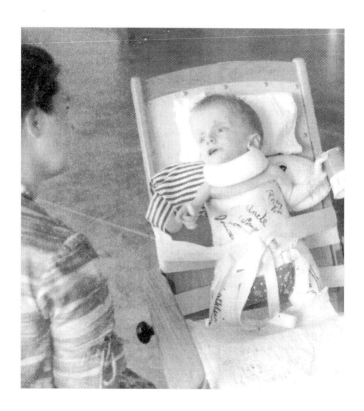

Jonathan's mother, Cynthia, visiting with Jonathan. Note the body cast and neck brace, plus the autographs on the cast. Shriners Hospital, Honolulu, Hawaii, circa 1970.

Sisters Amy and Becky, sitting with Jonathan in the front yard. Jonathan spent much of his early childhood in body casts. Family home on Nenue Street in Aina Haina, Honolulu, Hawaii, June 1970.

This is as close to surfing that Jonathan came. Unknown beach on Oahu, Hawaii, early 1970's.

Jonathan's 4th birthday with siblings Alden, Becky and Amy. Aina Haina, Honolulu, Hawaii, May 20, 1969.

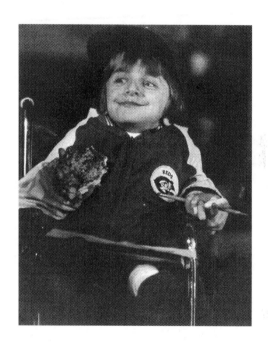

Jonathan, enjoying a piece of pizza while scoring a Hawaii Islanders baseball game. And, he's a Reds fan! Honolulu Stadium, Honolulu, Hawaii, early 1970's.

Jonathan, intently working on a project, wearing a Kansas City Chiefs jersey. The Chiefs were his favorite NFL team. Honolulu, Hawaii, mid 1970's.

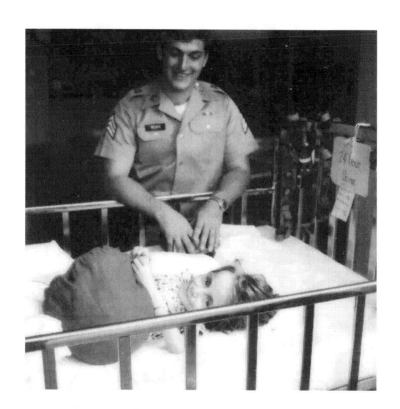

Sergeant Steve visiting Jonathan. Shriners Hospital, Honolulu, Hawaii. December 23, 1974.

Jonathan hanging out in his wheelchair. The Washington Redskins was his second favorite NFL team. Kapiolani Park, Honolulu, Hawaii, circa 1974.

Coach Paul Wiggin with Jonathan. Paul Wiggin was
the head coach of the San Francisco 49'ers, Kansas
City Chiefs, and Stanford University Cardinal football
teams. He was also Jonathan's football mentor. Unknown
location, circa 1983.

Jonathan, Becky, Amy, Ilio (dog), and Alden celebrating Christmas together. Stevensville, Michigan, December 25, 1979.

Jonathan sitting on the sidelines at the old Stanford Stadium (The Farm) in his role as the Honorary Head Coach of the East-West Shrine Game, a position he held for ten years. Palo Alto, California, January 9, 1982.

In his role as the Honorary Head Coach of the East-West
Shrine Game, Jonathan is offering inspiration to two
defensive players from the East Team. Stanford Stadium,
Palo Alto, California, early 1980's.

Players in the East-West Shrine Game would visit children at the Shriners Hospital in the days leading up to the game. In this photo, Jonathan is quite possibly showing a play he designed for player, John Elway, to use in the game. Shriners Hospital, San Francisco, California, January 1983.

Jonathan and the West Team group photo for the East-West Shrine Game. Stanford Stadium, Palo Alto, California, January 1988.

Jonathan was the ring bearer in his brother, Alden's, wedding. Top row: Bill Clink, Henry Studebaker, Alden Studebaker, Donna Studebaker, Nancy Miller, Becky Studebaker, Amy Studebaker. Middle row: Michael Smith, Judith Clink, Naomi Studebaker, Ruth Elster, Leonard Elster, Cynthia Studebaker, Georgina Smith. Bottom row: Robert Clink, Jonathan Studebaker. Unity of the Infinite Presence, Detroit, Michigan, May 18, 1980.

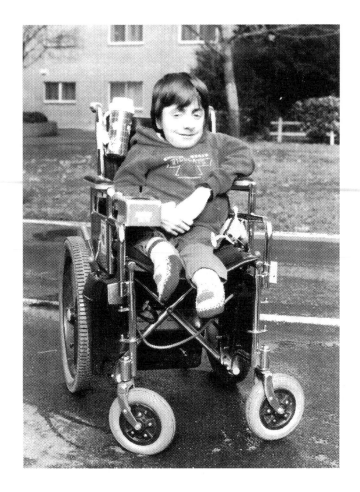

Jonathan's principal mode of transport was his electric
wheelchair. Chico, California, 1980's-90's.

Family Christmas gathering. Top row: James Downing, Henry Studebaker, Cynthia Studebaker, Scott Dennison. Bottom row: Rebecca Downing, Jonathan Studebaker, Amy Dennison. Foster City, California, December 1985.

Jonathan's parents, Henry and Cynthia Studebaker, celebrating Jonathan's graduation from California State University at Chico, Chico, California, May 1987.

Jonathan became president of the Lions Club. His grandfather, Leonard Elster, was also a Lion, and would have been quite proud of his accomplishment. Chico, California, late 1980's.

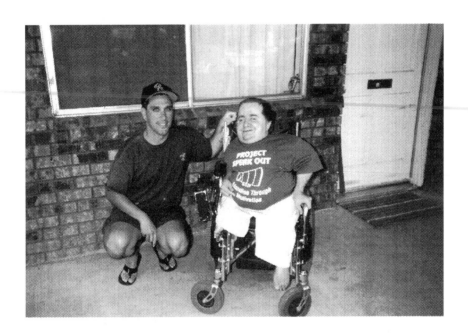

Jonathan and his best friend, Keith Cameron. In front of Jonathan's home on Orient Street, Chico, California, circa 1990.

"Farmer" Jonathan with his father, Henry, holding a super-sized zucchini. Jonathan had a small vegetable garden at his house on Orient Street. Chico, California, late 1990's.

Jonathan ran for Chico City Council, and had two of these billboards put up. Unfortunately, he lost the election. Chico, California, 1996.

Plaque in tribute to Jonathan. On the ground near a bench in Bidwell Park, Chico, California, 2001.

Printed in the United States
By Bookmasters